Borden Parker Bowne

Theory of Thought and Knowledge

Borden Parker Bowne

Theory of Thought and Knowledge

ISBN/EAN: 9783337220099

Printed in Europe, USA, Canada, Australia, Japan

Cover: Foto ©Thomas Meinert / pixelio.de

More available books at **www.hansebooks.com**

THEORY OF
THOUGHT AND KNOWLEDGE

BY

BORDEN P. BOWNE

PROFESSOR OF PHILOSOPHY IN BOSTON UNIVERSITY

NEW YORK ·:· CINCINNATI ·:· CHICAGO
AMERICAN BOOK COMPANY

Copyright, 1897, by HARPER & BROTHERS.

All rights reserved.

W. P. 8

PREFACE

THIS work does not aim to give an elaborate system of philosophy, but only to expound and recommend a certain way of looking at the problems of thought and knowledge. If we get the right point of view we can see for ourselves without waiting to be told. There are certain fundamental principles which underlie the problems in question, and the aim has been to bring them to light. The things which might be said are numberless, but, having due regard to the shortness of life, it has seemed to me that the discussion of principles is more profitable at present than the bulkiest collections of details. Besides, we have them already.

The root thought of the work is that thought is an organic activity which unfolds from within, and can never be put together mechanically from without. Persons on the sense plane perpetually seek to build up thought from without by the mechanical juxtaposition and association of sense impressions. This is the perennial source of that unthinking thinking which tends to deprive thought of all authority, and finally to dissolve it into a shadow of physical mechanism. This unprofitable, and sometimes pernicious, externalism can be overcome only by an insight into the activity and organic unity of thought itself. When this insight is reached, not a few crude and even gross fancies which underlie popular speculation in this field disappear of themselves, and the entire problem assumes a different aspect. Knowledge is no longer something originating outside of the mind, possibly in the nerves, and passed along ready-made into the mind; it is rather something built up by the mind within itself in accordance with principles immanent in the mental nature.

Nothing is nearer to us than thought, and yet nothing is harder to grasp. The reason is that spontaneous thought deals with its objects rather than with itself, and the work of reflection is difficult. Thought hides behind itself, and takes its own products for original data from without. Hence, for a long time, knowledge is taken for granted, and there is no suspicion of the existence, to say nothing of the complexity, of the knowing process. Then, when knowledge becomes a problem, it is solved in terms of the imagination, and without any careful analysis of the subject. In this way various theories of knowledge gain currency, being picked up on the plane of sense thinking and superficial reflection, and without being subjected to any searching criticism. Many of these are suicidal, but that does not matter much, so long as they can be pictured to the uncritical imagination and fall in with the prevailing fashion. Here, I conceive, is one of the great weaknesses of popular speculation, especially of the physiological type. It has not advanced far enough in reflection to see that the possibility of knowledge is a real problem, and that speculative theories must be tested, among other ways, by their bearing on this problem. In this connection attention is called to what is said concerning the speculative significance of freedom, the suicidal character of all mechanical systems of mind and fundamental existence, and the impossibility of any tenable theory of knowledge except on a theistic basis.

Apart from these deeper speculative questions I have emphasized two points the knowledge of which is of great importance, if not absolutely necessary, for our intellectual salvation. The first point is the volitional and practical nature of belief. Persons living on the plane of instinct and hearsay have no intellectual difficulty here, or anywhere else; but persons entering upon the life of reflection without insight into this fact are sure to lose themselves in theoretical impotence or in practical impudence. The impotence manifests itself in a paralyzing inability to believe, owing to the fancy that theoretical demonstration must precede belief. The impudence shows itself in ruling out with an airy levity the practical principles by which men and nations live, because they admit of no formal proof. These extremes of unwisdom can be escaped only by an insight into the volitional and practical nature of belief.

The second point referred to is the almost universal illusion arising from what I have called the structural fallacies of uncritical thought. Spontaneous thought is pretty sure to take its own operations as the double of reality. Thus arises the fallacy of the universal, the parent of a very large part of popular speculation. And when to this are added the omnipresent imposture and deceit of language, there results a great world of abstract and verbal illusion against which we cannot be too much on our guard, seeing that it is the source both of so much theoretical error and of so much practical menace and aberration. It is incredible, in advance of investigation, how much of what is said or written is pompous nothingness. Many a grave and dignified phrase when reduced to its lowest terms sinks to, or below, the wisdom of the nursery. Goldsmith gives two rules for becoming a connoisseur in art, one of which is always to remark that the picture would have been better if the artist had taken more pains. A great deal of current wisdom is equally cheap. Again, it is amazing on looking through philosophical speculation to discover how much of it is nothing but a shadow of our logical processes, in which the abstractions of logic are mistaken for the facts of existence. Finally, it gives ground for sober reflection, on listening to the heated discussion of social problems, to observe how largely verbal and abstract it is, having little contact with reality and being carried on mainly in a mirage of rhetoric and question-begging epithets. I doubt if students at present have any greater or more pressing duty than to strive to exorcise these logical spectres and verbal illusions, so that we shall see our problems as they are.

The theory of thought and knowledge and the theory of reality, or metaphysics, cover the field of fundamental speculation. And they belong together in such a way that neither can be fully discussed without the other. On this account some of the discussions of the present volume are preparatory, and must be handed over to metaphysics for final adjudication. This is especially the case with the ontological categories to which I have given little more than a formal treatment. They must first be seen as formal principles of thought before the question of their metaphysical significance can be dealt with. But the discussion must have an air of incompleteness until it is carried into the metaphysical realm.

Much of this work has been done in my earlier treatise

on metaphysics. I am now engaged on the revision of that work so as to adjust it to the present volume, and also with the aim of improving the discussion. This involves, among other things, some redistribution of the matter, and this in turn explains the appearance in the present volume of some matters treated in the earlier work. When the revision is completed, the two volumes will form a kind of whole, and will set forth a general way of looking at things which, I trust, will be found consistent with itself and with the general facts of experience.

BORDEN P. BOWNE.

BOSTON, *March*, 1897.

CONTENTS

INTRODUCTION . . . . Page 3

Aim of Philosophy, p. 3.—Classes of Philosophical Theories, p. 3.—Ground of their Division, p. 4.—Order and Division of Philosophic Study, p. 6.

PART I.—THEORY OF THOUGHT

CHAPTER I

THE GENERAL NATURE OF THOUGHT . . . Page 8

Definition of Logic, p. 8.—Thought Defined, p. 9.—Thought Distinguished from Sense and Association, p. 10.—Objectivity of Thought Defined and Illustrated, p. 13.

CHAPTER II

GENERAL CONDITIONS OF THOUGHT . . . Page 19

Consciousness Nothing by Itself, p. 19.—The Unity of the Mental Subject, p. 20.—Objections Considered, p. 21.—Substitutes for the Mental Unity, p. 25.—Tricks of Language, p. 28.—Law of Identity, p. 30.—Difficulty in this Law, p. 31.—The Positive Principle of Thought, p. 33.

CHAPTER III

HOW DOES THE MIND GET OBJECTS? . . Page 36

The Mind Active and Constitutive in Sensation, p. 38.—Recurrence of Experience Possible only to a Universalizing Intelligence, p. 41.—Work of Memory in Recurrent Experience, p. 44.—The Passage from Impressions to Things Impossible to Sense, p. 46.—Problem of Perception, p. 49.—Metaphorical Solutions, p. 50.—Perception as Due to Interaction, p. 51.—Perception as Mental Construction, p. 52—Idealism and Perception, p. 54.

CHAPTER IV

THE CATEGORIES . . . . . . Page 59

Difficulties in Recognizing the Categories, p. 59.—Time, p. 66.—Time a Principle of Thought, p. 68.—Number a Mental Product, p. 70.—Space a Mental Principle, p. 73.—Motion, p. 77.—Quantity, p. 78.—Being as Formal Category, p. 82.—Being as Metaphysical Category, p. 83.—Quality, p. 85.—Identity, Formal and Metaphysical, p. 87.—Causality, p. 89.—Interaction, p. 92.—Causality of Sequence, p. 93.—Empirical Causation, p. 96.—Freedom, p. 96.—Necessity, p. 100.—Possibility, p. 103.—Purpose, p. 104.—Relation of Purpose to the Mechanical Categories, p. 108.—Difficulties in the Empirical Perception of Purpose, p. 109.—How the Understanding Makes Nature, p. 113.

CHAPTER V

THE NOTION . . . . Page 117

Current Doctrine of the Notion, p. 119.—Antithesis of Individual and Universal, p. 119.—Inconsistencies of the Traditional View, p. 121.—The Concept and its Marks, p. 125.—Subject and Predicate Notions, p. 126.—The Concept as Symbol, p. 128.—Nominalism and Realism, p. 129.—Berkeley's View, p. 132.—Does Logic Deal with Thoughts or Things? p. 134.—Definition, p. 138.—Uncertainties of Classification, p. 141.—Thought and Language, p. 145.—Illusions Arising from Language, p. 147.

CHAPTER VI

THE JUDGMENT . . . . . . Page 150

Uncertainty in the Traditional Treatment of the Judgment, p. 151.—The Judgment Commonly Defined with Reference to the Syllogism rather than to Logical Fact, p. 153.—Categorical, Conditional, and Disjunctive Judgments, p. 157.—Conditions of Applying the Judgment, p. 162.—Symbolic Logic, p. 164.

CHAPTER VII

INFERENCE . . . . Page 166

Inference Defined, p. 166.—Classes of Inference, p. 167.—Principles of Inference, p. 169.—Traditional Rules of the Syllogism, p. 171.—Aristotle's Dictum, p. 172.—Mood and Figure, p. 174.—Peculiarities of Mathematical Reasoning, p. 175.—Objections to the Syllogism, p. 175. —Informal Reasoning, p. 179.

CHAPTER VIII

PROOF . . . . Page 182

Nature of Proof, p. 182.—Relation of Proof to Truth, p. 183.—Probability as the Guide of Life, p.185.—Calculus of Probabilities, p.186.—Misuse of the Doctrine, p. 189.—Difficulty in Application, p. 189.

CHAPTER IX

DEDUCTION AND INDUCTION . . . . Page 192

Nature of Deduction, p. 192.—No Deductive Science of Nature Possible, p. 193.—Problem of Induction, p. 194.—The Fruitful Principle of Induction, p. 196.—Inductive Methods, p. 200.—Difficulties of Inductive Reasoning, p. 201.—Induction and Deduction in Research, p. 206.—Hypotheses, p. 207.—Meaning of Law, p. 209.

CHAPTER X

EXPLANATION . . . . Page 211

Distinction of Fact and Theory, p. 211.—Difficulty in Reaching any Final Theory, p. 213.—Explanation as Classification, p. 217.—Scientific Explanation, p. 221.—Its Importance and its Superficiality, p. 223.—Metaphysical Explanation, p. 227.—Its Unprogressive Character when Mechanical, p. 230.—Source of the Illusion, p. 231.—Explanation by Intelligence, p. 233.—The Several Types of Explanation form a Series, p. 236.

CHAPTER XI

SOME STRUCTURAL FALLACIES . . . . Page 239

The Problem of Error, p. 240.—Suicidal Implications of Necessity, p. 241.—Only Solution in Freedom, p. 243.—The Fallacy of the Universal, p. 244.—Its Prevalence in Popular Speculation, p. 245.—Its Ravages in Psychology, p. 247.—The Fallacy of the Abstract, p. 251.—The Fallacy in Morals, in Philanthropy, in Social Questions, p. 252.—The Fallacy of Language, p. 259.

PART II.—THEORY OF KNOWLEDGE

CHAPTER I

PHILOSOPHIC SCEPTICISM . . . . . Page 267

Conditions of Rational Scepticism, p. 269.—Meaning of Scepticism, p. 272.—The Doubt of Reason, p. 274.—The Doubt of Sensationalism, p. 274.—Formal Doubt, p 275.—Doubt of Objective Knowledge, p. 279.—Its Foundation in Kantian Doctrine, p. 280.—Its Presuppositions, p. 281.—Its Suicidal Character, p. 285.—Relation of the Phenomenal to the Real, p. 290.

CHAPTER II

THOUGHT AND THING . . . . Page 296

Dualism in Human Knowing, p. 296.—Attempt of Materialism to Remove the Dualism, p. 298.—Ambiguity and Irrelevance of Idealism as Escaping the Dualism, p. 301.—Absolute Idealism, p. 302.—Its Origin and Development, p. 302.—Its Irrelevance, p. 305.—Its Failure, p. 308.—The Necessity of a Basal Monism, p. 311.—False Monisms, p. 312.—Active Intelligence the Only True Monism, p. 313.—Aids to Reflection, p. 316.

CHAPTER III

REALISM AND IDEALISM . . . . . Page 318

Many Forms of Idealism, p. 318.—Realism Admits of no Proof, p. 320.—Hasty Idealism, p 324.—Idealism Founded on the Knowing Process Alone Falls into Solipsism, p. 326.—What is Idealism? p. 328.—Extramental Existence, p. 330.—Difficulties of Transfigured Realism, p. 334.—Phenomena and Noumena, p. 336.—The Phenomenality of Space, p. 338.—The Contradiction in the Notion of an Ontological Space, p. 338.—The World as Thought and Act, p. 342.

CHAPTER IV

APRIORISM AND EMPIRICISM . . . . Page 344

Empiricism not an Inductive Study of Mind, p. 345.—The Empiricist's Conception of Experience Ambiguous, p. 347.—Mutual Incompatibility of Empiricism and Materialism, p. 348.—The Origin of Experience and the Warrant of Knowledge, p. 351.—Oversights of Empiricism, p.

353.—Empiricism and Race Experience, p. 357.—Empiricism and Mathematics, p. 362.—Knowledge of the Contingent Finds no Sufficient Basis in either Empiricism or Apriorism, p. 364.

CHAPTER V

KNOWLEDGE AND BELIEF . . Page 367

Knowledge and Belief Distinguished, p. 368.—Subjective and Objective Grounds of Belief, p. 369.—Practical Nature of Belief, p. 370.—Most Belief Necessarily a Matter of Hearsay, p. 372.—Demonstration Inapplicable to Reality, p. 373.—Practical Bearing the Test of Concrete Truth, p. 374.—Belief as Product of Life, p. 376.—Belief as Related to Will and Action, p. 380.—Distinction of Real Beliefs from Verbal and Notional Assents, p. 381.

CHAPTER VI

THE FORMAL AND RELATIVE ELEMENTS IN THOUGHT . Page 386

Part 1
THEORY OF THOUGHT

THEORY OF THOUGHT AND KNOWLEDGE

INTRODUCTION

PHILOSOPHY aims at a rational and systematic comprehension of reality. Or, since experience is the fundamental fact in all theorizing, and since reality can be known only in experience, in the largest sense of that word, we may say that philosophy aims at a rational and systematic comprehension and interpretation of experience.

This aim, however, is only an ideal which is very imperfectly realized. Philosophy is militant, not triumphant. As it has required the labor of many generations to bring the system of thought to its present development, so it will require the labor of many more to bring that system to anything like completion. Meanwhile only general outlines and partial views are possible. These, however, may be valuable, if they begin with admitted facts and make good their claims as they go along.

Philosophic theories fall into two great classes, theories of knowing and theories of being. This results from the nature of the case. The theory of being is the ultimate aim of philosophy, but that theory cannot be completed without a theory of knowing. A philosophic system is determined and characterized by its position on these two points.

In the doctrine of knowledge, the fundamental division of theories turns upon their conception of the mind as active or passive in knowing. However complicated the theories may seem in their application, the essential question is this, Is the mind active or passive in knowledge? Perhaps we may think that the term mind smacks too much of metaphysics, and then the question takes another form, Is knowing an active process determined by laws within thought itself, or is it only a mechanical reflection of objects in a passive consciousness? The answer to this question gives direction to our philosophy; and a long train of speculative consequences depends upon it.

In the doctrine of being, the deepest distinction of theories turns upon the conception of fundamental being, whether it be conceived as mechanical and unintelligent, or as purposive and intelligent. Unwittingly, often, but none the less really, philosophic debate revolves around the antitheses of freedom and necessity, of purpose and mechanism, of intelligence and non-intelligence. In addition, as already suggested, the theories of knowing and of being mutually affect one another.

There are, then, certain typical theories of knowing and of being, each of which has its peculiar implications; and whoever would understand the problems and the history of philosophy must master these typical theories. When this is done, particular systems may be understood in their essential worth, or worthlessness, as soon as we get their relation to the typical theory. When we know the logic of the general view we need not waste time in studying its particular forms. If they are logical we know where they must come out. If they are not logical we have no system but disjointed observations. They are systems only in the catalogue or advertisement.

Hence, epistemology, or the doctrine of knowledge, and

metaphysics, or the doctrine of real existence, are the two grand divisions of philosophy. As already pointed out, these do not admit of any absolute separation, as if the theory of one could be completed without a theory of the other. They are, then, different aspects of the whole question rather than mutually independent factors. At the same time, they are sufficiently distinct to make it desirable to treat them separately.

Historically, systems of philosophy have commonly emphasized one or the other of these two questions so as to become predominantly either theories of knowing or theories of being. Thus the systems of Locke, Hume, and Kant are pre-eminently theories of knowing. The systems of Spinoza and Leibnitz are fundamentally theories of being. In the historical development of thought, theories of being come first. This is due to the fact that the mind is objective in its first activities, and becomes reflective only at a later date. Knowledge is really determined both by the subject and by the object; but the object is the only determinant for unreflective thought. The full significance of the subject for knowledge was first proclaimed by Kant. Thought first goes straight to things, and if it stumbled on no contradictions among its conceptions it would probably never suspect the existence and complexity of its own processes.

In estimating, then, a philosophical system, we must get its position on these fundamental points of knowing and being. All else, so far as it is logical, results from that position. If we have a knowledge of the typical theories, we may spare ourselves the trouble of reading new works beyond the point necessary to determine their fundamental position. For instance, if one has mastered the logic of sensationalism in Hume, there is no need to waste time on the pathetic efforts of later sensationalists to galvanize their dead philosophy into some semblance of life.

Philosophy aims at a rational comprehension of reality. But the instrument of philosophy is thought itself. All systems of whatever kind, even systems of doubt and denial, must recognize the existence of laws of thought whereby the normal processes and results of thinking are distinguished from the abnormal. Without such recognition there is no distinction between rational and irrational, and naught remains but caprice, obstinacy, and infatuation.

Hence the logical order of philosophical study is logic, epistemology, and metaphysics. The first treats of the laws of normal thinking, or the science of thought. The second applies these laws to the problem of knowledge, and, by analyzing the idea of knowledge, aims to discover its general conditions and implications. These two are only different aspects of the one question. The third asks after the final conceptions reached by thought concerning real existence, or, more specifically, concerning man, nature, and the fundamental reality.

We have, then, as the most significant divisions of philosophic study the following:

1. Logic, or the Theory of Thought;
2. Epistemology, or the Theory of Knowledge;
3. Metaphysics, or the Theory of Being.

The first two divisions will be discussed in the present volume. The third will be postponed to a second volume.

The first topic, then, is logic, or the theory of thought. The treatment will differ somewhat from that of the traditional formal logic, because thought itself is differently conceived. We agree with the traditional logician that logic cannot deal with particular and concrete objects of knowledge, but should confine itself to the general forms and principles of thought which apply to all objects. At the same time, however, we conceive that thought has many forms besides those of the notion, the judgment, and the inference. The entire system of categories belongs to the forms of thought, and must be treated in any adequate exposition. Furthermore, unless logic is to sink into a barren shuffling of artificial notions, without any significance for truth or knowledge, it must take some account of its own metaphysical presuppositions.

A detailed and exhaustive discussion is not aimed at in the present work. The plan is rather to select such fundamental points for discussion as shall give the reader some idea of the essential nature of thought, and of the essential factors of the thought process. An insight into principles often dispenses with the discussion of details; and the study of details without a knowledge of principles can come to no conclusion beyond barren reflections and desultory observations.

CHAPTER I

THE GENERAL NATURE OF THOUGHT

THERE is no fixed definition of logic. Accordingly, its field is extended all the way from formal reasoning to metaphysics, according to the pleasure of the speculator. Even those who agree in defining it as the science of thought do not agree as to the limits of thought, and thus the difference reappears. This is due to the organic nature of reason, which forbids any hard and fast divisions. Hence, instead of engaging in barren disputes concerning the exact limits of logic, it is better to recognize that those limits must always have something arbitrary in them, and to aim at consistency, relevance, and significance in our speculations, whatever we call them.

We define logic as the science of thought, and proceed to show what we mean by thought. Of course, our immediate concern is with our human thinking. Whether "Thought," or "Consciousness," or "Cosmic Thought" be a presupposition of our thinking must be postponed to the Theory of Knowledge. Meanwhile, we limit our attention to our human thinking.

This limitation must be carefully noted, as oversight thereof has been a fruitful source of verbal disputes. It is plain that many things may be true for cosmic thought which are not true for our human thinking; and many limitations may be affirmed of the latter which must be denied of the former. The confusion of the two points of view can only result in further confusion.

For the present, then, we occupy the human standpoint; and our first work must be to gain some idea of what our human thought is.

The life of consciousness, as occurring, is neither true nor false, but simply fact. Misconceptions are as much facts as correct conceptions, and arise equally in accordance with mental laws. But this life has another aspect, according to which it is not merely a mental event, but an apprehension of truth. In this respect it is also subject to laws which claim to be the laws of normal thinking and the conditions of reaching truth. The mental life, considered as fact, belongs to psychology; the mental life, considered as apprehending truth, belongs to logic. This form of activity we call thought.

Thought, then, is that form of mental activity whose aim is truth or knowledge. The nature, laws, and implications of this activity are the subject of our study.

For the better understanding of this definition, it should be remembered that the term thought is often used with two entirely distinct meanings. Thought may signify the mental activity, and it may signify the contents grasped through that activity. In the latter sense, of course, thought includes everything which can exist for us. Sensations, feelings, the whole universe, indeed, so far as it is known, belong to thought. From this point of view, thought has no antithesis, but is all-inclusive. Oversight of this ambiguity has been the source of not a little sterile and tedious logomachy, something like that resulting from confounding thought and "Thought."

We have defined thought from the subjective standpoint as that form of mental activity whose aim is truth or knowledge. The reality and peculiarity of thought as a special form of activity will further appear if we contrast it with the affections of sense.

The human mind never rests in impressions of the sensibility, but works them over into forms inherent in its own nature. In so doing it transcends the sense fact entirely, and it does this on its own warrant. Thus, suppose I am struck by a stone. The sense fact is simply certain visual, tactual, and painful sensations. If I say the stone hit me, I have transcended the sense experience, and attributed objective existence and causal efficiency to the stone. Subtract these ideas, and there is nothing left but a succession of sensations in my own consciousness.

Again, if I suppose I see a moving body, the sense fact is only a continuous set of visual appearances at adjacent points of space in successive moments of time. To transform this into a moving body, I must pass from the fact of sense to the notion of an objective and identical thing. Or if I suppose I have successive experiences of the same thing, the sense fact is merely a similarity of successive sensations; and I should never get beyond this, unless I interpreted the sense fact by the notion of an abiding and identical thing.

Thus in these simplest and most elementary experiences we find a peculiar mental activity manifesting itself. There is a surplusage over the sensations. Here are ideas which are not sensations, nor any possible modifications of sensation. They do not admit of being sensuously presented, but belong to the unpicturable notions of intelligence. Yet the sensations become an intelligible object for us only as these ideas are superinduced upon them by the action of the understanding. This surplusage in experience beyond the contribution of the senses was recognized by Hume, and attributed to a mental "propensity to feign."

There is, then, a great distinction between what is in

sense and what is in thought. Of course, we at first suppose that all those things are in sense which we perceive through sense; but a small amount of reflection serves to dispel this illusion. In dealing with paintings and drawings, or with printed and written matter, the eye gives only lines and colors; the mind adds the meaning. But there can be no doubt that in all visual perception the meaning is contributed by the mind in like manner. What the eye gives is one thing; what we see or perceive is quite another. Since the publication of Berkeley's *New Theory of Vision* this fact has been a commonplace of psychology.

In hearing and the other senses the distinction is equally manifest. When we come to scientific study, the distinction between what is in sense and what is in thought is apparent even to the dullest. Even the sciences which have to do with physical objects live and move and have their being mainly in a world of rational conceptions which can be entered only by thought. Very few scientific conceptions admit of being sensuously presented or sensuously verified.

Thus, along with the receptivity of sense, but distinct from it, we see a special order of mental activity which works over sense data into rational forms. From this point of view, thought might be defined as the process whereby the mind works over the raw material of the sensibility into the forms of intelligence. This would not be a complete definition, but it would call attention to one of the most important aspects and functions of the thought activity in our experience.

Once more we may illustrate the reality and peculiarity of the thought movement by contrasting it with the associational movement.

We find two orders of movement and combination in consciousness. Many things or events are found together or occur together in experience without any inner connection.

But when they have thus come together in experience they tend thereafter to recur together by virtue of the laws of association. The most unlike things which have occurred together tend to recur together; and sometimes the connection becomes so intimate as to seem a matter of course. Language furnishes a good example. The words, spoken or written, have absolutely no likeness to the thought, and no fitness to express just that thought rather than any other; yet when once joined they seem to belong together, so that we even fancy we see or hear the thought itself. This fact underlies the order of reproduction. Memory reproduces the order of occurrence in accordance with the laws of association. This is the first order of movement. It is a mechanical grouping and reproduction of elements which have come together, and implies no internal connection.

The second order is of a different kind. It aims to reach not accidental conjunction, but rational connection. The distinction between the two is that in the former case the elements only come together, whereas in the latter they belong together. Thus, sound and idea come together; but the properties of a triangle, or cause and effect, belong together. The former might conceivably be separated; the latter are fixed in changeless relations. Now, the second order of mental movement referred to aims to transform the occurrences and accidental conjunctions of experience into rational connections, so that our thought shall represent not merely the chance order of coming together, but the fixed order of belonging together. The associational order repeats indifferently the conjunctions of experience; the thought order subjects them to a rational ideal.

This antithesis between thought and sensation, or between the thought movement and the associational movement, has not always been allowed. Thus, Hume recognized only conjunction and denied connection. In this he has generally been followed by the sensationalists. They have sought by means of association working upon sensations to evolve thought itself; so that finally all that is native to the mind is the passive sensibility and the laws of association. Given these, they aim to exhibit all else as product.

In so far as this claim admits the present existence of laws of thought, it is irrelevant to our present purpose. It is an attempt not to deny those laws, but to explain them on a psychological basis. The laws are evolved but valid. The thought life roots, indeed, in the sense life, but has its special forms nevertheless. In so far as the associational claim contains a denial of the laws of thought, we shall consider it in connection with particular cases. We shall see hereafter that, if the antithesis of thought and sensation is to be denied, it must be from the side of thought rather than from that of sensation. It may turn out that sensation itself is in a very important sense a thought product.

We come now to a point of the highest importance in studying the nature of thought. Reference has already been made to it in speaking of thought as related to truth. Some amplification is in order here.

Thought may be viewed as a mental event which ends in itself, and it may be viewed as apprehending or reporting a truth or reality beyond the mental event. Many of our conscious experiences are only mental events. They report nothing, and their whole duty is simply to be what they are. As such they are simply accidents of the individual, and have no relation to truth. As Ferrier has it, they represent or apprehend nothing which is "common to all"; they are simply an experience which is "special to me." But the distinguishing mark of thought is that, in addition to being a mental event, it claims to represent a truth which is independent of the mental event. Of course, thinking, as a process, is particular; and the entire contents of consciousness as mental events are particular; but our thoughts, though mental events, claim to be valid for an order of fact or reason which our thoughts do not make but discover, and which is common to all and not merely special to me.

But there are some mental events which are only special to me, as feelings, moods, and all mental states which end in themselves; yet in dealing with these the same fact comes out. For while these mental events are special to me in their occurrence, thought treats them as actual happenings in the total system of reality, and thus constitutes them a possible object of knowledge for all, and fixes them as actual components of the total reality.

How thought can do this, how the particular thought which, as mental event, is special to me can nevertheless affirm and apprehend something valid for all is no doubt a great mystery; but the fact is so involved in the nature of thought that thought vanishes altogether with its denial.

It is this fact which constitutes the universality and objectivity of thought, and distinguishes the judgment—at least, in its intention—from a subjective union of ideas.

Of course, this does not hinder that thought may often be mistaken. Chance conjunctions are put forward as fixed connections. Accidents of the individual are assumed to have universal validity. The special to me is mistaken for the common to all. But this very fact only illustrates once more that universality, or objective validity, is the essential form of thought.

This conclusion finds further support in a consideration of the judgment. What does any judgment mean? It always involves the assumption of objective validity, and would be absurd or frivolous without it.

Thus, suppose, for instance, that a geometrical judgment is in question—say, the sum of the angles of a triangle is equal to two right angles. No one would admit that by this judgment he meant only that in his own consciousness the subject and predicate come together. Possibly, under polemical stress, a sensational philosopher might momentarily take such a position; and then the sufficient answer would be, Well, what of it? The judgment being by hypothesis an accident of the individual, no one else need concern himself about it. But the bare fact of living together and of being mutually intelligible makes such a position impossible except as a verbal pretence. The geometrical judgment, then, carries with it a reference to a fixed order of reason which is common to all, and assumes to set forth some truth concerning that order.

Or we may take a judgment in physics—say, that water rises thirty-three feet in a pump under a certain barometric pressure. However many mental events may occur in reaching and announcing this judgment, no one would have the courage to say that it means only that certain notions cohere in his own consciousness. Even the most determined sensationalist or idealist would have to admit a world of coexistent minds and a universal order according to which all particular consciousness is determined. Without this admission the unlucky speculator would fall a prey to solipsism. Thus, the physical judgment contains a necessary reference to an order of fact which is not an accident of the individual, but is common to all. The nature of this common fact may remain highly mysterious, but its existence cannot be questioned without absurdity.

If, finally, we take an historical judgment—say, Washington crossed the Delaware—we see the same objective implication. Here an order of historical fact is assumed; and however necessary our thoughts as mental events may be for the grasping of the fact, they can never be identified with the fact.

Thus, in the essential nature and intention of the judgment, we see thought transcending itself as mental event, and positing a system for which our thought is valid, but which it does not make. The universality and community of the object have at bottom this meaning; not that every one grasps it, but that the apprehending thought reproduces an order which is independent of itself. If it should occur to some one of idealistic tendencies to suggest that this objective system is itself only a thought, the answer would be that, if it were so, it could not be identified with the thought of the finite individual, but would be independent of any and all of our thinking. For us, then, it would be something which we do not make but find. If, finally, any one should insist that thought cannot recognize anything beyond itself, that might well be true for "Thought," but it is not true for our thinking. For, whether philosophy can make anything of it or not, we are constantly recognizing an order of fact which we cannot view as dependent on our thinking, or as vanishing when we go to sleep.

This objective reference of thought is especially to be dwelt upon, as it is commonly overlooked by sensationalism and various cheap idealisms. They assume that impressions are the raw material of knowledge, and that all that has to be done is to group the impressions. But they fail to make clear to themselves either the problem or the data of their own theory. Now, in strictness, the data are particular, unqualified impressions; that is, they are impressions of nobody by nothing. If we relax the strictness enough to allow the passive subject, then we have particular impressions in the consciousness of a particular individual; and these admit of being variously associated. Then the problem is out of these data to generate the subjective form of knowledge and its objective validity.

The insolubility of this problem is manifest as soon as we comprehend what is to be done. If we succeeded in generating the subjective form of thought from particular impressions, we should still have made no provision for the objective reference and objective validity. For associated impressions, after all, are only impressions associated, and remain accidents of the individual after association has done its best or worst. A solipsistic group of impressions is the only outcome; and the judgment sinks into a mental event which reports nothing. We are freed from these whimsies by remembering the objective reference implicit in thought from the beginning.

But this affirmation of an objective reference in thought must not be mistaken for the claim that all parts of the thought process have their double in reality. Thought, the product, is objectively valid; thought, the process, is no part of the object. Hence a double inquiry. This concerns, first, the nature and laws of the thought process considered as a form of mental activity; and, secondly, the nature and extent of the validity of our thought for the independent object. In the latter part of the inquiry, logic passes into epistemology. Our immediate concern is with the thought process, its conditions and laws.

The thought movement, when it becomes self-conscious and reflective, rises into freedom, in distinction from the mechanical movement of association. The thought life is rooted in our nature, and begins without our reflective volition. But this spontaneous thought remains on the surface of things, and needs to be rendered more profound and exact. This is the work of freedom. All earnest study, all science and philosophy, rest upon a will to know, and a direction of our powers to this end. Science and all the higher forms of knowledge are no mechanical product, but a free achievement of the truth-loving mind. Nature presents us with a few things in the mental life; but only free work and devotion can make us rulers over many.

Thus, we have sought to show that within our experience there is a special order of mental activity with laws and aims of its own, which is to be distinguished from the mechanical order of association and from the passiveness of mere impressibility. If in our further study we find reason for doubting this conclusion we promise to withdraw it. Pending such discovery, we pass to consider the **general logical conditions** of thought.

CHAPTER II

GENERAL CONDITIONS OF THOUGHT

THERE are multitudinous conditions of concrete thought of an accidental sort, both physiological and psychological; and there are certain other conditions given in the very structure of thought itself. Only the latter concern us here.

And as consciousness is the absolute condition of all thought, it seems as if a discussion of consciousness were a necessary preliminary to the theory of thought. This seeming, however, is misleading. Since consciousness is an accompaniment of all mental states, it is easy to think that it is a distinct element by itself. This is a logical illusion. The spatial figures also in which we speak of consciousness lead to the fancy that consciousness is something which contains other mental states, or which furnishes the stage for their operations. But in fact consciousness is no simple, homogeneous mental state antecedent to objects, or apart from objects; it arises only in connection with particular objects, and is nothing by itself. When consciousness is empty of objects there is nothing left.

Consciousness may, indeed, exist in varying grades of clearness, from a vague sense of subjectivity and objectivity up to the distinct consciousness of self and the definite apprehension of an object; but in every case the vagueness of the consciousness is the vagueness of the apprehension; and an attempt to make the consciousness more distinct could only direct itself to making the conception more distinct. If there be a vague, undifferentiated, unrecognized somehowness of feeling which we choose to call consciousness, it is plainly nothing for intelligence so long as it remains in this state. In order to attain to rationality this general consciousness, which is a consciousness of nothing, must in some way become a consciousness of something. Hence the question, How we come to rational and articulate consciousness, is identical with the question, How we get objects of thought and knowledge.

Thought, as apprehending truth, exists only in the form of the judgment. The presence of ideas in consciousness, or their passage through it, is neither truth nor error, but only a mental event. Truth or error emerges only when we reach the judgment. The fundamental conditions of the judgment, therefore, must be fundamental conditions of thought itself. These are three: the unity and identity of the thinking self, the law of identity and contradiction, and the fact of connection among the objects of thought. The first is the condition of any rational consciousness whatever. The second is the condition of our thoughts having any constant and consistent meaning. The third refers to that objective connection which thought aims to reproduce, and without which thought loses all reference to truth. As the first relates to the constitution of the subject, it might be called the subjective condition; the second might be called the formal condition; and the third, as relating to the constitution of the object, might be called the objective condition. Or, without too great inaccuracy, they might be called, respectively, the psychological, the logical, and the ontological condition of thought. The name, however, is of no moment, provided we understand the thing.

We consider first the unity of the mental subject as the condition of thought.

Let us take the judgment a is b, where a and b are any two particular states of consciousness. How is this judgment possible?

The answer is, It is possible only as there is a conscious subject M, which is neither a nor b, but embraces both in the unity of its own consciousness. Then, by distinguishing, comparing, and uniting them in the unity of one conscious act, it reaches the judgment a is b. But so long as we have only the particular states a and b, they remain external to each other, and the judgment is non-existent and impossible.

A demurrer is sometimes raised against this conclusion. That the external juxtaposition of particular thoughts can never become a thought of the particulars in their mutual relations is manifest. A conception of all the parts of a watch in separation is not a conception of the watch. The conception of the watch is not a congeries of component conceptions, but it is rather a single, unitary conception. In like manner, it is urged, the judgment is also one. It is not built out of particular states, and needs nothing beyond the one judging act itself.

This claim is subtle rather than profound. There is a clear conception of the impossibility of building complex conceptions out of simple ones by mere juxtaposition; but along with this there is a confusion of logical simplicity with psychological simplicity. Psychologically, no doubt, the conception of plurality is as truly a single act as the conception of unity. The conception of a watch is as truly one as the conception of a single wheel. But logically the one conception has a plurality of elements; and there can be no true thought until the unity of the conception is distinguished into the plurality of its implications. Over against the plurality we must affirm a unity; and, equally, over against the unity we must affirm plurality. Analysis is as necessary as synthesis. The judgment, then, may be psychologically one, but logically it involves the distinction of *a* and *b* as well as their union. Without this distinction the judgment is impossible. And for this logical distinction and union alike we need something which is neither *a* nor *b*, but which comprehends and acts upon both. This something we call the self. By it we mean not anything sensuously or imaginatively presentable, but only that unitary and abiding principle revealed in thought, and without which thought is impossible.

The judgment as an act is unique and lonely. Physical images only serve to obscure it, or, rather, contradict it. The field of consciousness is spaceless and partitionless. Our objects are separated, but not in space or time. They are united, but not spatially or temporally. The relation is logical, not physical, and does not admit of being pictured. The attempt to construe it to the imagination misses its true nature, and leads to that mechanical externalism which seeks to build up mind from without. How the judging act is possible is the unparalleled mystery of consciousness. But then it is a fact; and the unity of the thinking self is not an hypothesis for its explanation, but its analytically necessary condition. Without this *a* and *b* fall asunder, and the judgment is impossible.

Over against the plurality of coexistent particular states the self must be one; over against the plurality of successive particular states the self must be both one and abiding. The latter necessity is as manifest as the former. For if we suppose the particular states to be in time, they vanish as fast as they are born; and if there be nothing which abides across this flow and unites the past and the present in the unity of its continuous and identical existence, once more the judgment becomes impossible.

We conclude, then, that the unity and identity of the

thinking self is an absolutely necessary condition of the simplest and most elementary judgment.

This account of the matter is not accepted by all. A very general claim of the sensational and physiological school is that a simple passive consciousness is possible which is made up of particular units of feeling or impressions; and these impressions, when united by association, are supposed to give us the judgment as a matter of course. On this view there is no unitary self which judges; but there are particular impressions grouped by association, and this grouping is the judgment.

We have already pointed out that this view overlooks the objective reference of the judgment, and that in its best estate it can reach only a fictitious objectivity, the reality always being only particular associated impressions in some particular consciousness. In addition, the view has no inner consistency. To begin with, its particular states of consciousness which have no reference to self in them are fictions of abstraction, and no data of experience, real or possible. By the time experience becomes anything articulate, it must be owned by somebody. Besides, if we allow those states, we are not advanced. For, by hypothesis, no one knows itself, to say nothing of knowing its neighbors; and thus the conditions of the judgment are not given. For this we need, not simply states of consciousness, but a consciousness of states; and this is a very different thing.

Nor will association help us. Indeed, association itself means nothing except for a consciousness which is not composed of particular states, but which in its unity comprises particular states as belonging to itself. In other words, the association of sensations is nothing in the intellectual world except for an abiding self. To see this we need only ask where, or for what, the sensations are associated. To say that they are associated for one another is to endow them with mutual consciousness. To say that they are associated in the nerves is to plunge into unintelligible cerebral mythology. If there were an independent consciousness which embraced them, we might say that sensations are associated in consciousness; but this will not apply to a view which recognizes only states of consciousness, and no consciousness of states. Thus the doctrine has no assignable relevant meaning whatever, except with reference to an abiding self.

Two naïve and traditional oversights have always helped this doctrine of association out of its chief difficulties. How to get particular impressions to recognize one another, and how from the juxtaposition of particular units of feeling to evolve a knowledge of their relations without invoking some superior principle, have always been problems of exceeding difficulty. The theorist, however, manages beautifully by mistaking his own knowledge of what is to be done for a development of that knowledge by the impressions themselves. Accordingly, when he has fairly confused himself with learned phrases about assimilative, successive, complicative, and other association, he announces that the work is done. But when we insist on walking by sight rather than by faith, it turns out that nothing is done, and that his apparent success is due to mixing himself up with the problem.

The other oversight is the one by which sensationalism saves itself from nihilism. The traditional means of escape from this collapse consists in the traditional ambiguity of the terms sensation and impression. Impression may mean a simple, unqualified, unrelated state of consciousness, and it may mean an impression of something by something. Sensation is similarly ambiguous. With the former meaning the issue is nihilism; with the latter meaning we have a fair set of rational ideas latent in the sense data. This ambiguity is sensationalism's most precious heirloom and its chief stock in trade. This has been shown with most painful thoroughness by Green in the introduction to his edition of Hume's works.

The necessity of the unitary and abiding self is stringent, but sometimes attempts are made to avoid the admission by changing the name. Thus, it is said, what is really necessary is not the unity of self, but the unity of consciousness. This turns out, however, to be only another name for the same thing. For this consciousness which is one is no sum or function of particular states. On the contrary, it has states, distinguishes itself from them, discriminates, compares, and unites them, and abides through them as self-identical. But that which does all this is precisely what we mean by the self. The names differ, but the meaning is the same.

Or suppose we venture a still airier abstraction and say that the only unity in the case is the self-distinguishing, self-identifying thought. Here again it is plain either that we have nonsense, or else an odd description of the self. So long as this thought is conceived as a particular and passing conception we have nonsense. That a particular conception, say inkstand, should so distinguish or identify itself as to become aware of other particular conceptions, as chair, table, tree, house, and have opinions about them, would be a performance worth seeing. But if our view is to escape this tedious imbecility, then our self-distinguishing, self-identifying thought must be conceived as something above particular thoughts, as having, comparing, and judging them, and as abiding through them. To be sure, we should have a very doubtful use of language, but this curious "thought" would be what we mean by the unitary and abiding self.

This fact deserves emphasis, as a weak dread of recognizing the self is a prominent feature of current psychological speculation. Ambitious clergymen and magazine scientists are fond of affecting an acquaintance with science for the sake of giving greater weight to their own rather cloudy utterances. The result is a body of doctrine which, in distinction from science proper, might well be called pulpit and magazine science. Latterly psychologists have been falling into the same bad way. Doctrines like the conservation of energy have been picked up by hearsay and verbally exegeted without any suspicion of their limitations. In this way we have been forbidden to think that our thought, or purpose, or volition, has anything to do with the direction of our bodies, under penalty of being unscientific. Again, a good many physical inquiries may be pursued on a phenomenal basis; and metaphysical questions are rightly excluded as irrelevant. Accordingly the half-educated, with whom a little learning has been unusually disastrous, give out that metaphysical notions are unscientific; and unscientific in turn passes for fictitious.

Under the pressure of such verbal intimidations, some of the weaker brethren among the psychologists have such fear of the "scientist" before their eyes that they are ready to ignore facts in order to be scientific. It is supposed to be metaphysical, and hence unscientific, to speak of a real self; and hence they hesitate to do so for fear of losing caste with the "scientists." These weak brethren need to be both enlightened and encouraged by being told that it is a false science which owes allegiance to anything but fact and logic, and that it is metaphysical to speak of a real anything. A real world, a real atom, a real force, a real energy, a real existence are highly metaphysical notions; and it excites surprise to find persons who are devout believers in such things suddenly shying at the notion of a real self on the ground of its being metaphysical.

Only a theoretical prude, therefore, or one so anxious for the purity of science as to forget that science itself must be subordinated to fact, will take offence at the notion of the self if the facts call for it. But in affirming the self we affirm nothing picturable or sensuously presentable, but only what we mean and experience when we say "I." And this self, so far from being a questionable fact, is one of the surest items of experience. The sun in the heavens, as objective reality, is far more questionable. If science is to deal with facts without distortion, no fact can well be more scientific than the one thus described by Thomas Reid: " I am not thought, I am not action, I am not feeling; I am something 'that thinks and acts and feels.' The self or I is permanent, and has the same relation to all the succeeding thoughts, acts, and feelings which I call mine." However we may change the name, we are forced to retain the thing, or the thought life falls asunder and vanishes.

Sundry metaphysical questions may indeed be raised concerning the nature of this self and in what its permanence consists; but they do not touch the fact of permanence. The fact is revealed in thought itself; and no one has ever succeeded in more than a verbal denial of it. Moreover, the metaphysical questions apply equally to all reality, and are no special difficulties of psychology. On the plane of ordinary thinking, where for action we demand an agent, and for changing states an abiding subject, there is nothing which can show a better title to be called real and abiding than the thinking self. And if we raise the deeper metaphysical questions we find the apparent realities of sense perception vanishing into phenomena, while selfhood seems to be the only thing that can show any claim to abiding existence. But these deeper problems we hand over to metaphysics. Here it suffices to point out that, whatever mystery the reality and permanence of the self may involve, they cannot be denied without wrecking thought altogether. As to the fact, the uninitiated will find some help in deciding from remembering that the claim is simply that I am not thoughts but I think, and that I who now think am the same who thought yesterday.

That the self is not independent of all conditions in the performance of its synthetic function of consciousness is known by experience. Here belong all the facts of mental dependence on normal physical conditions. But the unity of the mental subject is demonstrated by the fact of any rational consciousness. It is not the consciousness that we are one which is decisive, but that we are conscious at all.

The oversight of this fact, common among sensationalists, is due to several reasons: (1) The unity denied is commonly restored in some figure of speech, or is assumed in the language employed; (2) the speculator performs the synthetic acts involved in the judgment himself, and mistakes this for their performance by the sensations; (3) he mistakes the external union of sensations by association for their logical union in a judgment. Thus he is led on to a naïve denial of the self; a denial which, in one way or another, he is perpetually recanting. It is interesting to trace the figures of speech whereby the exiled self is recalled from banishment. Indeed, the abiding self has never been denied except verbally.

The trick of language whereby the self denied is assumed in order to express its own denial is well illustrated in the following passage from Hume, in which he proclaims the reduction of the self to a flux of impressions:

" For my part, when I enter most intimately into what I call *myself*, I always stumble on some particular perception or other, of heat or cold, light or shade, love or hatred, pain or pleasure. I never can catch myself at any time without a perception, and never can observe anything but the perception. . . . If any one, upon serious and unprejudiced reflection, thinks he has a different idea of *himself*, I must confess I can reason no longer with him. All I can allow him is that he may be in the right as well as I, and that we are essentially different in this particular. He may, perhaps, perceive something simple and continued, which he calls *himself;* though I am certain there is no such principle in me." *

We shall get a realizing sense of the advantage of expressing a theory in language which hides its true nature if we will be at the pains to substitute for the personal pronouns in this passage the vanishing impressions required by the theory. As none of these abides beyond the instant of its occurrence, and all are perpetually dissolving into something else, it follows that the first I is not the same as the second I, and that of the later I's no one has any identity with any other. The Hume of the beginning of the passage dissolves into any number of other Humes before it ends. But the humorous nonsense of the doctrine is concealed from the reader by the language employed, which throughout implies the denial of the theory. Indeed, the view cannot be set forth in any form of human speech without hopeless contradiction. If Hume had been compelled to use the language of his own theory it would have needed no other criticism. When with such a conception of mind he can write, "The mind has the command over all its ideas, and can separate, unite, mix, and vary them as it pleases," one can hardly resist the impression that Hume is trying to see how far the game of logical hide-and-seek can be carried with human dulness.

* *Treatise of Human Nature*, Part IV., Sect. VI.

We conclude, then, that thought exists only in relation to a conscious and abiding subject. Apart from this relation it is an unreal abstraction.

The second general condition of thought is the law of identity and contradiction; that is, our conceptions must have fixed meanings and must be used consistently therewith. This we express symbolically:

First, positively, A is A.

Second, negatively, A is not B.

In its positive form it is called the law of identity; in its negative form the law of contradiction. These are not separate and independent laws, but opposite sides of the one fact that no valid thought is possible without fixed conceptions and consistency in their use. And the forms are always to be interpreted with reference to this principle; otherwise they become barren or misleading. That A is A, or that everything is equal to itself, is a tautology. That everything is its own predicate is a form of empty words. That A is not B is generally false; for the great mass of affirmative categorical judgments have for their formula A is B. But we readily find our way through these verbalisms by remembering that the logical law in question only demands fixed meanings for our conceptions and consistency in their use.

A second law is commonly given as the law of the excluded middle. According to this law, a given subject must either have or not have a given predicate. Any third possibility is excluded. But so far as logical form is concerned this is no independent law, but only an implication of the law of identity and contradiction.

In concrete application these laws are often in appearance rightly violated; and thus it might seem that they are not really laws of thought. A is often not A; and between

B and non-B there are often many middles which are not excluded. This is due to the fact that, in actual thinking, both affirmation and negation are often limited and relative. In such cases the contradiction is only apparent, and in no way affects the validity of the logical law. Living speech abounds in such contradiction, but only the unhappy verbalist finds any difficulty therein. All others take the language as it is meant, and regard the implied limitations.

The law of identity in its double aspect, and with its implication of the excluded middle, is the only one recognized by the traditional formal logic—a logic which has nothing to do with truth or knowledge, but only with formal consistency in statement. Such logic may be good as far as it goes, but that it does not go far is evident.

This formal principle of consistency is to be distinguished from the metaphysical category of identity. The failure to do so is at the bottom of some confusion in the history of thought. The Eleatics made it affirm the impossibility of any change, and Hegel denied that it is a law of thought at all. However this may be metaphysically, the necessity of the law as a formal condition of thought is manifest, as without it nothing would mean anything, and both affirmation and denial would be emptied of all significance or distinction.

The real difficulty in the case is this: If our thought absolutely created its objects, it could fix and define them on its own warrant; or if our thought were concerned only with a system of changeless ideas, the law of identity would present no difficulty. But this is the case with us to a very slight degree. For the most part, our thought is engaged in grasping an existence which it does not make and which is constantly changing. In order to do this the mind must of course impose its own laws upon the independent existence. And here the fact appears of a certain antithesis between the laws of our thought and the nature of many of its objects. In thought itself there must be no flow. The contents of ideas must be constant quantities. If there be change in reality the mind must stiffen even the change into fixity. The thought of change must be as changeless as the thought of the unchanging. It was this fixity of the ideas with which Socrates overcame the scepticism which sprang out of the dissolving flux of the sophists; but in turn it gives rise to the problem how to express a changing existence by changeless ideas, and this problem involves some special puzzles.

For instance, what fixed conception would truly express the reality of any developing thing—say, a human being? If the conception had no parallax with the fact at the age of thirty, what of it at the age of fifteen? or fifty? It would seem that we should need a new conception for each new increment of change, and in that case each conception would become invalid as soon as formed. Of course spontaneous thought recognizes no difficulty, for it does not even understand the problem; but reflection finds it difficult. If we think to mend the matter by including the entire cycle of development in the conception, and saying the thing is all that it is to become, we unwittingly take a long step in the direction of idealism, besides seriously scandalizing common-sense. The boy is allowed to be the father of the man, but how can we say that the boy is the man? or that the acorn is the oak? To be sure, we cannot adequately define the acorn without reference to the oak; but the acorn is just acorn, and all else is idea. But when we declare that the idea of the completed thing is its true reality, then the reality lies in a world of changeless ideas; and the world of changing things, where most of us find reality, becomes only a temporal manifestation of the changeless ideas.

The problem here is simple, almost elementary; but the solution lies pretty deep. We shall find an advantage in postponing its further consideration for the present. Having looked the difficulty boldly in the face, we pass by on the other side. Meanwhile it is plain that no valid thought is possible unless A equals A, and no knowledge is possible unless the changing things allow themselves to be grasped by fixed ideas.

The law of identity is but the negative condition of thought. If it were the only law, thought would come to a standstill. This was early shown by the Megarians. The law sets objects apart in hard and fast isolation. A is A, B is B, C is C. And the Megarians claimed that only such identical judgments and the negative judgment, A is not B, are possible. Thus they shut thought up to identical and negative judgments without motion or progress.

This necessary result of the law of identity, when taken abstractly and alone, leads us to the third fundamental condition of thought, or what we have called the objective or ontological condition. If the law of identity be the negative principle of thought, we may call this the positive principle.

The need of some principle beyond the law of identity has long been apparent; but the principle has never been satisfactorily formulated, or reduced to a single and adequate expression. Leibnitz called it the law of the sufficient reason, but this is generally recognized as an unsatisfactory formulation. But whatever the formulation, the positive principle which is necessary to enable thought to move at all is the assumption of rational and systematic connection among the elements of that independent order which thought must assume, if it is to be more than a meaningless mental event; that is, the objects of thought must not be isolated and unrelated, but must be variously connected in rational relations. The mind is impelled by its nature to seek such connection, and without assuming it thought cannot begin at all. This is simply our old assumption of belonging together once more in distinction from simply being or happening together.

This connection on which thought depends may be of various kinds. It may be (1) of objects in a class, (2) of different classes, (3) of substance and attribute, (4) of cause and effect, (5) of ground and consequence, (6) of the successive states of a thing, etc. The necessity of such connection is apparent if thought is to be possible. Without the connection of objects in a common class, every judgment becomes singular. Without the connection of inherence, the attributive judgment is baseless. Without the communication of classes, the subsumptive judgment is impossible. Without the connection of cause and effect, the causal judgment is worthless. Without the connection of reciprocity or mutual determination, existence breaks up into unrelated elements, and no judgment can find its way from one thing to another. Without the continuity of existence, past and future fall hopelessly asunder, and nothing is left but vanishing and groundless shadows.

From all this we can understand the significance of Hume's denial of connection between coexistent properties in what we call things, and between antecedent and consequent in time. Thus the outer world of coexistences broke up into groups of qualities without any inner union, and the world of cause and effect vanished into an unconnected series of groundless events. Thus science was made impossible, as its fundamental notions of law and causation were denied. Finally, even the externality of the world and the existence of other minds disappear, and nothing is left but a groundless and vanishing phantasmagoria in the consciousness of nobody. Hence we conclude once more that, if there is to be any thought, the objects of thought must form a system or exist in systematic connection.

It is a tradition with the formal logicians that this law of connection belongs to metaphysics rather than to logic. Of course one may limit logic to suit himself, and logic may be limited to the one law of consistency in statement. Such logic is good in its place as a pedagogical discipline, and is always negatively valuable. But it ought not to be called the science of thought, as it ignores the most vital feature of thought. Such a conception of thought is a relic of the period when it was held that perception is a simple process complete in itself, and independent of thought altogether.

If it be said that the law of connection is a law of existence rather than of thought, the answer is that it could never be known as a law of existence if it were not also a law of thought. Since the time of Kant it cannot be questioned as a law of thought; the only doubt is to what extent it is a law of existence. This objection also rests on a precritical conception of knowledge. The mind is supposed to grasp the reality directly without any mediation of thought; or, rather, the reality is supposed to report itself without any mental activity whatever.

Thought, then, which has any relation to truth and knowledge, or which concerns itself at all with its own presuppositions and implications, can never escape making a general metaphysical assumption about its objects and their systematic connection.

The unity of the self, the law of identity, and the fact of objective connection are the fundamental conditions of thought. In themselves, however, they give us no objects, but only the conditions of having and dealing with objects in general. How the mind gets objects is our next inquiry.

CHAPTER III

HOW DOES THE MIND GET OBJECTS?

A MIND is conceivable which should create its objects outright by pure self-activity and without dependence upon anything beyond itself. Such is our conception of the Creator's relation to his objects. But this is not the case with us except to a very slight extent. Our mental life itself begins, and we come only gradually to a knowledge of things and of ourselves. In some sense our objects are given; that is, we cannot have objects at will or vary their properties at our pleasure. In this sense we are passive in knowledge, and no idealism can remove this fact. But in some sense, also, our objects are our own products; for an existing object becomes an object for us only as we think it, and thus make it our object. In this sense knowledge is an active process, and not a passive reception of ready-made information from without. Formal logic only tells what we do with objects after we get them, but not how we get them. Empiricism tells us that we get objects only by experience, but fails to perceive that experience itself rests upon a complex rational activity.

We have, then, to study that activity of thought whereby rational consciousness and articulate experience are made possible. Our study, however, has nothing to do with the temporal order of mental development, but only with its immanent logical principles. These remain the same, whatever the order and rate of development. The present chapter aims only to give a general conception of the process of getting objects as a form of internal activity. The next chapter will treat of the factors of thought more in detail. The trained reader will lose nothing in passing at once to that chapter. But the natural man has such difficulty in grasping knowledge as anything but a passive reception of knowledge completely determined from without that the more general discussion seems pedagogically necessary. This misconception also is the prolific mother of so much confusion and misunderstanding in popular philosophy that some prolixity and repetition may be excused if they even tend toward its removal.

At the base of our thought life is the life of sense. This is something given. By no effort of ours can we produce this life or modify its laws. This, however, does not mean that sensations are poured into the mind from without, as if things threw them off, or as if they were produced by the nerves and furnished ready-made to consciousness. On the contrary, the sensation itself is purely a mental product, an elementary reaction of our sensibility against external action. But these reactions are no products of thought. They result from the structure of our sensibility, and are strictly a datum for the rational nature. If they were not given they could never be produced.

Because of the elementary and factual nature of the sense life, most theories of human thought have started from it as a common ground; and the sensational theory has aimed to exhibit the thought life as only a modification of sense. The untenability of this view has already appeared. Even in the simplest judgment of sense we have found not an interaction of sensations, but an action upon sensations, a unique synthesis by thought. It is, however, a very natural view that the sensations are already completely determined in themselves, so that thought does not

constitute them in any sense, but finds them ready-made.
If, then, we can find some principle of movement and grouping among the sensations whereby they may be united into orders of coexistence and sequence, we need not look beyond them for any special thought principle.

This view of the complete passivity of the mind, at least in sensation, is about self-evident to all minds on the sense plane. Nevertheless, it is mistaken. The constitutive action of thought penetrates even into sensation as an articulate experience; and sensations become anything for thought only through the action of thought itself. This is to be shown.

A sensation in itself, or apart from thought, is simply a peculiar affection of the sensibility. But the sensation as occurring has no unity and no identity. As temporal, its successive phases are mutually external and mutually other, or different. Like an exploding catherine-wheel, the occurring impression sputters all around the circle; and when we attempt to grasp it only a mental blur results, unless the mind fixes the dissolving impression into a single and abiding meaning. Only thus can a sensation become an object for thought.

We have, say, a color sensation, and in this the mind seems to be purely passive and receptive. Of course we cannot have sensations at will, and in this sense we are passive. But even in this passive experience the mind does more than simply read off what is given. For in calling it a sensation, whether in distinction from the self or from other sensations, we already posit it as a definite and self-identical content. The impression, apart from this act of fixation, involves an indefinite multiplicity in itself, just as the motion of a body from A to B is no simple and single thing, but an indefinite number of movements through all the intervening points. And as this motion becomes a single one only as the mind constitutes it such, so the indefinite manifold involved in a sense-impression becomes a single and simple sensation only as the mind constitutes it such. Hence the experience of a single sensation as anything articulate implies, as its absolute condition, that the mind constitute it one and identical. Until this is done the impression is as good as nothing for us. Sensations must be fixed and defined with reference to a permanent meaning before they can be anything for thought. In other words, the color sensation must become a sensation of color.

Now to the sense-bound mind this must seem to be the veriest trifling. The sensation is one as a matter of course; for who would think of calling it two? As to the distinction between a color sensation and a sensation of color, nothing could well be imagined more utterly verbal and barren.

Without doubt so it must seem; for the work of thought is so quick and subtle that it requires some care to recognize it. Thought is amazingly successful in hiding behind itself. We must make an effort to unmask it and bring it to self-recognition.

And, first, as to the unity of the sensation. Let us suppose the impression to last through a certain time. It is plain that the earlier parts of this time are not the later parts. The time, therefore, as occurring is not one but an indefinite manifold. Left to itself it would never become one, for it has no unity in it. Such unity as the time has it owes to the intellect.

But the impression as occurring is equally an indefinite manifold. The impression as occurring in the earlier parts of the time is not the impression as occurring in the later parts of the time. Each impression as existing vanishes with its date, and as the time admits of indefinite division the impression becomes indefinitely many. Where, then, is its unity? Manifestly it has none in itself; it acquires it only through the act of thought which constitutes it one. The impression as occurring is a continuous flow, and thought transforms it into a fixed idea.

And now it should not surprise us to hear common-sense claiming that it is one and the same impression throughout the whole period of its occurrence. But this only illustrates once more the difficulty which untrained thought has in recognizing itself. For the impression is not the same as occurring; it is the same only in the sense that a fixed intellectual meaning is illustrated or expressed in all its phases. But before this can be recognized the fixed meaning must be distinguished from the flowing impression; that is, once more the color sensation must become a sensation of color, which is really a very different thing. The former is the color impression as occurring; the latter is the color impression as the bearer of an abiding and recognizable meaning. The former is a flowing affection of the sensibility; the latter is a timeless idea of the intellect.

This conclusion we reach by a simple analysis of the facts and their implications. It is not claimed that there is no period of passive sensibility preceding the action of thought. A great deal is imagined about that, but not much is known, and the imaginings are largely inconsistent. But whatever the fact may be in this respect, those sensitive states become something for thought only through the constitutive activity of intelligence. For any who think otherwise we propose the problem: Given a flow of states, each of which perishes as fast as it is born, to deduce, or in any way reach, any articulate conception whatever. It is respectfully suggested that all who undertake the problem should carefully refrain from falsifying the question by importing their own knowledge of what is to be deduced into the data of the problem. If this care be exercised it will appear that the temporal, as such, eludes all knowledge until it is brought under the control of a timeless idea.

There is, then, an implicit logical activity in the simplest sensation by the time it is anything for intelligence. This activity finds further and more manifest illustration in the fact of recurrent experience, of which the associationalist makes so much in his theory, and which common-sense finds quite a matter of course. It appears that this fact involves a complex logical activity, and is possible only for an intelligence which has transformed its particular experiences into general conceptions of abiding significance.

How is recurrence in experience possible? The answer is that on the plane of fact, or as a psychological event, recurrence is not possible. All that is possible on this plane is the occurrence of similar experiences, the similarity remaining unrecognized. Recurrence, however, implies identity or continuity, and there is no identity between the sensation occurring yesterday and the similar one occurring to-day. As the recurring day is another day, so the recurring sensation is another sensation. In the field even of simple sensation recurrence is impossible for a merely registering intellect—it is possible only for a universalizing intellect; that is, for an intellect for which the simple experiences are not merely particular vanishing mental events, but also bearers of an abiding rational meaning which is common to all and identical in all. In other words, they must be at least implicitly classified and distinguished from the universal as its concrete specifications.

If, then, we speak of recurring sensations, we have, at least tacitly, risen above the sensations as particular impressions, and are operating with the logical universal. We have reached the universal, unwittingly indeed, but we have reached it nevertheless. This is equally true when we speak of associated sensations. A sensation as event admits of no recall. The actual sensation in its own particular existence can recur as little as past time can recur. The new sensation also which, as event, is here for the first time has never been associated with anything, and could never recall anything. The new event has as little association with past events as the new day has with past days. Thus the doctrine stands still, or vanishes into a grotesque psychological mythology, unless we transfer our thought from the vanishing event to its abiding logical equivalent; and in order to do that we must already have passed beyond the particular to the universal.

Now all this is so foreign to our spontaneous thought that it might easily seem absurd. The work of thought, we have said, is so subtle and so quick that we fail to recognize it. How foreign this is to uncritical thought appears especially from the course of the associational philosophy. That philosophy operates from the start with universals, but it naïvely supposes it is dealing with the unmodified particulars. Its apparent success depends largely upon this confusion.

But a scruple remains behind and presses for utterance. One is uneasy at this liberal attribution of logical work of which we are by no means conscious. One is inclined, then, to lessen the amount of this work by saying that in recurrent experience the particular experiences are all, and that the only further fact is a certain similarity among them. Recurrence in experience means simply the occurrence of similar experiences.

There are cases where this seems to express the objective fact fairly well. It could not, indeed, be applied to our successive experiences of the same thing without landing us in the abysses; but it seems to describe the objective fact in recurrent sensation well enough. But it does not describe the subjective fact at all. The assumed similarity of the occurring experiences implies all that has been said about the implicit presence of the universal. The similarity itself can only mean that an identical or common content finds expression in the many experiences; and however much it may be in the things, it can exist for us only through a logical activity whereby the one element in the many is abstracted and fixed as an abiding meaning.

And thus it turns out that recurrence, even in sense experience, is not the simple, unmediated thing it appears to be, but involves a deal of implicit logical work.

But, we may further ask, considering the separateness of all experiences as events, how can there be any recurrence whatever in experience? As the same thing cannot happen twice, it would seem that recurrence is altogether impossible. This conclusion, as we have pointed out, is correct on the plane of fact, or of a simply registering intelligence. Recurrence is possible only on the plane of the universalizing intelligence. Even recurrence of thought is possible only to a universalizing intelligence; and then it depends on our distinction of thought as a mental event from thought as having contents and validity. Thought as an event can never recur; but the logical contents may be reproduced. Thus, suppose I think triangle in the morning and again in the afternoon. The two acts are not identical. They are separated by time, by their psychological context, and by their own individuality; but the contents are the same. The acts are double as events; they are one in their significance. As events, they are two occurrences; as having meaning, the second occurrence is a recurrence of the first. But the recurrence consists entirely in the identity of meaning. It belongs to the ideal world of logic, and is impossible in the factual world of psychology.

So much for the recurrence of experience. It is almost disheartening after all this to learn that even yet we have made no provision for the experience of recurrence. This demands, in addition to the previous work, that we relate the experiences to self and to one another under the form of time.

This work is commonly supposed to be provided for by memory. Sensations occur in succession, and hence are known in succession, and hence are reproduced in succession as a matter of course. But succession in experience is so little an experience of succession that the former by itself would make the latter impossible. Memory also, as a mental event, is in the present, and all the contents of consciousness are in the present. To introduce time distinctions into consciousness would make consciousness impossible. Hence, if we are to have any experience of recurrence, the mind must first give the form of time to its experience, and by relating the elements of its experience under the form of time, make the distinction of past and present possible.

Thus it appears that for an experience of recurrence, even of sensation, we need (1) to relate our sensations under the form of time, (2) to raise the sensation from a particular event into an abiding logical meaning, and (3) to assimilate the later experience to the earlier by identifying the contents common to both.

Thus in this most elementary experience—so elementary, indeed, as to seem to lie below thought altogether—we find a subtle logical activity implicit. The work is not reflectively done, but is really done, nevertheless. The mind does not yet possess reason, but reason possesses the mind. Under the guidance of the immanent reason we see the mind lifting itself above the flux of impressions into a rational world which, while potential in it from the beginning, only slowly becomes its conscious possession.

What has been said thus far applies to impressions simply as states of consciousness; and we find that they become anything for intelligence only through a constitutive, organizing, classifying activity of thought upon the impressions. These as occurring have to be transformed before they are usable by thought. Thus it appears that articulate sensations are by no means data of passive experience which deliver themselves unmodified in a passive consciousness; and thus it further appears that sensations, which are often looked upon as the elements out of which, by association, intellect is built, are really products of intellect, so far as they are anything intelligible. The raw material itself must receive a mental form before it can enter into the mental structure.

Succession is pre-eminently the law of the cosmical and psychological fact considered in abstraction from intelligence. It is now clear that such a fact can never be an object of knowledge, except through the mediation of some superior principle. Two fixities are needed to make a knowledge of the successive possible: the fixity of the self and the fixity of the idea. With the denial of either of these the knowledge of the successive vanishes altogether.

Here it may occur to some one who has heard of the ideality of time that there is no real succession because there is no real time. This is at best an unfruitful refinement at this place, and, moreover, the doctrine is not very clear in its bearings on the present question. For whether time be ontologically real or not, apparent time is an undeniable element of experience, and the present problem would receive no simplification. For supposing that events are really successive, we have only to explain how a knowledge of succession is possible. But if we suppose that events are not successive we have to explain the appearance of succession, as well as the possibility of knowing it.

Besides, it is not easy to admit that day and night occur together or that the earth is on all sides of the sun at once. The ideality of time must have some other meaning than this, and that meaning lies too deep in the obscurities of metaphysics for present discussion. The relation of the absolute being to the cosmic order is involved, and our present concern is with our human life and knowledge.

The immanent activity of thought in sense experience finds further illustration in the interpretation of the impressions. For thought does not rest in the apprehension of sensations as having simple and identical qualitative contents; it proceeds to relate them variously and interpret them. Only thus does thought reach a world of reality and of rational system.

And here again untrained thought finds it hard to recognize itself. As it seems a matter of course that sensation should be complete in itself without any qualifying action of intelligence, so it seems equally a matter of course that sensation should interpret itself. And so it is, after thought has given sensation a rational significance. After thought has projected sensation as the effect or quality of a thing it is very easy to find the notions of thing, quality, and causation in sensation. After thought has related sensation to self, there is no difficulty in abstracting the notion of self from the sense life. But to get these ideas from the impression as occurring is a problem of another order of difficulty. It is, however, the real problem for those who view mind as the passive recipient of sensations completely qualified from without.

The insolubility of this problem has been manifest to all with eyes to see since the time of Hume. The immediate outcome of such a view is nihilism, in which both subject and object disappear in an indistinguishable haze. Even solipsism is impossible; for the mind reaches itself only through its own rational activity. But crude thought never dreams of distinguishing between the original properties of the impressions and the qualifications they receive from the mind itself. Hence it seems to find a great many things in passive experience which were never there. Sensationalism recognizes the distinction only in a hesitating and uncertain way. From the naïve empiricism of Locke to the more sophisticated associationalism of our day the doctrine has found its chief support in the verbal ambiguity thence resulting. We have already referred to this ambiguity as the traditional means of escape from the nihilism implicit in a consistent sensationalism.

Impressions organized and interpreted by thought may well be a source of information; but impressions left to themselves are nothing intelligible, and reveal nothing intelligible. Articulated sound when informed and interpreted by thought becomes rational speech; but in and by itself it is only noise. Whatever meaning it has is given to it; it can have no meaning for itself. If, now, some speculator should propose to develop language by allowing sounds to associate and evolve meaning for themselves, we should have an exact parallel of the philosophy which aims to build intelligence out of sensation. And if our speculator should be chronically uncertain whether, by language, he means articulated noise or speech informed by thought, he would perfectly illustrate the ambiguity of the sensational philosophy. If, finally, he should conclude from the rationality of speech that the thought is in the words and needs no mind to put it there, since any one with ears can hear the thought, he would also illustrate the difficulty crude thought is under in recognizing itself. It requires more wit than is always present to distinguish between sound and sense, and to see that noise, however loud or long, can never of itself become rational speech.

If we should suppose sensations universally qualified by reference to self as their subject, and to fixed ideas as expressing their qualitative contents, we should still remain within the sphere of the individual consciousness. But a large part of the interpretation of impressions consists in transcending this subjective circle by relating our sensations to a world of real objects which exist apart from our consciousness or knowledge of them. How this is possible we have now to consider.

How do we pass from subjective and discontinuous impressions to objective and identical things? A formal answer is that we get objects by perception. But this is only a name for the process; it does not tell us how perception arises or is possible. In popular thought perception is only a passive reflection of objects; in opposition to this view we seek to show that perception is really an active process by which the mind builds its objects for itself.

Perception is no problem for spontaneous thought; it becomes such only on the development of reflective speculation. Here again thought hides behind itself; and thus it comes to pass that perception, which is a marvellous achievement of thought, is looked upon as a matter of course. Things exist, and the mind reflects them as passively as a mirror reflects the objects before it.

This concentration of the mind upon its objects rather than upon its own processes is a most fortunate circumstance for both mental health and progress. Because of it, the mind is taken out of itself and introduced to the world of things without being delayed among the obscure and intricate processes of knowledge. Had we been left to argue our way from the self to the not-self we should certainly have made sorry work of it, as especially appears from the fact that we are not over-successful in speculatively construing the passage after it is made. If we had to learn to walk from a knowledge of our muscles, we should certainly never get under way; and if we had to learn to perceive by a speculative analysis of the process, we should never progress. Fortunately the elements have been kindlier mixed. Our objects seem so immediately reflected in our passively receptive consciousness that we assume that the system has only to be in order to be both knowable and known. We also seem to be entirely passive in perception, and the object appears to impose itself in its objective reality upon the mind. As for any mysterious processes underlying perception, they so little manifest themselves in consciousness that we must view them as fictions of speculative fancy.

This is how the matter presents itself to spontaneous thought. But a little reflection serves to disturb this easy faith. The existence of the object is not a knowledge of the object. The object itself cannot pass bodily into consciousness, and consciousness cannot expand itself and embrace the existing object. The mind can do nothing but think, and the object can do nothing but be. Hence, unless perception is to be viewed as pure magic, we must contrive some way of bringing the subject and the object together. Thus perception becomes a problem. Our first care must be to get a clearer conception of the problem.

Common-sense assumes that a world of things exists in space and time, altogether apart from mind and consciousness, and we know this world by perception. The assumption itself may be open to doubt in the form given, but it becomes impregnable when changed to read that a cosmic order exists apart from our individual thought and consciousness. The first form is a natural exaggeration of the objectivity of thought, which crude thinking is sure to fall into. The modification proposed rescues the assumption from the objections of the idealist, and leaves it open to us to believe upon evidence that that world, which exists apart from our intelligence, after all exists only in, for, and by a supreme intelligence, instead of existing in hard and fast lumpishness, and externality to all intelligence as common-sense dreams.

But admitting the existence of an order beyond ourselves, our knowledge is not explained. The question remains, How it can become an object for us; and the answer is, Only by thinking it, or constructing it in thought, and thus making it our object.

Two questions are to be kept distinct: first, the existence and nature of the independent order; and, secondly, the process by which it becomes an object for us. Only the latter question is now under discussion.

This problem has difficulties which do not exist for our knowledge of states of consciousness. There we needed an activity of fixation, definition, and classification, but we were not called upon to transcend our consciousness by passing to a world beyond it. But here we have to reach a world of things from states of consciousness which are not things. This demands some new categories, and gives rise to some special difficulties.

There are two general conceptions of the nature of the object—realistic and idealistic; but both alike compel the assumption of a complex constructive activity by the knowing mind as the condition of knowledge.

Naïve realism generally solves the problem by figures of speech. For a long time men amused and confused themselves by speaking of images which are thrown off by the object, and which pass into the mind and mediate a knowledge of the things from which they proceed. This is intelligible only when applied to visual objects. When applied to the other senses, and especially when applied to the rational relations which exist among, if they do not really constitute, objects, the conception has no intelligible meaning, even as a figure of speech. The image of sound, of hardness, of causal relations has no meaning whatever. And even for visual objects, the notion is not to be taken literally. No one could tell what he means by the passage of such images into the mind except as a figurative way of describing the fact of knowledge — a way, moreover, which throws no light upon the process.

Equally worthless are the theories which describe the object as impressing, or stamping, or photographing itself upon the mind. These too are figurative descriptions of the fact, which throw no light upon the process. If we should take these figures in earnest, we should need to know where is the extended mental surface upon which the stamps or impressions are made, and how an impression on the mind, conceived as extended substance, becomes an impression in the mind, conceived as knowing subject. Such views lose all credit, except as rhetorical devices, as soon as we reflect upon the physiological conditions of perception and upon the fact that knowledge can never be passed along ready-made, but arises and exists only in and through the cognitive act.

In all developed realistic views which do not call in God as the mediator of knowledge, perception rests in some way on an interaction between the mind and the object. We get from subject to object, it is said, by the category of cause and effect. This is open to many doubts when, by the object, we understand not merely something independent of ourselves, but the apparently perceived object. To all appearance, the latter is in the passive voice; and it requires some ingenuity to make it the cause of its own perception. We pass over these scruples, however, and point out that in all interaction nothing passes between the agents; but each reacts according to its own nature, so that the reaction in every case is nothing carried into the agent from without, but is rather an expression of the agent's nature under the circumstances. If, then, a mind react against external action by generating feelings, thoughts, and knowledge within itself, these are not to be viewed as carried into the mind, but as generated by the mind. This is true even for sensations.

This abstract argument is not strengthened, but is made concrete for the imagination by considering the physical antecedents of perception, as they are reported by the physiologists. By universal agreement these antecedents consist in some form of nervous change; and this is totally unlike things, on the one hand, and thoughts, on the other. If, then, thought does actually follow upon the nervous change, we can only view it as something generated by the mind within itself. As the spoken word or the printed page contains no thought, but is only the occasion upon which a living mind thinks out of itself, so the nervous changes contain no thought, but are only the occasion upon which a living mind thinks out of itself. One who does not know how to read would look in vain for meaning in a printed page, and in vain would he seek to help his failure by using strong spectacles. Language has no meaning except for one who furnishes the meaning out of himself. Where the mental insight is lacking, eye-glasses and ear-trumpets are of no avail.

And here is a great wonder. That a mind, without pattern or copy, upon occasion of nervous changes, of which, moreover, it knows directly nothing and commonly knows nothing whatever, should develop out of itself the vision and knowledge of the world is the wonder of wonders. But we hide it from ourselves for the most part by ignoring it, or, rather, by being ignorant of it. If the fact be called to our attention, we seek to reduce the wonder, first, by identifying the nervous change with the subjective impression, and, secondly, by regarding the impression as already the impression of things. But the impression itself, so far as subjective, is already a mental reaction; and the interpretation of its objective significance is the wonder in question. The naïve notion that we know reality immediately and compare our thoughts with it, and thus find a standard for our copying needs no consideration.

Even if we should view perception as an immediate revelation there would be the same necessity for a constructive activity on the part of the percipient; for a revelation can take place only by stimulating the mind to think the thought to be revealed. Nothing could be revealed to a stone, even if the matter were chiselled into it. No high truth could be revealed to an idiot, however fluent he might become in the repetition of the verbal forms. In order to the reception of any knowledge whatever the appropriate activity of the subject is as necessary as the existence of the object.

And yet, in spite of this exposition, common-sense continues uneasy. The object seems so immediately and undeniably given, and we are so little conscious of any complex activity in perception, that we conclude there must be some mistake. It cannot be that we have been talking prose all our lives without knowing it.

The difficulty here arises from a double oversight. First, we suppose that the existence of the object is in question. Hence we suppose that, if we are sure of that existence, there is no further question. The illusion is apparent. No conviction of the reality of the object throws any light on the process of perception.

Secondly, we fail to distinguish what is in the sense from

what is in thought, and thus we easily delude ourselves into thinking that the unaided sense puts the object bodily before us. But a glance at any painting or drawing, or even at a mirror, serves to dispel this illusion. Here the thing seen—that is, the thing that is in the sense—commonly drops out of perception altogether, and thought busies itself with the meaning. In such cases we have a clear illustration of how the mind puts before itself a group of related objects which are not in the sense at all. The objects are before the mind, but they are not in the sense; and they are before the mind through its own constructive activity.

Thus far on the realistic view of the object.

In the idealistic view there is no thought of an interaction between the mind and its object. The object itself is already conceived as a thought; not yours or mine, indeed, but a divine thought. But this view as little explains perception as the previous one. The problem how to make that thought ours forthwith emerges, and we are as badly off as ever. Vague references to an eternal or absolute consciousness contain no solution as long as that consciousness is other than our own. We have a new theory of the object, but not much light on the problem of knowledge. The dualism inherent in human knowing is untouched; for, whereas on the realistic view we have a world of things over against our thought, on the idealistic view we have an objective divine thought over against our thought. On both views we have the problem of reproducing in human thought the objective fact, be it real or ideal; and this problem admits of only one solution on either view. That the world should exist as a divine thought does not imply its existence for my thought any more than the possession of knowledge by the teacher implies its possession by the pupil. Some provision must be made for impartation.

And here idealism has too often contented itself with figures of speech. We are said to share or participate in the divine thought, or to enter into it; but we are not told how this is to be done. There can be no sharing in the sense that the thought is broken up and parcelled out. The only way in which I can share or enter into another's thought is by thinking his thought for myself; and until I do this the thought is non-existent for me. In conversation no thoughts pass between the speakers, but each mind thinks and thus grasps the other's thought.

With similar unclearness it is said that the eternal consciousness reproduces itself in the finite consciousness, and sometimes the divine thought and our thought are identified outright. Different mathematicians have not many geometries, but only one; so all thinkers have not many truths, but the one truth, which is the divine thought common to them all. But this identity at best is only a logical one; i in no way removes the fact that the common truth can be grasped only through a series of special activities by each individual thinker. If we should venture the further suggestion that each thinker and all his thinkings are phases of the divine thinking, we should lose ourselves in hopeless nonsense. All our confusion, blundering, and error would thereby be made divine.

If, then, the world be essentially God's thought, it becomes our thought only as we, by our own mental activity, build up that thought for ourselves, and thus share or participate in it. This work can never be done for us by any outside party, and still less by any figure of speech.

The difficulty with all views which deny or ignore the activity of the mind in perception is that they turn thought into a kind of thing which can exist apart from thinking, and can be passed bodily along. Such views find ready acceptance in that stage of thought where only sense forms are conceivable; but they vanish of themselves as soon as it is seen that knowledge arises and exists only in and through the knowing act, and that this act can be performed by no one for another, but only by each for himself.

The conclusion is that a world of things can exist for us only as the mind reconstructs it as a world of thought. If we prefer to say that the real world is already a world of thought, then the conclusion is that the world of objective thought becomes anything for us only as we rethink it and thus constitute it our object. However real or ideal the world may be, it becomes an object for us only as the mind builds up in consciousness a system of conceptions, and relates their contents under the various forms of intelligence.

This conclusion is valid for even the simplest forms of perception. Not even the sense elements of knowledge pass bodily from the object into the mind. Primarily, they are only reactions of our sensitive nature against external action; and, in fact, it turns out that there is nothing corresponding to them in external reality. They are only projections of our sensitive states, and have no existence apart from consciousness.

In organized knowledge the constructive mental activity is still more manifest. This knowledge is so far from passing ready-made from the object into the mind, that it is not given even in our perceptions themselves, but is constructed only at great expense of time and labor. Simple perception rests on the surface and grasps only appearances. It reaches no science and no system. Reflection, on the other hand, seeks to pass behind the visible forms, and in so doing it profoundly modifies all our spontaneous convictions. To see this we need only reflect on the difference between the physicist's, or chemist's, or geologist's, or astronomer's thought of reality and that of the child or boor. The conceptions are incommensurable. In all of this work we see the mind constituting, correcting, revising, enlarging its conceptions, and thus building itself into a truer knowledge of its objects.

In its perceptive activity the mind finds its objects in the world of things. But it also finds a highly complex system of objects in itself, or in its own subjective, social, and historical manifestations. The great sciences which belong to this field, as ethics, economics, law, politics, philosophy were not discovered ready-made, but are rather the slow product of generations of mental activity, in which the mind has sought to fix, define, and systematize its conceptions for the better expression and understanding of its own experience.

An abiding order, independent of our finite and individual thinking, and in this sense a real order, is the necessary presupposition and implication of our thinking. And this order becomes our subject or our mental possession only through our own activity. In this way existence slowly passes into knowledge.

And now we must have a parting word with the child of the dragon's teeth, as Plato calls the disciple of the senses. After all, he asks, does this complex activity you speak of mean anything more than this, that we are able to know things? The reply is that it means nothing more than that. At the same time it is worth while to add that this ability to know things, which our friend thinks so simple, really implies this complex activity.

In leaving this subject, however, it must be pointed out that the previous discussion is not meant in any way as an explanation of knowledge, as if it were a recipe by following which knowledge might be compounded. It describes the process and some of the implications of knowing; but no reflection and no analysis of notions will ever enable us to deduce knowledge from that which is not knowledge.

Knowledge is knowledge, and knowledge must be its own vindication. But knowledge has conditions and implications, and these may be discovered. In the deepest sense of the term, we must be content with knowing, not how knowledge is possible, but that it is possible.

Nevertheless, the thought activity involved in knowing is beyond all question. We pass now to consider the leading forms and laws of this activity more in detail.

CHAPTER IV

THE CATEGORIES

WE have now to study those immanent mental principles which underlie articulate experience and make it possible. They are the norms by which the mind proceeds, implicitly or explicitly, in fixing, defining, and relating its objects. They constitute the framework of thought, and form the contents of the pure reason. These principles, in accordance with a philosophic tradition of long standing, we call the categories; but any other name will do as well, provided the thing be understood. In adopting this name, however, we assume no responsibility for any historical scheme of the categories such as that of Aristotle or Kant. The only contention is that there are immanent principles underlying experience, and these we proceed to study.

The recognition of the categories as immanent principles determining mental procedure is exceedingly difficult to two classes of persons, the naïve disciples of common-sense and the professional empiricists. The former think it sufficient to say that, on looking over our system of objects, we find them existing in certain general relations, as space and time, cause and effect, quantity and quality. These classes are the categories; but instead of being principles which determine experience, they are manifestly given in experience, and, as formal principles, they are only abstractions from experience. Many empiricists would agree with this view; others would simply add the claim that the categories are products or precipitates of sense experience under the principle of association.

Both of these views rest on an inability to grasp thought as an organic activity. Common-sense finds no activity in thought whatever, but only a passive reflection of existing objects and relations. Empiricism attempts to reach thought by a mechanical juxtaposition of mutually external elements, and fails to see that there can be no thought without an organic synthesis within the unity of the mind itself. Both of these views have been already set aside.

Apart from this fundamental difficulty, another obstacle to insight on the part of these classes arises from a mistaken expectation. There seems to be a demand that the categories as principles should reveal themselves as such in consciousness. This is a mistake. As we walk in entire ignorance of our muscles, so we often think in entire ignorance of the principles which underlie and determine thinking. But as anatomy reveals that the apparently simple act of walking involves a highly complex muscular activity, so analysis reveals that the apparently simple act of thinking involves a system of mental principles. In neither of these cases is the appeal to the uneducated consciousness, but to the indications of analysis. The anatomist shows the muscles and the part they play, although they do not reveal themselves in consciousness. In like manner, the anatomist of thought shows the implicit principles by analyzing the products of thought. The validity of his results can never be tested by appealing to the "natural or unsophisticated consciousness," but only by examining his analysis. It is important to bear this fact in mind in the present inquiry, as it often happens that superficial students fancy the categories, as determining principles of intelligence, are sufficiently discredited by the fact that they are not revealed in the unreflective consciousness.

The exceeding difficulty which minds on the sense plane experience in grasping the immanent principles of intelligence leads us to attempt another illustration. A law of growth cannot be sensuously presented; it can only be intellectually apprehended. Nevertheless, the facts of organic growth cannot be understood without affirming an immanent law in the organism which determines the order and kind of development. The law cannot be seen in itself, but it is manifested in its results. The law is not something in the organism which the organism uses to grow with, but it is rather that immanent principle of growth without which the unfolding of the organism could not be understood. It is indeed conceivable that some one, low in the scale of mental development, should call for a sight of the law, and, in default of such vision, should denounce the conception of a law of growth as fictitious or mythological; but even common-sense would recognize that his difficulty was purely subjective.

The categories are such immanent principles. They are nothing which can be shown to the senses; they are manifested in the mental product. They are not principles which the mind uses to know with, but they determine the form of knowing. They are not empty forms of the pigeon-hole type into which the mind sorts its experience; but they are the organic principles by which experience is built up. They are as necessary to the understanding of experience as the law of growth is necessary to the understanding of organic form, and they are equally unpicturable.

Whoever will duly reflect upon these things will see that the categories are not set aside by inventing terms and phrases of dislike and impatience, or even by inflicting upon them the indignity of inverted commas. For thinking does involve a highly complex activity of determination and relation, and the norms of this activity must be immanent in the activity itself.

With expressions of apology to those who feel the tedium of this incessant repetition, we venture to set forth the old claim from a slightly different angle of view.

Thought is to a very great extent a relating activity, and the progress of thought consists largely in establishing rational relations among the raw materials of our experience. Indeed, our objects are so largely defined and constituted by their relations that nothing articulate would remain if the element of relation were eliminated. But the natural assumption of spontaneous thought is that objects are given without any qualifying action on the part of the mind, and these objects exist in relations and are known in relations as a matter of course. The existent relation explains the known relation.

This view is at once natural and erroneous. The relations of things, so far as they exist for thought, are instituted by thought, and the relations instituted can only be viewed as objective expressions of principles immanent in thought itself.

Two questions are to be distinguished here: (1) How do objects come to be related in existence? (2) How do they become related for us or for our thought?

The former question does not now concern us. Respecting it many metaphysical scruples might be raised. We might claim with Locke that relations are only the work of the mind, and are non-existent apart from mind, so that things in themselves are unrelated. Or we might hold with others that relations are the work of mind, and that things are really related; and then the conclusion would follow that the world of related things can exist only in and through a relating cosmic intelligence. Locke drew the wrong conclusion from his premises. But we forbear to raise these questions, and consider solely the condition of things being related for us, whatever they may be in themselves, or however they came to be related in themselves.

In answer to this question we must say that, as the existence of objects is not a knowledge of the objects, so the existence of objects in relations is not a knowledge of the relations. Things can be related for our thought only as they are related by our thought. If we insist that our thought grasps relations already existing we must also insist that it does so only by reinstituting them, just as the mind grasps thoughts already existing only by rethinking them. The fact of relation is revealed only in the act of relation.

This would be true if all the relations of thought could be found in the sensations themselves. As existing objects become known objects only by constructing them in thought, so existent relations become known relations only by constructing them in thought. But, in fact, the most important relations by which knowledge is constituted do not exist among sensations as mental states at all; neither are they like the simple relations of qualitative resemblance or difference which we might think the mind simply reads off from sense experience; they are rather contributed by the understanding to the formation and interpretation of experience. Thus, relations of space, causation, identity do not exist among sensations as mental states; they are the form which the mind gives its experience in passing from impressions to objects.

In treating the categories several ways are open to us. We might begin with (1) the logically first, (2) the psychologically first, and (3) the logically simplest. In the first case, we should begin with being as the basal conception upon which all others depend, and should then proceed to the other categories in the supposed order of their dependence. In the second case, we should have to guess a little, but should probably begin with being under the special form of thing. Sensations may be temporally first in the history of the individual, but they certainly are not the primary objects of consciousness. Indeed, until the power of abstraction has been developed to some extent, the conception of a sensation except as the quality of an object is impossible. In the third case, we begin with categories which are involved in our mental tastes themselves, and then proceed to the metaphysical categories which lie outside of the mental states altogether.

The psychological method is here irrelevant. Whatever the psychological order of development may be, the significance of the thought factor is unchanged. As between the other two methods, the question of chief importance is not which category we discuss first, but what we say, whichever we discuss first. The third method, however, has the advantage of enabling us to begin with categories on which all agree, and to note the parting of the ways when we reach it. On this account we adopt it. We are not to be understood, however, as holding that the categories are really unfolded in a corresponding temporal order. On the contrary, the organic nature of reason would lead us to expect that all the categories are implicit from the start. And this expectation is justified by analysis. The simpler phenomenal categories admit of no application except in connection with the deeper metaphysical principles. We treat them successively, but they really coexist.

The simplest relation possible among our objects is that of likeness and unlikeness. Not even this is passively received from without, as it involves an activity of fixation, discrimination, comparison, and judgment. There is no likeness which delivers and registers itself upon a passive consciousness. There may be feelings which accompany the perception of likeness, but such feelings would not be the perception. Without raising the scruple whether likeness as such can even exist apart from intelligence, it suffices here to point out that in any case the existence of likeness is quite distinct from its recognition. The latter is possible only through the activity of intelligence.

The judgment of likeness may be in very simple matter, and the likeness itself may be only vaguely qualitative, as in the case of many sensations and feelings. A mind which could form such a judgment would be said to have the power of perceiving likeness and difference. Or the judgment may be in very complex and abstract matter, as in scientific or historical analogies. Such a judgment also might be said to rest on a power of perceiving likeness and difference; and hence it might be concluded that the essential power of the mind is the power of perceiving likeness and difference. This has seemed to many a great simplification, and to make it simpler still they have fixed their thought on the perception of likeness and difference in the field of simple sensation, and here it seemed to be almost a matter of course.

But this simplification is illusive. The power of perceiving likeness and difference is no simple, homogeneous faculty; it is as complex as the mind itself. Likeness and unlikeness are not independent ideas; they imply some special relation under which they are discerned. Things may be like in form, or date, or quality, or quantity, or function, or causal relation; and no one can discern these several kinds of likeness who is not furnished with the corresponding ideas. There is, therefore, no simplification in declaring that the mind has simply the power of discerning likeness and difference, for the points in which they are discovered may form a highly complex system. It is like the claim sometimes made that the essential mental faculty is that of generalization. This claim may be allowed if we recognize that this faculty acts in incommensurable fields, producing temporal, spatial, causal, and other generalizations. But with this rider the claim reduces to a purely verbal simplification.

Resemblance, then, may be the great category of science. Knowledge may be only a detection of likenesses and differences. Science itself may be but the discovery of the one in the many, or of the identical in the different. But such propositions, however true they may be, or whatever their rhetorical value, contain no real simplification of logical processes, and are barren of any valuable insight.

Time

Time is the first independent relation we consider. It is, in brief, the form under which we relate events. Its essential elements are antecedence and sequence; and its dimensions are past, present, and future.

Concerning the relation itself there is very general agreement. All are content to accept this category as simple and irreducible. Disputes concern chiefly the source of the idea and the metaphysical nature of time.

On the former point there are several views:

1. It is said that events occur in succession, and hence are known in succession as a matter of course. The mind simply reads off the succession as given in experience.

2. The idea of time is derived by abstraction from the experience of objective sensation revealed in memory.

3. Time is primarily a law of thought whereby the mind relates events under the form of antecedence and sequence, and thus makes the temporal experience possible. Given the temporal experience, we may by abstraction get the idea of time; but the temporal experience itself is possible **only** through a peculiar relating activity of thought.

Of the first view it is to be said that the occurrence of events in succession does not provide for our knowledge of them as successive. However real the objective relation may be in itself, it must in some way become real for us before it can become an object of knowledge.

But this seems provided for by the second view. The succession in the world beyond us gives rise to successive impressions in consciousness, and this succession of impressions is of course temporal, and nothing is needed but to read off the fact as revealed in memory.

This is so sun-clear that it seems almost like an affront to good sense to question it. And yet upon reflection the clearness proves to be an illusion. It is plain to any one on a little thought that simple succession in experience is far from being an experience of succession. If each event were forgotten with its date, no conception of the past could ever arise. There would be succession of experiences, but no experience of succession. Thus even common-sense can be made to see that without memory there could be no temporal experience for us, whatever there might be for lookers-on from the outside.

But memory becomes memory proper only as the temporal relation is presupposed. Memory as an act or event, if it be in time at all, must be in the present, and all its data must be in the present. There is no temporal relation among these data considered as states of consciousness. To admit such relation would make consciousness impossible. The fact can only be some qualitative feature of the states of consciousness, and this feature becomes the stimulus to the mind to relate the contents of consciousness to the self and to one another under the temporal form. Until this is done we have no memory and no temporal experience. And this relating act can never be done for the mind; it must always be done by the mind and by each mind for itself. However time may exist by itself, it can exist for us only as we relate our objects to the unity and identity of self-consciousness under the temporal form.

Of course this does not mean that the temporal category is applied to events already known as such. This would indeed be a work of supererogation. It rather means that the events become known as such only through the act of relation. Apart from this act, they are non-existent for thought.

Thus the second view of the source of the temporal idea breaks down. The experience from which the idea of time is abstracted is one which contains it, and it contains it only because the mind has already given its experience the temporal form.

We are shut up, then, to the third view. The essential relation of antecedence and sequence is established by the mind itself, and only thus does it become a relation for mind. The necessity of the relation does not lie primarily in the events, but in the mind; and the properties of time are to be understood from the side of this relating act. As all events are related by the same law and in a common scheme, time is said to be one. The unity consists entirely in the fact of a single system of relations according to the same law, so that from any point whatever in the system we can find our way to any other by a continuous process. If there were any events which could not be related in one scheme, time would not be one. But as no event can be conceived which cannot be thus related, time is not only one; it is also infinite and all-embracing. But the unity and infinity of time are only consequences of the fact that the law of synthesis is one and extends to all events.

Ordinarily we do not extend the temporal synthesis beyond adjacent events. We give these the relation of antecedence and sequence, and ignore their relation to other events or groups of events. The unity and infinity of time commonly lie latent in the background of our thought.

The consciousness of time, then, is not a passive mirroring of an objective succession. It rests ultimately upon a mental activity whereby the contents of consciousness are temporally related to one another and to the abiding self. This gives us the consciousness of subjective time. This form of relation is next extended to the cosmic order, and thus the belief in objective time arises.

It would be hard to announce a view more scandalous to uncritical thought. Do not events really succeed one another? it will ask; and do we not remember events in their succession? Is not, then, this notion of a law of synthesis, or relation, immanent in intelligence, purely gratuitous, to say the least? It will certainly seem so, in spite of our exposition, to all who are naturally a little dull. The difficulty which others, more favored, feel is due to a failure to grasp the real problem. It is not now a question whether events really succeed one another, but what is involved in their being successive for us. It is not a question whether we can remember events in their succession, but what such memory implies. The objector takes as data the results of our mental activity, and when we point out that these alleged data are possible only through previous mental processes, he seems to fancy that the data are in some way denied. When finally he is brought to consider the problem how to transform succession in experience into experience of succession, he promptly confuses his own knowledge that the sensations are successive with the emergence of that knowledge among the sensations themselves, and the problem is victoriously solved.

Questions concerning the nature of objective time we postpone to metaphysics. There are a good many reasons for thinking that time is only a category of experience and not an ontological fact. But here it suffices to have shown that time is primarily a law of mental synthesis whereby we relate events. If there be no objective time, of course it is a mental product; and if there be an objective time, we can know it only through a subjective activity according to a subjective law.

The determination of the units and measures of time belongs to the special sciences.

Number

Relations of time make possible the development of the relation of number. The succession of moments and events gives us the basis of number. On this account Kant called number the science of time, as geometry is the science of space. In this view he was led on by his desire for symmetry rather than by the facts themselves. The objective basis of number is the distinctness of objects, and not merely the sequence of moments or events. The discriminated difference is the essential thing, and this is as possible with differences in space, or degree, or unpicturable consciousness as with differences in time.

It is a very natural fancy of crude thought that number exists in the objects, and that all the mind has to do is to read off the existing number. Number adheres so closely to the objects that to know them seems to be the same as knowing their number. But this seeming is illusory. However countable experience may be in itself, it becomes the counted only through a new and peculiar form of action upon that experience. This involves the establishment of a unit and a process of counting. Neither of these operations is anything which does itself.

The unit does not establish itself; for one and the same object may be one or many, according to the point of view or the mental aim. Even spatial objects have no inherent unity, while in most cases, as in scientific measurements, the units are purely arbitrary. The unit of work, of temperature, of time, of space, not only does not determine itself, but its determination is a matter of great difficulty.

Supposing units established, they do not count themselves. Eyes cannot see the number. Simple staring at a group of objects will never report their number. Number is grasped only through a process of counting, and number exists only as things are united by the mind in numerical relations.

And here two sets of very worthy persons will begin to grow uneasy if not impatient. First, the naïve disciple of common-sense will ask if counting things does anything to the things—if it makes their number or reveals it. To which the reply is that these questions reveal once more the chronic difficulty common-sense has in recognizing that thought is an active process. Accordingly, when the claim is made that counting is a mental activity, and that number exists not for sense but for thought, common-sense fancies that number has been denied. Then it proceeds to count the objects in order to prove that things really have number. Schelling was quite right in saying that philosophy is not everybody's affair.

The traditional empiricist also insists on getting the floor. He has quite a list of stories about savages who cannot count beyond their fingers, or who cannot even count at all, but, like the lower animals, remember each thing independently. Now what, he asks, is the significance of these facts in their bearing upon the origin of number? We answer, Their significance is nothing. For the question is not how the numerical activity begins, or whether it always begins, or whether it often has only a crude and obscure development. These are psychological questions which concern only the temporal order of development; they do not touch the logical question as to what is involved in the numerical activity, whenever and however it may begin. Our claim is simply that whatever the temporal and psychological history of the numerical function may be, it is something forever distinct from any passive affection of the sensibility. Its source and its law are to be sought within.

In numerical science the unit is the abstract form of an act of position, and number arises from the repetition of this act under the synthetic form of counting. In this way we reach the numerical series of the so-called natural numbers, and by varying the processes we reach the elementary numerical operations. These, however, soon become so complicated that special processes have to be invented. In this way the mind builds up a great ideal world of number where the notions, processes, methods, and tests are all purely mental creations without any analogue in objective experience. Powers, roots, logarithms, differentials, integrals, limits, and rates are illustrations. Here the mind creates its own data and processes and problems, and tests them all by its own insight. Sense is so far from being the source of these matters that it cannot even test them after they are created.

To develop the idea of number and unfold its forms and implications belongs to arithmetic and algebra.

The concrete application of number presupposes classification. Otherwise there is neither one nor many. The determination of the unit also is a difficult matter when number, which is essentially discontinuous, is used to measure the continuous. Units of time, distance, energy, intensity, work are illustrations. Such units are relative and formal only. This is the case, indeed, with most of our units. They are units only with reference to our aim or standard of reference, and may be one, or many, as the point of view changes. This is particularly the case with spatial and temporal units. The mutual externality of parts and the resulting indefinite divisibility of any assumed unit forbid us to find any ultimate unit in space and time. What constitutes real substantial unity in distinction from formal and relative unity is a metaphysical problem of some difficulty.

A history of the units employed in weighing and measuring would be a large part of the history of physical science and an important chapter in the history of civilization.

Space

The relations of time and number may be said to be founded in the mental states themselves. These states are events, and they are a manifold. In the temporal and numerical synthesis, therefore, the mind may seem to add nothing to the events, but only to read off what is there. It is otherwise with the relations of space. These do not exist among our impressions as states of the sensibility, but only among our objects. That is, impression a is not alongside of impression b, but the objects a and b are projected in mutual externality.

Of course, unreflective thought identifies the existence of things in space with a knowledge of the same. But here again reflection on the general fact that a relation can exist for the mind only in and through the relating act disposes of this view. Reflection also on the physiological conditions of perception shows that if out of them a conception of objects in space relations is ever to emerge, it can be only as the mind posits its objects and gives them space relations on its own account.

The possibility of doing this, even when there is no question of a real space and real objects, is seen in every vivid dream. Dream objects are not in space, but have the form of space; and the space in which they appear is not something which contains them; it is rather the form of the dream. In such cases we have a perfect illustration of the space-relating activity of thought whereby spatial experience is produced. We need a space to hold things as little as we need a space to dream in.

However real, then, space may be as an objective fact. it can exist for the mind only as we give our objects space relations. Until we relate them spatially they are not in space for us. Space, like time, is primarily a law of mental synthesis, whereby the mind relates its coexistent objects under the form of mutual externality. Secondarily, space is the abstract form of external experience. What space is ontologically we leave to metaphysics.

The fact that space relations do not exist among states of consciousness but only among objects has caused the sensationalists no small embarrassment. For all those who identify existence in relations with a knowledge of the relations, the claim is plausible that the temporal idea may be deduced from the successions of experience. But to deduce a spatial externality from sensations which are not mutually external is a task of another order of difficulty.

Those who need it may find some help to a better appreciation of the problem and its difficulties in the following exposition: The stream of thought as a psychological process has no spatial qualities. There may be ideas of bulk, but there are no bulky ideas. There may be ideas of distance, but there are no distances between ideas. The thought of triangle is as little triangular as the thought of sugar is sweet, or the thought of fire is hot. To introduce spatial qualities bodily into consciousness would, of course, be incompatible with the unity of consciousness—that is, with the possibility of consciousness; and it would lead to such nonsense as that the thought of the distance of the earth from the sun is ninety-five millions of miles long.

Plainly, we have to distinguish between the qualities of the thought, considered as a mental act, and the qualities of the object which the thought grasps. The stream of thought, then, as conscious process, has no spatial qualities; and thus the problem arises, How can the ideas of bulk, distance, direction, emerge in that which has no bulk, or distance, or direction? We have to deduce spatial properties and spatial relations from that which is spaceless.

In this strait, sensationalism has had recourse to two devices. One is to identify the idea of space with the idea of time, complicated with certain muscular and tactual sensations. The other is to evolve the idea as a resultant of interacting temporal sensations. Neither device has been clearly conceived or steadily distinguished from the other. Both alike are failures. There is no way of expressing a logarithmic spiral, or a cycloidal curve, or an elliptical function in terms of time and touch; and there is no assignable reason why sensations which are purely temporal should ever give rise to something incommensurable with them.

The conclusion is that space relations exist for the mind only as it establishes them among its objects, and the necessity for their establishment lies primarily in the mind itself. How the mind can do this of course there is no telling. How non-spatial thought can have spatial intuition is quite beyond us. We have to content ourselves with recognizing the fact that it can have such intuition because it does have it, and with showing the fatuity of looking for the source of the intuition elsewhere than in a law of the mind itself.

We have, then, in space and spatial qualities, not a reading off of the properties of sense impressions considered as qualitative states of the sensibility, but a peculiar form imposed upon them by the mind itself.

What was said of the unity and infinity of time applies

equally to space. We relate our objects in a common scheme, and thus space appears to be one. We relate all our objects in the one scheme, and thus space appears to be all-embracing. Finally, the form of relation admits of indefinite repetition, and thus space appears to be infinite. But the unity is simply the unity of the law. The all-embracing character of space means simply the applicability of this law to all external objects. The infinitude of space is only the inexhaustibility of the spatial synthesis. None of these properties is a direct apprehension of objective fact, but only an implication of the space law.

In daily experience we seldom extend the spatial synthesis beyond surrounding objects. These we relate in mutual externality and relative position. Beyond this we seldom go. The unity and infinity of space lie latent in thought and only emerge upon occasion. Often we leave our objects so unrelated that we do not seem to be in space at all. At other times we fail to relate our several groups, and seem to have several spaces. The objects of successive creations of the imagination are alike spatial in that they have the space form, but they cannot be united in any common space. We experience something of the same kind in travelling when we drop out the intermediate links between successive spatial groups. We believe that they could be united in a common space intuition, but so far as the experience itself goes there is nothing to compel it or even to suggest it. For this there is needed a certain continuity of experience, and it is quite conceivable that our experience should have been such that we should never have united our objects in a single spatial scheme.

It seems amazingly clear that things are in space rather than in space relations, but when we attempt to tell what the deeper meaning is in the former expression we find ourselves groping. The truth seems to be that the two expressions reduce to the same. The fact, however, is to be noticed that the actual relations of objects do not exhaust the possible ones; and thus arises the conception of infinite possible relations, of which the actual are only a limited number. This conception of other possible relations may be the underlying thought in saying that things are in space rather than in space relations.

As in the case of number, the spatial synthesis may go on in pure abstraction from concrete objects. In this way we reach the conception of space as a whole. In the continuous synthesis of abstract positions we become aware that the process has no end, and that from any point in the scheme the way is open to any other. Thus we come to the consciousness of the unity and all-embracing nature of space. In this same abstract activity the mind generates the conceptions of pure geometry—the point, the line, the angle, the surface, the solid, etc. To unfold the contents of the pure space intuition in this abstract sense is the function of geometry in its various forms.

In our every-day determinations of space there is a curious relativity due to the fact that we make ourselves, and more particularly our own heads, the centre of our space, or the origin of the axes of reference. Here and there, up and down, right and left, before and behind, are illustrations. These terms have no meaning for the pure space intuition, but only for that intuition as modified by the experience of a physical organism.

Motion

A mixed category, implying both space and time, yet not given in either or both, is motion. It implies both; for motion is unthinkable apart from space and time; and yet it is undefinable in terms of anything but itself. If we think only of coexistent points of space, we have no motion. If we think only of successive moments of time, again we have no proper motion. If we define motion as change of place, or as the passage of a body from one place to another, we only give the meaning of the word; the idea is implied in the definition.

Quantity

In comparing some experiences we become aware of a qualitative likeness or unlikeness. In comparing some others we become aware at once of a qualitative likeness and of another order of likeness or unlikeness. The experience of this second order is the fundamental fact in the experience of quantity. Quantity refers to an order of likeness and difference within qualitative likeness, and the changes within qualitative constancy are quantitative. When there is no qualitative likeness there can be no quantitative comparison. A noise is neither greater nor less than a color; the two are incommensurable. We might possibly think a clap of thunder greater than a flash of lightning, but only as we subsumed both under a common point of view—say, the amount of subjective disturbance or shock.

Quantity cannot be defined in terms of anything but itself, and we have to go back to the original comparison of experiences of like quality to get the fundamental meaning. This is true for quantity itself, and for its three dimensions of equal, greater, or less.

The quantity of anything is primarily its magnitude, whether of extension, duration, or intensity. In this there is nothing relative any more than there is in a simple quality. Without quantity in this sense the conception of both being and quality would vanish. In this general sense we may say that all concrete things and qualities are quanta. But when we come to measure quantity then an element of relativity appears. This is seen in the fact that there is no absolute unit of quantity, and that nothing is absolutely great or small. All magnitudes depend for their numerical value upon the unit of measure; and this is relative to our aim, or convenience, or some feature of our experience. From this it further follows that in any concrete case of continuous quantity the magnitude is really a ratio of one quantity to another, for the assumed unit is itself quantity.

It is common to speak of quantity as continuous and discontinuous. Continuous quantity exists in the three forms of extension, duration, and intensity. The first two forms relate respectively to spatial and temporal magnitudes, the third relates to whatever qualities have degree. All three of these forms are measured by number. How much? means, How many? When no definite number is given there is an implicit reference to some standard, and the quantity is simply determined as large or small, or as equal, greater, or less.

Discontinuous quantity consists of numbers and of discrete objects which may be counted. These have all the dimensions of quantity. They may be large or small, equal, greater, or less.

In the study of social and economic questions quantity appears in the form of statistics, giving rates, ratios, averages, etc.

The notion of quantity moves entirely within the field of qualitative likeness. When, then, unlike qualities appear, they defy any common quantitative treatment unless they can be reduced to quantitative variations of a common unit. Hence the joy in the scientific world when apparently unlike phenomena are reduced to phases of one quantitative process.

When the notion of quantity can be applied, and the quantity itself accurately measured, an exactness of conception becomes possible which is otherwise unattainable

It is then possible to apply the science of number to the matter and develop our data to any desired extent. It is this fact which makes quantity so prominent a category in physical science, and which leads to the hasty assertion that nothing is science which is not quantitative. It is not, however, the bare notion of quantity which is so fruitful, but rather the possibility of exact measurement. Where this is not given we may still insist that all things and qualities and activities are quanta, extensive or intensive, but we are no better off than before. We must also be on our guard against a false show of quantitative accuracy when the case does not admit of it, as when one reports his health on a scale of one hundred. Number is exact, but it cannot make vagueness accurate or sense out of nonsense.

The development of the units, measures, and relations of quantity belongs to the special sciences. It suffices here to have shown the significance of the category, and to point out that the great quantitative sciences, pure and applied, are not picked up ready-made on the field of sense experience, neither are they the precipitate of any random association. On the contrary, they are the magnificent product of thought in its effort to master experience and rise into self-possession.

Space, time, motion, and quantity, with number for their measure, are the great elementary categories of mechanical science. They contain the basis of pure mathematics and kinematics, and thus furnish the groundwork of physical science.

But all of these categories resemble the law of identity, in that they set the objects apart without any internal connection. The events which are formally related in time have no inner bond. In like manner the phenomena united in space are left mutually external without any substantial bond or reciprocal connection. These categories alone would not carry us beyond groundless events and disconnected appearances. If we leave out the metaphysical categories the visual world is not a world of things, but a set of shifting and dissolving appearances without unity or identity. The temporal world also has no continuity, but is a ceaseless and groundless flux of beginning and perishing events, and, as such, is strictly nothing for intelligence. Motion too becomes a delusive phantom, without the notion of a continuous and permanent subject. We should have successive appearances at adjacent points, but no motion. This is the point to which Hume reduced sensationalism, and beyond which it cannot go. The mind, however, saves itself from this collapse through its metaphysical categories.

In treating first of the categories of phenomena, then, we do not intend to imply that they come first, or that they can be applied apart from metaphysical principles. Any category by itself is an abstraction from a rational whole of which all the factors coexist.

The metaphysical categories, such as being, identity, causality, cannot be presented in sense at all. They are rather the unpicturable notions of intelligence, and are the chief means whereby the mind transforms the fleeting and unintelligible impressions of sense into an abiding object for thought. Of course, formal logic insists on turning these categories over to metaphysics, on the ground that they concern existence rather than thought. But it is plain that they concern existence for us only because they are primarily thought principles. In the articulate conception of objects they are the leading factor. It is only the logic of formal consistency which is absolved from considering them, and this logic is a small matter.

Being

Being, or existence, or reality, is the first of the metaphysical categories. In the world of events all occurrences are real; their occurrence is their reality. In the world of ideas any conceptual object whatever has a sort of existence. In this sense the centaur and chimera, Rosinante and Alborak, exist. In the world of consciousness actual thoughts and feelings are real, in distinction from others which, as not actual, are unreal. In this sense, also, error and confusion exist as well as truth and clearness; that is, they are actual forms of experience. In the broadest sense, then, being includes everything, thought and its objects alike; for all of these do in some fashion exist.

In this general use of the term, the mind only posits itself and all its acts and objects as members of a system of reality without further specification. All that is involved in it is a possible objectivity for thought. This act of positing results necessarily from the antithesis between thought and its object. Thought as act does not make, but reveals its object; and even when thought grasps itself, it reveals itself as a real activity. Even the special to me has an aspect which makes it, at least potentially, common to all; for it is one phase or factor of the real system of things and events. In this sense thought presupposes being, and has no significance without the reference to being. In this reference we have the most general expression of that objectivity which we have seen to inhere in the nature of thought.

This use of the term being implies a possible objectivity for thought, but it does not necessarily imply any substantiality or identity in the object; neither does it carry us beyond solipsism. These objects might all exist only as phenomena of the individual subject; and thus we should miss anything substantial, or any abiding ground. Hence, another and more metaphysical use of the term, in which the mind distinguishes between being as substantive existence and being as applied to events, between being as the abiding reality and being as objective appearance which exists only in its perception. We deal now with being in the metaphysical sense.

Of the subjective demand for this category there can be no doubt. It is the fundamental category with spontaneous thought. Even causation is secondary. Qualities are qualities of something; attributes are attributes of something; and that something is commonly supposed to be in sight. The manifest objectivity of things leaves no room for question. Doubt on this point is simply unintelligible to common-sense. For popular thought things are undeniably there, apart from our thought, and continuously existent, whether we think of them or not. This is the form which the objectivity of thought necessarily takes on in spontaneous thinking.

Of the logical necessity of this category there can be equally no doubt. Our objective experience is absolutely inarticulate and nothing for intelligence until it is fixed and defined with reference to an abiding and independent meaning. The distinction between the real and the imaginary, the actual and the fantastic, depends upon the same reference. As long as the thinker remains shut up with only his own mental states as his objects, he not only never emerges from solipsism, he never emerges into articulate thought at all. For this he must have at least the form of independent objectivity and permanence. This is the truth in Kant's otherwise rather unsuccessful disproof of idealism.

Of the metaphysical validity of this category, finally, there can be no question other than a verbal one. Perhaps it might occur to us to claim that, while the form of independent objectivity and permanence is necessary to thought, the fact itself is not thus necessary; and the world of objective but unsubstantial phenomena might be offered in illustration. But this illustration would only show that the category of being may be applied to unsubstantial phenomena, not that it is unreal or unnecessary. For if we deny the category outright, not even solipsism is left; and even if we should allow the solipsistic subject and his phenomena, those phenomena would reveal nothing, would have no ground or bond or inner connection whatever, and would thus elude all rational apprehension.

By the form of objective existence the mind transcends itself and reaches a common to all. By affirming the metaphysical reality of objective existence the mind secures, in addition to objectivity, real ground and connection. The former is given in the essential nature of the judgment. The latter is necessary to save thought from disappearing in a mirage of dissolving phantoms. Thus the objectivity of thought and the demand for ground and connection meet in the notion of being.

The category of being appears in three leading forms— thing, soul, and God. But in all three it stands for the real ground and principle of unity in the manifestations of the respective realms.

The critical misgivings concerning this category which now and then appear in speculation arise from a misconception, or they relate to its application. Sometimes being has been identified with extended substance and limited to material things. Sometimes search has been made for the extended substance in distinction from properties, and the failure to find it has led to a denial of being. Such difficulties vanish when being is understood as the abiding ground and source of manifestation.

Other scruples relate to the application of the category.

In our experience being falls into the two classes of minds and things, both of which for spontaneous thought seem equally real; or if there be any difference it is in favor of things. But the idealists have given a good many reasons for thinking that the world of things has only a phenomenal existence, and hence is without substantial reality. But this only concerns the location of the category. Being is still affirmed, but it is limited to personal existence. Impersonal things are said to exist only in and for thought; but all the more are the mental subjects affirmed, for without mind there would be no world at all. The objection, too, is metaphysical rather than epistemological. For, in any case, being and quality are the great forms under which we comprehend even the alleged phenomena of the external world, and this distinction is contributed by thought.

Quality

The thought of being in abstraction is only the empty form of objectivity and ground. Considered as actual, the thought vanishes entirely unless we proceed to give the being qualities or attributes. Pure being, or being without attributes, is objectively nothing. Subjectively it is the bare category of objective position. In the concrete act of position there is always a double aspect. First something is posited as real, and thus being is affirmed. But if we ask what this real thing is, we can only tell in terms of its qualities. The act is not complete without this double aspect, as a judgment is nothing without both subject and predicate. In the judgment we posit a subject which we unfold in the predicate, and neither is anything apart from the other. So reality is conceived only through its attributes, and the attributes exist only in the reality. Either is an unreal abstraction apart from the other.

This relation of being and quality, or of substance and

attribute, underlies our attributive judgments. We get some idea of its importance when we remember that the relation of thing and quality underlies all of our spontaneous thinking about the outer world, and in its grammatical form of noun and adjective is one of the fundamental factors of language.

The category of being has been a source of great anxiety to the sensationalists, and they have oscillated somewhat uncertainly between denying it and reducing it to terms of quality. As the senses do not give it, an equivalent has been sought as follows:

The senses do indeed give us only qualities; but these qualities form groups by association, and all that we mean by a thing is simply such a group. The contents of a sense object are expressed in a series of sense qualities. Primarily, these qualities were unrelated, and there is nothing in any one that implies any other; but from frequent coming together they are united by contiguous association into a fixed group. Hence, instead of saying that the thing A has the quality B, we may say that B is one member of the group we call A; and this is really all the attributive judgment means.

This claim has some plausibility when we are dealing with purely sense objects, but none when dealing with rational objects. And even in the case of sense objects the claim overlooks the intention of the judgment. The association of sensations can only give associated sensations, and these are necessarily special to the individual. They contain no common to all; and even the fictitious objectivity ascribed to them can be explained only by invoking a mental "propensity to feign" to account for the surplusage. Association, too, expresses merely a coming together of subjective states in a particular experience, and not a belonging together in a common reality. But this objective connection is the meaning of the judgment. If there be no such connection, the judgment is baseless; and if there be such connection, it can be reached only by thought. If, however, these groups of qualities exist objectively and are objectively connected, then, like Mr. Mill's "permanent possibilities of sensation," they are only strange names for things.

If, then, we are asked what the notion of being adds to the sense contents, we reply, It adds nothing that can be sensuously presented. It adds only independent objectivity, or an objective principle of ground and unity. The form under which the principle is to be thought is a problem for metaphysics, but the principle itself cannot be questioned without destroying thought altogether. Metaphysics finds reasons for thinking that the category of being can be adequately thought only in the form of free personality, but being in some form is a necessity of thought.

Our thought is primarily and largely occupied with sense objects. Hence our conceptions of qualities are mainly of the passive and spatial type. But as the thought of being grows more dynamic, or as we rise to the conception of spiritual being, our thought of qualities takes on the form of powers, energies, capacities, faculties, etc.

Identity

Identity may signify sameness of meaning, or equivalence of logical value, and it may signify metaphysical continuity of existence. In the former sense we affirm identity of ideas, however separate in time they may be, considered as mental events. But when things are separate, no matter how identical their definition might be, we affirm similarity, not identity. Chemical elements are not made identical by the exact similarity of their properties. The principle of consistency, also, which we have treated as the law of identity, provides only that our thoughts shall have fixed meanings, not that things must be metaphysically continuous. Hence the distinction between the principle of consistency and the category of identity. The former might suffice for dealing with a system of changeless ideas, but we need the latter when treating of concrete reality.

The necessity of this category is plain. Without it experience would vanish into a groundless flux of perishing events. There would be no connection between the past and future of a thing; in fact, there would be no thing. Thus the thought of being itself would vanish. If we think to help ourselves by saying that the thing is while it lasts, we fall into the puzzle of the infinite divisibility of time, and our things become infinite in number if not infinitely various in quality; and each of these is groundless in its coming and going.

From this abyss the mind saves itself by its category of identity. When there is temporal or spatial continuity of manifestation the mind affirms sameness of existence. Thus it is the same sun day after day, and matter is the same under all phenomenal changes. The meaning of this sameness admits of some debate, but it certainly implies at least continuity of existence. In this sense it is an implication of the law of connection, and in this sense it is a necessity of thought.

Scruples similar to those attaching to the category of being attach also to the category of identity, and the same general reply must be made. Either they concern the application of the category, or they are metaphysical rather than epistemological. Thus, it may be said that there is no ontological identity in the physical world, but only a phenomenal similarity in the successive manifestation. A continuously produced musical note is not the same for any two instants, but it has throughout an equivalent acoustic value. This equivalence of value is its only identity. In like manner the world of things is only a phenomenal process, and has no identity beyond its constant form.

This scruple is not wholly gratuitous. Metaphysics shows that the notion of real identity in distinction from formal identity abounds in obscurity. Yet still the objection concerns primarily the location of the category, and not its reality. For if we reduce nature to a flowing form with no proper identity, all the more must we affirm metaphysical continuity somewhere to make this flowing form possible. And this flowing form, again, becomes manageable by us only as we reduce it to the form of an abiding thing. If, then, there be no true identity in things, a question we postpone to metaphysics, all the more does the category of identity appear as a mental imposition necessary to any articulate conception of the flowing world of change.

Spontaneous thought never has any question about the identity of things. Its only difficulty is, first, in seeing how any question as to its meaning can possibly arise, and, secondly, in seeing that the relation is not found in sense, but is contributed by thought. It will help to insight to reflect upon this problem: Given discontinuous sensitive states to construct an objectively existing and continuous thing; or given discontinuous subjective experiences to infer a continuously and objectively existing thing. Crude thought, of course, will have no difficulty; for the experiences will be assumed to be experiences of things from the start, and thus the problem will be solved with neatness and despatch.

Causality

It is a very natural illusion of spontaneous thought that we can think of being independently of all other categories. But if we eliminate from the notion the ideas of quality, identity, and permanence, being itself vanishes. Being as thus conceived is only an abstraction, or the empty form of thought without contents, or the beginning of a thought which awaits completion. And for this completion the further category of causality is needed; without it being vanishes into a baseless phantom. Causality is not something added to the notion of being, but something contained in that notion.

The disaster involved in denying the causal element appears from the following considerations: Things, if real, would be mutually indifferent and non-existent. Events would be groundless, and experience would fall asunder into chaos. Perception, if it were otherwise possible, would become solipsism; for our perceptions, having no cause, could never be related to a real world. Indeed, even the idea of being itself, as anything beyond the individual and momentary presentation, would vanish, and thus nihilism would be the outcome.

The essential meaning of causation is dynamic determination. It may be illustrated (1) by the self-determination of a free agent, (2) by the determination of the consequent by the antecedent, and (3) by the mutual determination of different things. In the first form we have freedom; in the second we have the causal connection of sequences; and in the third we have the causal connection of coexistences, or the interaction of things.

Several questions may be asked concerning this idea. They concern (1) its source, (2) its validity, and (3) the form of its application.

On the first point we must regard the mind as the source of the idea. Even Hume admitted this in a left-handed way. A mind with no category but time can discern only sequence; but since our mind does affirm more, this excess, along with many other excesses, Hume ascribed to a mental " propensity to feign."

As to the second point, to deny the reality of causal connection would cancel objective thought entirely, and, moreover, would vacate sensationalism altogether; for all its explanations consist in showing how the past has determined belief according to the laws of association. Of course if there be no determination, all this is hopelessly inconsistent. Some beliefs were and some others are; but to think of any ground or connection is to abandon our theory.

The third point remains in uncertainty until this day. The necessity of affirming a causal ground is stringent, but it is by no means easy to fix the form and place of that ground, or to fix the form in which causality itself must be conceived. The traditional intuitionalist has rightly affirmed causal connection, but has been a little hasty in locating it. In particular he has located it with all assurance between the physical antecedent and the physical consequent. Under the influence of his crude realism he has regarded both of these as things in real space, and as he could see nothing else in the neighborhood of course the antecedent must be the efficient cause. But metaphysical considerations make this assumption doubtful. All that we see in such a case is the temporal order; and when one has sufficiently reflected upon the antithesis of the phenomenal and the real, it becomes a question whether true causality can be found in the phenomenal at all, and not rather in a power beyond the phenomenal order which incessantly posits and continues that order according to rule. Thus the seasons, or day and night, do not cause one another, although they succeed according to rule; they are rather all alike resultants of another order which is the ground of their changes. In the same way, we might possibly view the physical series as being only a temporal order without any causal connection between its members, and as having its causal ground in something beyond it. These considerations show that the absolute certainty that an event has a causal ground somewhere by no means enables us with equal certainty to locate that ground and determine its nature. Popular thought on this subject rests entirely on crude realism. The physicists speak much of the antithesis of the phenomenal and the real, but they have attained to no consistent thought or expression on this matter.

Again, both the problem of interaction and that of causal sequence have some special obscurities. In thinking of an ideal system, the unity of the mind is the supreme condition of the system. The members exist only in and through the unitary thought. The members also are determined with reference to one another, and thus may be said to exist in reciprocal relations. Without such reciprocity there would be no system at all, but only disjointed ideas. But this reciprocity is merely logical and not dynamic, and is possible only in the unity of consciousness. But when we think of a real system we understand a system which exists apart from our thinking, and then the question arises, How shall the reciprocity which the thought of system demands be realized in actuality? If the real system were also a thought system whose members are produced and related by thought, there would be no difficulty; but common-sense finds such a view altogether too airy. All the more, then, must we ask what it is beyond our thought which takes the place of the unity of consciousness and binds the system together.

The common answer is that the unity of consciousness is replaced by the dynamic interaction of things, and thus they reciprocally determine one another. But this is a hasty application of the idea of causality; for it is conceivable that, instead of reciprocally determining one another, they are reciprocally determined by something which is not the things, but which embraces all the things, as the mind embraces all its thoughts. Of course, if we are to think of the system at all, the reciprocal logical relation is necessary. The members must be thought in mutual relativity; but how this relation is dynamically founded is not easily discerned. Indeed, the difficulties of the popular view are so great that thought has long been drifting about among mere verbal solutions, as that things are united by forces or exercise mutual influence, or else oscillating confusedly between the pre-established harmony of Leibnitz and some monistic doctrine of causation. In fact, this is a problem of such grave difficulty that science and even logic do well to leave it to metaphysics, and confine themselves to observing the laws of reciprocal change among things, in the full conviction that the ground of these changes will find out for itself how to solve the problem.

For practical purposes, then, the fact of reciprocal change among things may be called their interaction, and the laws of that change may be called the laws of their interaction. In this way the practical and inductive problem will be simplified; and no harm will be done, unless we mistake this postponement of the speculative problem for its theoretical solution.

Thus all that we bring away from the consideration of the interaction of things is the conviction that there is a causal ground for their reciprocity, but without having decided the form under which that ground is to be thought. We have also found a practical problem to which logic and science may devote themselves without raising the metaphysical question. Meanwhile they remain under bonds not to declare that question answered because, in practice, it may be ignored.

The causality of sequence has similar puzzles. Confining ourselves for the present to the field of necessary causation, we have the following specimen difficulties:

First, it is plain that if the future is to be the product of the past, or is to be explained by the past, it must in some way be included in the past; otherwise it is a groundless becoming, and the law of connection vanishes. If we could exhaustively think the past without finding the future in it, the future would be groundless; and if, on the other hand, we find the future in the past, we are at a loss to know what the difference between past and future may be.

Out of this puzzle the mind seeks to help itself by the notion of potentiality. The future was potential in the past. But unless this potentiality is an actuality of some kind, it can do nothing; and how to represent a potential as actual, or what the difference would be between a potential actual and an actual actual, is quite beyond us.

If, now, we have recourse to description and say that potential means only that future conditions develop out of past conditions, we see at once that "develop out of" in a strict sense has the same difficulties, for how can that come out which was in no sense in? But if we mean only that new conditions temporally follow old conditions, then we affirm mere succession and miss the idea of ground and connection altogether.

These difficulties meet us whether we try to work the problem with one or several causes. In both cases we oscillate between connectionless succession and unintelligible potentialities.

This consideration of the causality of sequence leaves us with the conviction, first, that some bond of connection must be found, and, secondly, that it is by no means easy to determine in an off-hand way the nature and place of this bond. The theories of spontaneous thought are mainly expressions of the former conviction without any insight into the deeper mysteries of the problem. The same is true of the traditional intuitionalism.

Finally, the notion of causality itself is not perfectly transparent. To many it will seem enough to say that causality is action, and that is the end of the matter. We trace effects to causes, and there we must stop. But this satisfaction is somewhat disturbed by the reflection that the action must at least be grounded in, and conditioned by, the nature of the agent; else it would not be explained by the agent, and anything might be the cause of anything. Hence we have to describe and define our causes in terms of their effects, and we get effects from causes only by including them in the notion. If we can think the cause exhaustively without finding the effect in it, the effect is not provided for; and, on the other hand, how to find the effect in it is a problem of exceeding difficulty. The necessity of thinking the effect in relation to the cause is no more stringent than the necessity of thinking the cause in relation to the effect.

Thus the law of identity avenges itself upon the law of connection. The former, in its conviction that A is A, forbids us to say anything of A which is not contained in the notion of A. The latter also has to admit that no motion is possible unless A be really $A + X$. Without this admission the new phases are groundless, and with this admission the only progress is from potentiality to actuality, which progress, moreover, is a very obscure affair.

Luckily, life can go on without solving this riddle, but it is doubtful if there be any speculative solution on the plane of necessary causation. Necessity has clear meaning only as rational necessity; that is, where we see that the premises imply the conclusion, or that the antecedents contain the consequent. But metaphysical necessity is an exceedingly dark notion; in fact, it is purely negative without any positive content. Men are led to it by the fancy that the alternative is chance and the denial of connection, and hence they link event to event by necessity. It is conceivable, however, that the alternative is not chance, but uniformity administered by freedom.

In like manner potentiality is a clear notion only on the plane of freedom. Here it means the self-determination of the free agent. But on the plane of the necessary it is pure opacity. It must be something which is at once real and not real, actual and not actual. Unless we can master this, the alternative is to refer all motion, progress, development, evolution, to a supreme self-determination which ever lives and ever founds the order of things. In that case the past is not potential of the future any more than the summer is potential of the winter, or the setting of the sun is potential of the rising of the moon; but both past and future are phases of a movement which abuts on freedom, and of which the successive phases are but implications and manifestations of the one thought which is the law and meaning of the whole.

For practical purposes these metaphysical difficulties may be outflanked by an empirical theory of causation. We find that events occur under certain empirical conditions. The total group of conditions may be called the cause, and any member of the group, upon occasion, may be called the cause. Again, we find an order of concomitant variation in different things. This we may call their interaction, and may study its laws. It is this conception of causation which underlies inductive science and a great deal of popular language. It is not properly efficient causation at all, but only a rule of being or happening. This limitation of field must not be forbidden, and it must not be mistaken for a solution of the metaphysical problem.

The causality of freedom means self-determination. This is a causality which looks to the future and is not driven by the past. It is a causality which forms ideals and plans, and devotes itself to their realization. Instead of being snoved out of the past, it is self-moving into the future. It may posit an order and maintain it. It may conceive purposes and realize them. Our experience of such causality is limited to the inner life, but it is in fact the only form of proper causality of which we have any experience whatever. And there are reasons for thinking that, instead of being a special case of causation, it is really the typical form to which all cases of real causation must be assimilated. Metaphysics shows that the metaphysical categories elude any real apprehension or presentation, except in terms of personal experience, and this is especially the case with the category of causality. When we do not conceive it under the volitional type we have the bare form of ground without any possibility of representing our meaning.

Several facts make this conception difficult. First, we tend to think causation only under the form of time. We seek the ground of that which is in something that was; and thus the idea of the new beginning, involved in volitional causality, is rendered strange and portentous. That the other view loses itself in the infinite regress escapes us.

Secondly, our reflective activity is largely directed to material and spatial relations, and our notion of causality takes on a corresponding character. Dealing with material and impersonal phenomena, we naturally conceive the causality to be of a material and impersonal type. Here we mistake our certainty that there is a causal ground for a conception of the form in which that ground must be conceived. But the progress of speculation is making the notion of physical causation increasingly difficult, and is reducing the physical to a phenomenal order whose cause must be sought beyond itself.

Thirdly, volitional causality itself is commonly conceived in connection with a variety of psychological and even physiological limitations, which are no necessary part of the notion. In this way it acquires a certain grotesqueness when applied to cosmic causality. But mental illumination will disperse these whims.

Because of these facts a one-sided conception of causality takes possession of the mind, and is not easily ejected. However, when thought becomes more critical and profound, it not only appears that the conception of free or volitional causation is as possible as that of necessary causation, but it becomes at least doubtful if it be not the essential type of causation proper, in distinction from those uniformities of sequence which are popularly called causation. With this conception, if we seek for explanation we are not sent toiling back along a line of infinite regress, as in the case of necessary causation, but we find what we seek in the free and purposive agent, the only real explanation of anything. From this conception, also, the difficulty concerning actual potentialities disappears, and some provision is made for progress. Of course it is impossible to tell how such causality is made or is possible, but no more so than to tell how any causality is made or is possible. Any ultimate fact is mysterious—that is, it is something to be admitted rather than comprehended; but still there is a choice in mysteries. Some may be forced upon us by the facts and may illumine all other facts, while some may not be required by the facts, or may leave the facts as opaque and unintelligible as ever. It ought not to be hard to choose between the two classes.

The general conception of causal determination is one with which the mind can in no way dispense in rationalizing its experience. The extent to which it enters into our thought appears when we reflect upon the dynamic substantives and adjectives in language, and especially upon the active verbs which make up so much of speech. All of these are but specifications of the causal idea and relation. The same may be said of the science of mechanics. But the establishment of the formal relation by no means involves an insight into its metaphysical nature. We content ourselves with showing the general significance of the relation for thought, and its origin in thought rather than in sense. The deeper inquiry we leave to metaphysics. It is with this category as with that of being: there is practical unanimity as to the necessity of the formal category, with much uncertainty as to the metaphysical form in which it is realized.

Among those who have defined causation as invariable sequence there has been chronic uncertainty whether such sequence is the meaning or the mark of causation. This ambiguity has greatly increased their speculative resources.

These are the categories which underlie our elementary objective experience. Experience becomes experience, or becomes articulate, only as these categories appear in the flux of impressions. They are not applied to a something given to consciousness, but the mind gets objects or consciousness acquires definite contents only as they are applied to the raw material of impressions. Of course they are not to be viewed as primarily conscious possessions of the mind, but rather as immanent principles. They become conscious possessions at a later date, when the mind, by reflection on its own work, finds that it has been constituting its objects under the categories, and then, by abstraction, gets them in the form of ideas.

These categories also give the form or framework of elementary experience. If we conceive the specific contingent contents of experience removed, there would remain the framework of space, time, number, quantity, quality, substance and attribute, cause and effect, etc., and all possible experiences would necessarily take on some of these general forms in becoming anything for us.

Necessity

This is a much more doubtful category than the preceding ones. Its prominence, however, in uncritical thought, both popular and scientific, is patent to every reader. That necessity rules in nature, that natural laws are necessary, that all things are included in a system of necessity, are among the most familiar propositions. That the meaning of this necessity is sun-clear is assumed as beyond question.

Yet, after all, it is not so clear. As we have before pointed out, the only clear necessity is rational necessity; that is, necessity of thought. But uncritical thought demands more than this: it insists upon a necessity of things, or a metaphysical necessity.

It is plain, however, that if there be any such necessity it must manifest itself to us as a necessity of thought. We must, then, examine the latter to see if we find any trace of the former.

Necessity of thought may mean simply a factual condition of thought without which thought could not go on.

Again, it may express merely a logical relation, as of premise and conclusion, or of subject and predicate. The premises necessitate the conclusion, or the subject implies the predicate.

Or a necessity of thought may be a proposition which cannot be denied without contradiction or without violating some clear intuition of reason.

In none of these cases do we certainly come upon anything metaphysical. We are concerned only with thought itself.

But necessities of thought may involve necessities of things, and the mind seeks to import necessity into things themselves. This has been attempted in two ways—by way of logic and by way of explanation.

In the former case the argument has always been from the necessity of an affirmation to the affirmation of a necessity. This is a hopeless fallacy. The utmost possible conclusion from a set of conditioned facts is an unconditioned fact. A basal and absolute necessity is simply a spectre evoked by bad logic.

The introduction of necessity into things by way of explanation appears in connection with our conception of the nature of things and in our thought of the laws of things. Neither of these represents any absolute necessity, for there is no assignable necessity for the things. We may fancy, however, that there is a necessity in the things. This fancy is a fiction.

In the case of the laws it is plain that all that experience gives is uniformity. How this is produced is a problem. The uncritical mind assumes necessity as a matter of course; but all that it means is the negative conviction that the fact could not be otherwise. Of course it might conceivably be otherwise, but there is some hypothetical necessity which forbids it.

In the case of the nature of things the thought of a necessary connection has apparently more justification. Here it is closely connected with the thought of identity. To think of a thing at all we must think of it as what it is, as A; and hence it seems as if there must be some necessity whereby A is A. To be sure, A need not be at all; but so long as it exists there is some necessary principle whereby it is A and not something else. This, however, is a question which cannot be solved without some conception of the relation of A to the unconditioned reality. A might conceivably be the expression of an unpicturable necessity, and it might be the expression of a thought.

In short, this category of necessity in its metaphysical use is simply a superficial application of the principle of ground and connection. The general assumption has been that the alternative is to deny connection, and hence the notion of necessity has taken possession of uncritical thought. Our thought also is vacillating, our wills are capricious, our effort weak and discontinuous; and thus again it is easy to fall into the notion that some impersonal necessity is the only adequate administrator of existence both in its details and in its totality.

The ease with which the uncritical mind satisfies itself finds striking illustration in this fancy. Will and intellect are not thought to be deep enough and steady enough to maintain the system and its constant on-going, and hence we fall back on necessity. But this necessity is not only hypothetical in its existence, it is equally hypothetical in its contents and direction. That the present order is necessary we know by hypothesis. That it will continue we know by hypothesis. So far as any insight is concerned, the future is absolutely hidden from us; we can only be sure that the fact, whatever it may be, will be necessary. So far as the rational founding of objective knowledge is concerned, no doctrine of chance or arbitrariness could leave us in a worse plight. But we escape these difficulties by naïvely mistaking our psychological expectation for a logical warrant.

An additional reason for care in the application of this category of necessity is found in its bearing upon the problem of error. We have already pointed out the element of freedom involved in the nature of thought itself. Hereafter it will appear that the denial of freedom leads to the collapse of reason itself. Meanwhile it is plain that, while reason is impelled by its own nature to seek for fixed connection, the nature and ground of that connection form a deep speculative problem which can by no means be settled in an off-hand manner.

Possibility

Possibility is another of the doubtful categories. Its only clear meaning is based upon the self-determination of a free agent; apart from this it is metaphysically nothing. As used in popular speech it has a variety of meanings.

Thus, that is possible which involves no contradiction. This is logical possibility, and means only conceivability.

Or, that is possible which, for all we know, may happen or may have happened. This possibility is only an expression of our ignorance.

Or, that is possible which would happen if certain conditions were fulfilled. This possibility is merely an expression of the order of conditioned events. But as long as the condition is unfulfilled the event is impossible, and when it is fulfilled the event is not only possible but actual.

In reality, apart from the sphere of freedom, the only possible is the implications of the actual. Many other things may be conceived, but they are impossible as not founded in the real. If, then, we would know what is concretely or really possible we must have a complete insight into the nature and implications of reality itself.

A good deal of wild work has been done in the field of speculation through confusing these several forms of possibility. A favorite confusion has been the fancy that all possibles must finally become actual; for, it was sagely questioned, how can anything be called even possible if it will never become actual? *Ever* is the symbol of positive necessity, and *never* is the symbol of negative necessity. What will never happen is impossible. This wisdom vanishes when we decide which possibility we mean.

Purpose

The categories of being, space, time, causation, are necessary in order to have any articulate experience whatever. It is through them that we reach intelligible objects, or that world of facts which seems to be given to us ready-made in sense perception. But these categories alone would keep us among isolated things and events. Space and time separate rather than unite; and causality, at least in its mechanical form, provides for no system. For the further systematization and unification of our objects a higher category is needed; and this we find in purpose, or, rather, in the elevation of causality to intelligent and volitional causality, with its implication of plan and purpose.

Kant pointed out that the application of the categories of the understanding under the conditions of space and time reaches no totality and comes to no end. The temporal and spatial synthesis can never be exhausted, and leaves us toiling hopelessly in the infinite regress. In the same way the joining of sequences under the law of causation is an endless process, and hence an irrational one. As a relief from this sterile task, Kant proposed ideas of the reason above the categories of the understanding. These were to enable thought to reach some systematic totality and thus find some rest. For objective experience the ideal proposed he called the world. This ideal is no datum of experience, but the conception of a completed whole, by means of which thought is enabled to give, at least formally, systematic completeness to its labors.

Kant's deduction of this ideal of the reason leaves much to be desired, but in the fact itself he is by no means so far from the beaten track as it might seem. The terms "Nature," "Cosmos," "Universe," are familiar expressions of the same idea. In all alike there is the notion of a finished whole, whose parts or factors exist in systematic relations determined by the nature of the whole. The part played by "Nature" in the history of thought is patent to every reader, but it has not been equally plain that this "Nature" is primarily the shadow of our systematizing and architectonic thought.

The demand of thought for systematic totality is manifest, and that this demand will always get itself recognized, wittingly or unwittingly, is clearly shown in the history of speculation. But, as in the case of the other categories, the form in which the demand shall be met is not immediately evident. Kant has simply given a name to the demand rather than a proper conception. He saw, indeed, that time and space and causation, as the linking of events, neither singly nor collectively could meet this demand; and after he had furnished a name for the higher principle he left its nature and ground quite undetermined, except to suggest its purely regulative character. Had Kant written the *Critique of the Pure Reason* after he had thought his system through to the *Critique of the Judgment* he would probably not have been content with the verbal unity and totality reached in the notion of the world.

The principle we need here can never be found in any impersonal or mechanical conception whatever. Metaphysics shows that every such system fails to reach any true unity, while mechanical causation loses itself in the infinite regress. Verbal classifications from without are only external impositions and hang in the air. The unity and system demanded must be internal, and this true inwardness can be found only in self-determining, self-conscious causality, guiding itself according to plan and purpose. Thus only do the unity and totality of the system become possible. Until we advance to this conception we either contradict ourselves or wander among verbal solutions.

The necessity of affirming purpose has a double root—theoretical and empirical. The former consists in the dialectic of thought, whereby reason is found to be in unstable equilibrium, or, rather, in no equilibrium, until it elevates itself above the mechanical categories and rises to the conception of self-determining and intelligent personality as the supreme category in being and causation. Of course this necessity can be appreciated only when there is a good degree of original reflective power combined with some critical development. Hence it is commonly undreamed of by spontaneous thought, which never suspects the shortcomings of its mechanical categories when viewed as absolute and final. The higher categories, like the Copernican astronomy, do not commend themselves to one on the sense plane of mental growth. In both cases some intellectual range and flexibility are needed to make the truth acceptable.

The empirical ground for affirming purpose lies primarily in our experience of intelligence, and, secondarily, in sundry peculiarities of objective experience which are said to point to intelligence as their cause. Both points call for a word of exposition.

Several questions must be distinguished: (1) Is purpose a category of thought? (2) Is it so self-evidently such a category as, say, the law of causation? (3) Has the subjective category objective validity?

To the first question the answer must be affirmative. Purpose is a category involved in the nature of free intelligence. The great distinction between mechanical and intellectual causality is that the former is driven from behind while the latter is self-determined towards ends which lie before. As looking towards future ends it is called final causality—that is, it is purposive. Final causality is the causality of will informed by intelligent purpose.

Hence in our experience of intelligence we find its activity taking on the purposive form. The whole range of volitional activity, whether in ourselves or in others, is otherwise unintelligible. And everywhere the mind seeks to relate its objects as means and ends, or to comprise them in a scheme of purpose or an all-embracing plan. Moreover, we experience a peculiar satisfaction when we are able to trace relations of purpose. The universal teleological impulse has never left itself without a witness. This is nowhere more marked than in the writings of antiteleological thinkers. Nature is driven out with a fork, but ever comes running back. Thought must become teleological before it can complete itself.

To the second question the answer must be that the categories are not all on the same plane. Some are necessary to even elementary experience, while others are necessary only for the reflective systematization of experience. Hence it is easy to think that only the former are properly necessities of thought; but the fact is that only the former are necessities of certain phases of thought. When thought is complete, however, it may even appear that the higher categories are the supreme laws of thought, and that the lower categories vanish unless they are taken up into the higher.

The category of purpose is not so prominent in elementary experience as in reflective thought. All objects are in space; all events are in time; every change demands a cause; but comparatively few things suggest a purpose. When we take things in isolation, and as they exist for sense perception, it is easy to ignore the relation of purpose altogether; and commonly it is difficult to suggest any purpose whatever. Thus we are led to deny that purpose has any essential relation to thought and to question its application to reality.

Here again our difficulty is double. First, we remain on the plane of the lower categories without suspicion of their implications; and, secondly, we fail to note that the tracing of purpose is necessarily a far more complex matter than the tracing of causation.

As to the first point, it is only when thought becomes systematic and aims at completeness that the rational significance of purpose is seen. Then it appears that the antithesis is not between causality and non-causality, but between mechanical and volitional causality. And then it further appears that mechanical causality is entangled with unintelligible potentialities which remove all progress from it; that without these it stands still; that it cancels itself in an infinite regress; and, finally, that it involves reason itself in hopeless disaster. Thus volitional causality at last appears as the only form which can be made basal without speculative collapse.

The necessity of purpose as a principle of thought, then, is reflectively rather than intuitively reached. Though apparently outranked in authority by the law of causation, reflection shows that the latter is unable to maintain itself in the form of mechanical causality, and reaches equilibrium only as it advances to the form of volitional and purposive causality.

From this point of view the affirmation of purpose is made solely to enable thought to maintain itself and to attain to systematic completeness. It would remain valid even if we were unable to trace the purpose in reality. As we must maintain the fact of law even where we find chaos, so we must maintain the fact of purpose even if we find the purpose inscrutable. In both cases alike we live in the faith that growing knowledge will reveal the existence of that in which meanwhile we believe.

From the empirical standpoint also the negation of purpose is not entirely without apparent support, as the tracing of purpose is commonly far more difficult than the tracing of causation. In our human activities, as soon as our purposes become at all complex or take on the character of plans, the aim can be discerned only from a comprehensive survey of the whole. In such cases it is easy for ignorance to miss the governing law so as to see in the means no relation to the end, and even no hint of any end. In the construction of a great building, or in the carrying out of the plan of a campaign, the subordinates very generally work in accordance with a plan not revealed to them. Their whole activity is governed by the relation of means and ends; but they remain in ignorance, for the relation is not objectively revealed until the work converges towards completion. To one standing in the midst of the work, and especially in its raw beginnings, or to one studying the details singly and not in their relations, the end may well be missed altogether.

From the nature of the case we must be largely in this position with regard to the purpose in nature. Our own brevity makes it hard to believe in purpose when it is slowly realized. The distress which many theists have felt at the doctrine of the slow development of cosmic forms is largely due to this fact. In the same way an ephemeron would miss the purpose in the mass of human activity, because its range of knowledge and rate of temporal change would not enable it to get any vivid impression of movement converging towards an end. Add to this the fact that we may easily determine our objects according to the lower categories without rising to the thought of purpose, and we readily comprehend how purpose should seem to be no category of thought at all, but only at best a doubtful induction from experience.

The question concerning the objective validity of purpose is really double, according to the standpoint. It may be raised from the Kantian point of view which makes all the categories subjective, and in this sense we remand it to metaphysics. It may also mean that purpose is only a superstition of uncritical thought and has no validity in fact. This view has its foundation partly in the facts already mentioned, and partly, and more especially, in the supposed antinomy between purpose and necessary causation.

This puzzle is not altogether gratuitous, but has its roots in the crude metaphysics of common-sense. A purpose as such is only a conception, and demands some means for its realization. But those means, of course, must be adequate to its realization if they are to realize it. Hence, when the means are given the end results as a matter of course; and then it becomes possible to look upon the end, not as purposed but only as unintended product.

In dealing with human combinations of means this puzzle could never arise. The realization of our purposes through mechanical means, so that the result is an expression at once of purpose and of mechanical necessity, is one of the most familiar facts of our experience. Here the antinomy between causation and purpose cannot arise because we know the causation is determined with reference to the purpose. But in dealing with cosmic combinations the puzzle is pretty sure to arise in the superficial stage of reflection. We find effects emerging in a system of law, and the order of necessary causation appears to provide for all the facts. Nature is tacitly or explicitly erected into a mechanical and self-enclosed system, and thus the facts, which at first impressed us as intended, now seem to be only the unpurposed products of mechanical causation.

In the last paragraph we have the natural history of atheism, so far as it has an intellectual origin. So long as matter was regarded as inert, causation had to be sought outside; but by the dynamic theory of matter, causation was provided in matter itself. A principle of order was next found in the notion of law, and nothing more seemed needed. Matter furnished the being, force furnished the causation, and law provided the order. These three together formed the one Nature or system of the world, and beyond this there was nothing. Matter and force are already seen to do much, and are daily doing more. No one can set a limit to their possibilities. The reign of law is fast becoming all-embracing, and the more law the less God.

The way out of this puzzle must lie in a criticism of its assumptions. The fundamental antithesis of purpose and causation is incorrect. The true antithesis is that of mechanical and volitional causality, and this question is purely a speculative one. Again, allowing the mechanical causality, purpose is not excluded unless it be shown that the mechanism cannot be viewed as founded in or directed by intelligence. The conception of nature as a self-enclosed and self-sufficing mechanism has no support in reflective thought. The necessity which rules in nature turns out to be uniformity unwarrantably transformed into necessity, and is, in fact, only a shadow of our own crude thinking. When all these considerations are mastered, and the self-destructive implications of necessity are also grasped, the antiteleological objections are seen in their superficiality.

And, in general, all that is needed is that thought shall understand itself. Crude thought tends to rest in the lower and mechanical categories, and when it becomes reflective it seeks to test all things by those categories. In this way space, time, material being, and mechanical causation become its supreme categories and its final tests of reality. Of these it has no doubt, and it applies them unhesitatingly.

This necessarily results, when at all thorough-going, in casting doubt or discredit on all the higher forms of thought and on spiritual conceptions of existence. Then we have the conflict of science and religion, or of reason and faith. But this conflict, so far as it is real and not fictitious, rests entirely upon the mutual relations of the categories; and it can be removed only by a better understanding of thought itself. We must see that the lower categories imply the higher, if indeed they have any application beyond phenomena. The reconciliation of science and religion can never be effected by a special chair established for that purpose; the reconciliation is to be found and effected only by an adequate study of thought itself. If the subject is to be referred to any chair, it must be the chair of logic. The ease with which untrained thought misses its way, the practical importance of right thinking, and the practical mischief of wrong thinking make philosophy an important practical discipline.

Thus we have sought to give a hint of the fundamental categories and relations of pure thought. They constitute the framework of intelligence, and when experience is built into them they give the form of experience. As immanent principles, they underlie experience. As abstract ideas, they are reached by abstraction from that experience which, as principles, they make possible.

Thought seeks system, not only in dealing with its objects, but also in dealing with itself. Hence the attempt to connect the categories as necessary implications of one principle. Aristotle picked up his categories empirically, if not at random, in the field of grammar; and his conception of their function has little in common with the modern one. Kant framed his system of categories from an analysis of the table of judgments furnished by formal logic. His procedure has been much criticised, especially on the ground that there is no deduction from one unitary principle, but only an enumeration. Fichte and Hegel made great efforts to remedy this defect by deducing the categories from a single root and showing their inner connection. These efforts were not crowned with complete success. There is connection among the categories. The attempt to stop with the lower categories reveals, upon reflection, inadequacies and inconsistencies which cannot be removed until we advance to the higher categories, or to the highest. In so far the analysis of reason is fruitful. But it is not shown that reason admits only of the existing categories, no more, no less, and no others. Reason—that is, our reason—is not able to complete its own system, and is compelled to accept itself in many respects as a fact which is by no means transparent, but rather abounds in opacities and mysteries. We make no attempt, therefore, at deduction or systematic completeness. We content ourselves with showing that the mind does work according to these principles, and reaches knowledge only through them.

From all these considerations we can understand the importance of the Kantian question, How is experience possible? Locke had claimed that mental principles are got from experience; but it was an experience in which those principles were implicit. Hume saw this, and sought to reduce experience to its true dimensions; and these he found in impressions. It was reserved for Kant to show that such an experience can never be, or become, anything articulate without an organizing activity on the part of the mind according to principles immanent in the understanding.

Again, we can find a tenable meaning for the Kantian statement that the understanding makes nature. Much of Kant's writing is so obscure or ambiguous that, in determining his view on particular points, there is often danger of losing the philosophical question in a sterile exegetical squabble. Commentaries on Kant are burdened with this unprofitable matter. We do not pretend, therefore, to tell just how much Kant meant by this utterance; and still less do we consent to become responsible for the Kantian deduction and conception of nature. Nevertheless, the statement admits of an interpretation at once true and important.

Of course, for us, the meaning cannot be that any one of us or all of us make the cosmic reality. So far as we are concerned, that reality exists in its own right. But we may still ask how the existent nature becomes an object of knowledge for us. And when we remember that sense alone can give us nothing but discontinuous sensations, and that unaided sense perception at best could give nothing more than discontinuous presentations, we must ask, What weaves this rather flimsy and unsubstantial material into a solid and abiding world? It is the mind; and the mind can do it only because the pattern of nature is implicit in the mind. For known nature is primarily our own product; as another's thought, so far as grasped by me, must be immediately my own thought. It has in it, indeed, the necessity of referring to another's thought, of which it grasps the contents; but, nevertheless, the thought is mine. In like manner, my thought of nature has in it an objective reference, so that I am grasping a content independent of my thought; nevertheless, both the form and contents of nature, so far as they exist for me, are my own product.

The understanding, then, makes nature in a real and important sense. It is only through the laws of nature immanent in the understanding that any knowledge of an objectively existing nature can possibly arise. Whether, corresponding to the reason by which nature exists for us, there is a Cosmic Reason by which nature has its real existence is a question we postpone for the present.

Before leaving this subject a word must be said concerning a pair of scruples which may well have arisen in the reader's mind. Might we not, it may be asked, by a similar style of reasoning, deduce any number of categories, so that finally we should have as many categories as we have objects?

There is something in this, but not what the objector thinks. If we take the matter in strict exactness, the fact is the mind having a multiplicity of experiences and reacting upon them in a variety of ways. None of these exists except through a special mental activity. Even the reactions of sensation are a special form of mental action, and for different classes of sensation we have to assume a corresponding qualitative difference in the sensibility to explain the difference in the product. In this sense we may speak of apriori faculties of sensation, and we may multiply them as long as we find any qualitative difference. The same is true for the reactions of the understanding. There is no reaction in general, but there is a special reaction for each particular thing. In this sense the knowledge of anything and everything is apriori; that is, it is not something passed into the mind, but involves a special activity of the mind. However, in looking over these activities we find that they fall into certain classes, and these classes can only be looked upon as expressing general forms of mental action, and as founded in the nature of the mind itself. When any of these forms can be subordinated to others, we have only subordinate principles of intelligence; but when they are incommensurable and defy further reduction, then we have the elementary and essential principles of intelligence. But even in this there is a certain departure from the fact, which is always and only the mind acting in various ways. There is, then, no objection to one's making as many categories as he pleases, provided always they represent real forms of mental activity; and there is also no objection to making as few as one pleases, provided, again, the categories do not put incommensurable things together, and do not overlook real forms of mental activity. The point to be observed is that it is not a question of importing ready-made knowledge into a passively receptive mind, but rather of best expressing the forms and principles of a complex mental activity.

The other scruple referred to is this: In all that we have said about the mental activity involved in knowing, the object has not appeared as a determining factor at all. But certainly the object is the most important factor in knowing. Knowledge is of the object, and the object must determine knowledge. But in our exposition it seems as if knowledge were determining the object, and thus it seems as if there were no object, but only a projection of our own conceptions.

This scruple is not entirely groundless. For spontaneous thought the object is everything and thought is nothing. It was therefore necessary to show that, however real the object may be, it becomes an object for us only through our own activity. The thing world must be reproduced in the thought world, and the forms of the thing world must take on the forms of the thought world. This cannot be escaped on the most realistic theory. And if the thoughts which arise do really grasp existing things, this is possible only as there is essential identity between the fundamental forms of thought and those of things. That thought working according to its laws should yet rightly apprehend things existing according to their laws is impossible without this identity, and also without a profound adjustment of the interaction of thought and things. This smacks a little of pre-established harmony; but no theory can escape it which does not lose itself in a blind materialism on the one hand, or in a solipsistic idealism on the other.

CHAPTER V

THE NOTION

WE have delayed thus long to treat of the traditional logical forms because of the importance of the logical principles which condition thought. Formal logic of the traditional type begins with "terms" or "names," which are supposed to be found ready-made in consciousness, and then proceeds to unite them according to the principle of consistency, and never suspects, meanwhile, that the most important and vital work of thought must be done before this work can begin. Thinking about a given world is something, but getting a world to think about is a great deal more; and it is precisely this latter feat in which the chief work of thought appears. Hence the need of the preliminary discussion.

In treating of the traditional forms we take for granted a certain acquaintance with them on the part of the reader. We shall attempt, therefore, no detailed exposition, but shall confine our attention rather to important points and to some general criticism. In this way we hope to get some insight into the rational principles which underlie the logical forms, and to escape the barren wastes of fruitless distinctions and meaningless details which make up so large a part of traditional logic.

Conceiving, judging, and inferring are not three successive forms of mental activity, so that the first form can be complete in itself without the others. On the contrary, each form enters into and implies the rest. Of course there is some conceiving which precedes some judging, and some judging which precedes some inferring; but as general forms of our thought activity each involves all. The intellect which could not judge could never conceive. The intellect which could not infer could not judge. Conceiving, judging, inferring, then, are only different phases of one indivisible process. We treat them successively, but they are simultaneous in existence. Of course it is understood that we are speaking of human thinking. An intuitive reason would have no need of inference.

From this standpoint the three factors of thought are the notion, the judgment, and the inference. These, however, are not independent of the constitutive activity of thought, but rather depend upon it. The present chapter will treat of the notion.

For thought, of course, terms are primarily nothing but vocal or visual signs of ideas. The meaning behind the sign is the important thing. This is variously called the notion, the concept, the idea, the conception. We begin with the thought element, and postpone to a later paragraph what we have to say about terms or language.

The logical aim in the formation of the notion is perfectly simple. It is merely to form fixed conceptions which shall enable us to master and express experience. The presupposition is that experience admits of being reduced, at least to some extent, to such fixed forms. The difficulties which arise concern the realization rather than the aim.

And here at the start it may be well to explain away an apparent contradiction running through our discussion of the notion. It is spoken of as fixed, and yet its changing nature perpetually appears. This inconsistency vanishes on remembering that this fixity is the ideal form of the notion. $A = A$. It does not forbid that A may be increased by a new factor, B; but even then the same law holds. The new idea $A + B$ must be $A + B$ and not something else. The contents of many notions undergo great changes, in which case the real fact is that a new idea has taken the place of the old; but new and old alike are under the necessity of being fixed in their meaning or identical with themselves.

The common doctrine of the notion is as follows: The mind begins with particular things, or events, immediately given in experience. This work precedes thought. These particulars are then compared, and are seen to have some element in common. This common feature is next separated by abstraction from the particular cases, and thus appears as the notion, or concept, which is defined as the common element in many individuals. Later on this concept is extended by generalization to all similar individuals, and the work is complete. This is the sum of the theory; all else is application.

That some concepts arise in this way is clear enough; and for some purposes and from some standpoints the view is sufficiently accurate. Many things are known as individuals long before they are classified; and often enough new facts compel reclassification. The botanists and zoologists are constantly redistributing their facts so as to create and uncreate classes, yet without any modification of the individuals dealt with. These facts seem to show that individuals are known independently, and that the knowledge of classes and class terms is necessarily a later product. And we might even claim that a moment's reflection shows that it must be so. The knowledge of man can arise only from a knowledge of men.

This seems conclusive; but, on the other hand, when we attempt to tell what these individuals are, the answer always consists of general terms. If we would describe Socrates we have to call him a man, a Greek, a philosopher. Indeed, language has no significant terms which are not universals; and any mind which is developed enough to use language is necessarily moving on the plane of universals. When proper names have no connotation they merely denote an object and mean nothing. Hence any individual object whatever, by the time it is anything for thought, is included in a system of classification, and is known only as it is subsumed under some general notion. Articulate perception involves assimilation. Cognition is completed in recognition. The presence of this generalizing tendency is manifest in the early development of children, who are perpetually assimilating new objects to previous experience. It would seem, then, that the knowledge of man is an important factor in the knowledge of men, and that any articulate knowledge of men must be a knowledge of man.

These things show that the antithesis of individual and universal is not so simple and manifest as we at first suppose. In fact, it has only a limited validity. Some conceptions are, indeed, individual with reference to some others; but these singular conceptions are themselves either universals or functions of universals. The universalizing process and the universal element are present in every individual by the time it is anything for intelligence. The relation of the categories to consciousness makes this necessary. They furnish the fundamental classifications without which thought cannot even begin. Hence no strictly unclassified thing can be an object of knowledge. The sense impression itself, we have seen, becomes an object of thought only for a universalizing intelligence. Finally, even if an utterly singular conception of a thing were possible, that conception must at least be a universal with reference to the successive phases of the thing. Nothing is one in sense experience. A thing becomes one only

through the formation of an abiding conception which is
the truth or meaning in the successive experiences. Without this conception there would be only a flux of impressions which would elude thought altogether, and this one
conception is plainly a universal with reference to a plurality of experiences.

We conclude, then, that the current conception is mistaken, according to which the knowledge of the singular is
something complete in itself, while the universal is reached
by abstraction from the knowledge of individuals. And
the professional logicians themselves have never succeeded
in being consistent on this point. After insisting that logic
has to do only with concepts and classes, that the concept is
the point or points in which many objects agree, that the
application of the concept to a knowledge of individuals
is a logical abuse, they do not hesitate to speak of concepts
of individuals, of singular concepts; and, when treating of
the extension of concepts, they not infrequently hold that
when the extension of a concept becomes a minimum it
is called an individual. All of these inconsistencies are to
be found in the logical writings of Sir William Hamilton
himself. Such uncertainty and contradiction necessarily result from the failure to see that a proper knowledge even
of the singular is possible only to a universalizing intelligence. A conception may indeed be singular with reference to some other conception, but it can never be absolutely singular without vanishing from thought altogether.

But do we not always begin with the knowledge of individuals, and thence advance to the knowledge of universals? Here it is worth while to make a distinction. The
mind creates some of its objects by definition and invention,
and some of its objects it discovers through perception. In
the former case the universal precedes the singular as its
law. The universal is the law for forming and dealing with

individuals. The watch preceded watches. The definition of the parabola preceded parabolas. And wherever the mind acts creatively the general conception precedes and determines the particulars.

But on the perceptive side we may hold that we certainly begin with individuals, and that universals are necessarily a later product. If we allow this, the question what the knowledge of individuals implies still remains open. The common assumption is that either individuals must be known before universals, or universals must be known before individuals. But a third possibility remains, that the knowledge of the two should grow together. And it is this third possibility which is realized in the case of our developing intelligence. The knowledge of the singular commonly develops along with that of the universal. If the universal is realized only in the singular, the singular is understood only through the universal. Without particular experiences, thought is empty; and without the universal form, thought is chaotic and unmanageable. This interpenetration of the two elements compels us to regard the singular as a specialized universal, and the universal as a generalized singular. If, then, we admit that knowledge is of individuals, we must also admit that this knowledge is possible only to and through a universalizing intelligence. Again, if we admit that individuals are the only realities, we must also admit that these individuals become anything for us only as they are comprised in a general rational scheme.

Hence the antithesis of singular and universal, in any form in which it can exist for articulate thought, is by no means the antithesis of non-logical data and logical abstractions. On the contrary, the conception of the individual is as truly a logical product as the conception of the universal, and the true antithesis is that of singular and general concepts. In the case of complex objects, these two classes agree in having the same number of marks united in the same way, or by a common law. They differ solely in the form in which the marks are given. In the singular concept the marks have specific values, and in the general concept they have general values; but in both cases the internal structure and law are the same. This relation finds perfect illustration in algebra. A formula with general quantities represents the general concept. The same formula with specific values substituted for the general quantities illustrates the singular concept. If we begin with the universal we specialize it and reach the singular. If we begin with the singular we generalize it and reach the universal. In both cases, however, the internal logical structure is the same.

The traditional logic has contented itself with some very superficial work in this matter. First, it has supposed that the individual may be articulately known apart from and before the universal. Secondly, as a specification of the same error, it has supposed that the conception of the individual involves no proper logical work. Thirdly, it has supposed that the concept has arisen by simply abstracting from individuals their elements of likeness and dropping their differences. The mistake of the first two suppositions has already appeared. The individual exists for thought only as it is defined and fixed in a logical scheme. The mistake of the third supposition appears on reflecting that, by such a process of abstraction, thought would reach only a zero result. Things which are alike are still different in those points in which they are alike, and if all the elements in which they differ were eliminated there would be nothing left. The actual procedure of thought in passing from individuals to universals does not consist in dropping differences, but rather in substituting for the particular marks of the individual the general marks of the class. For instance, particular animals have particular forms of nutrition and reproduction, and these differ greatly from one another. But in forming the concept, animal, it would not do to leave out the marks of nutrition and reproduction, although animals differ in these respects. On the contrary, the mind retains the marks, but gives them a general form; as when we generalize a particular problem in algebra we retain all the quantities and relations, but give them a general form.

These considerations apply only to the mutual relation of the singular and universal as elements of the thought process. Their metaphysical relations form a separate question. But with regard to the former our conclusion is that thought exists only through a process which is at once a generalizing and a particularizing one. Without either element our thought would come to a standstill. From some points of view the traditional doctrine presents the matter well enough. Some individuals are known before some universals, and some universals are won by abstraction from previously known individuals. This is admitted and even insisted upon. At the same time, these individuals are functions of other universals; and this fact must not be lost sight of in estimating the relation of the individual to the universal, considered as elements of the thought process. Their metaphysical relations will be treated in a later paragraph.

The essential nature of the concept, whether singular or universal, consists in its abiding thought content. This conception of an abiding significance is the central element. When the experience is simple, as in our elementary sensations, the concept itself is correspondingly simple. Here the logical work consists in giving the form of thought to material which it does not produce. In this way the unmanageable flow of non-rationalized sense impressions becomes something for intelligence. When the concept is complex the mind unites the elements into a complex whole whose parts belong together, or it analyzes the complex whole into its implications. The former is especially the case in dealing with external objects; the latter is the rule when dealing with subjective creations. When the marks which go to make up the concept of a subject may be separately experienced, as in the reports of the different senses concerning an object, the mind unites these marks into one complex conception. But when the conception is grasped as a whole from the start, as in a mathematical definition, the mind analyzes it into its implications. Thus the concept, triangle, is not made by adding sides, angles, and area: but the complex conception, triangle, is analyzed into sides, angles, and area, as implied in the notion.

Here again the traditional logic has been too easily contented. Confining its attention mainly to concepts of external things, it has tended to regard the concept as merely the sum of its marks. $S = a + b + c + d +$, etc., would be the form into which the conception would fall, where S stands for the concept, and a, b, etc., stand for its marks or factors. But it is plain that such a formula can have no application to those cases in which S is not built up from the marks but rather implies them, or in which S precedes and determines the marks. Not even the formula $S = f(a, b, c, d)$ would be adequate to these cases; for S is the prior notion, and the marks are functions of S rather than conversely. The concept, watch, is not a sum, nor even a function, of its parts; but, conversely, the parts are rather functions of the one law-giving concept, watch. It is only for certain arbitrary or artificial concepts that the marks are simply co-ordinated, as in the traditional scheme. We shall find this superficiality underlying the empirical theory of predication.

In spontaneous thought everything turns on the basal

antithesis of things and qualities. This arises naturally from the form of our sense experience. Corresponding to this fact we find our notions falling into two great classes, subject and predicate notions. The former primarily represent things which have a substantive existence; afterwards they come to stand for any conception which serves as a subject for predicates. Predicate notions are those which have only an adjectival existence; that is, they represent qualities or activities, and can be conceived as existing only in connection with a subject.

In language, substantive notions are represented by most common nouns, and the predicate notions by adjectives and verbs. Predicate notions often take on a substantive form in the abstract and verbal nouns of a language, and then they become prolific sources of error. The substantive form gives a false show of independence to the adjective idea. We can guard against this illusion only by returning to the realities or concrete relations from which the ideas were abstracted.

Predicate notions are simple. The logical work in getting them consists in recognizing the one in the many, and in fixing it as a unit of thought. These notions also form the contents of our subject notions; for we define or express the latter only by their attributes, or predicates, or marks, as they are indifferently called. Without predicate notions subject notions could never be formed, and without subject notions predicates would be a flight of groundless adjectives. The necessity of finding ground and connection forbids us to rest in the thought of externally juxtaposed qualities without any internal bond, and thus we are forced upon the subject notion. And the impossibility of grasping or expressing being, except in terms of quality, forces us upon the predicate notion. The subject notion is only a special form of the general demand for rational connection.

What it contributes to the predicates is just the notion of a unitary ground which transforms their external juxtaposition into a fixed and complex unity. The attributes, then, are not attributes of one another, and they do not coexist by chance, but they form a group whose members belong together in the unity of a common subject.

In the empirical view of the subject notion, as in most logical discussion, there is almost exclusive attention to the objects of sense perception. These, as sense objects, seem to be sums of qualities, and there seems to be no other connection between these qualities than that of mere external adherence in space or time. Hence the statement often made that things are only bundles or groups of qualities; and hence, also, the claim that the subject notion is but the sum of its marks or attributes. Predication, then, means not the affirmation of a mysterious inherence of a predicate in a subject, but simply the declaration that certain predicates so come together that where one is found the rest are found. When, then, we say A is B the true meaning is that A and B are always found together, so that from one we can infer the other. And for this result nothing but experience and association are needed. Experience gives us simple qualities; association unites them; and the judgment simply declares the result.

The shortcomings of this view have already appeared in discussing the empirical doctrine of being. The simple qualities themselves are logical products by the time they are anything for intelligence. There is, further, a mistaking of subjective association for objective connection, and thus the essential aim of the judgment is missed altogether. Of course the view has no application to the large body of notions where the marks are not expressed in sense terms, but in terms of the understanding. This is increasingly the case even in physical science, where there is a growing insignificance of sense terms, and a constant attempt to turn them into conceptions of the intellect. The view is equally inapplicable to those conceptions which the mind creates for itself by definition, as in most of the subjective sciences.

The general notion expresses in one thought the contents of many things. Man stands for all men. As such the concept becomes a shorthand expression for all the individuals comprised under it. This fact, which makes the concept a great convenience and a great time-saver, does not depend altogether on our thought. The classification involved in the categories does indeed depend on the structure of reason, but to have any validity it must reproduce the structure of things. This classification, too, is so general that, if it were all, the mind could never attain to any but the most elementary development. The fact that a more complex classification is possible depends, not on the mind, but on the nature of its objects. These are such as to admit of a complex system of classification, and thus provision is made for a higher mental development. It is quite conceivable that our objects should have been such as to be as incommensurate as the data of different senses. In that case the mind would have lost itself in the unmanageable multiplicity and incommensurability of its objects.

We need the concept as a shorthand expression for the many. We also need a shorthand expression for the concept. We have already seen that the adequate concept of a class must contain all the marks common to the individuals of the class, and that the difference between the general and the singular concept does not consist in the number of marks or in the order of their union, but in the manner in which they are given. This relation we have illustrated by algebraic formulas with general and specific quantities.

Thus the concept itself, when the object is complex, becomes equally complex when thought out into completion.

But in actual use the concept is rarely thus completed. The finished concept, whether singular or universal, is an ideal rather than an actual possession. Instead of thinking it in its full contents, we rather abstract some single feature or factor and let that stand for the rest. This is the case with all complex singular concepts as well as with universals. When we pass from species to genera the thought becomes more and more a bare outline, which is filled out only upon occasion. All complex thought tends to become abbreviated, and, in that sense, symbolic. The shorthand expression or symbol carries the thought with sufficient accuracy, and we need only regard the proper treatment of our symbols, as in algebra we need not regard the meaning of our symbols, but only their logical manipulation. In this way a great economy of time and strength is secured, and, indeed, without it thought would break down from the cumbrousness of its own operations. On the other hand, this fact is a most prolific source of error, as the mind easily loses itself among its symbols and misses reality altogether.

The nature and meaning of the notion have been the subject of much not over-intelligent debate from very early times. It seems incumbent on us to glance at the matter in passing. The debate concerns, first, the objective or metaphysical nature of the notion, and, secondly, its subjective or epistemological nature.

The first question led in early philosophy to the dispute between realism and nominalism. The former held that universals are realities of which individuals are only accidents. The latter held that universals have only a mental existence, and that individuals are the only proper realities.

There is much in the order of thought that lends itself to the realistic view. We have seen that particulars become clear to us only as they are regarded as specifications of a general conception. Definition proceeds through the higher genus. The singular, then, for our defining thought, is always an accident of the universal. From this it is easy to conclude that the universal precedes the singular and constitutes its essence. And in an age when the theory of thought was undeveloped, and the order of thought was unhesitatingly taken for the order of things, realism was a very natural illusion.

At the same time the claim could be held, even in that undeveloped state of thought, only so long as attention was exclusively directed to the species of natural history. So long as we speak of man, cow, horse, and similar strikingly distinct species, there is a kind of plausibility in the notion of essences or types; but when we pass to genera and higher orders there is not even a semblance of meaning. The universal animal or organism would be hard indeed to typify. Besides, as Plato saw and said, there are many concepts which are artificial and relative to our own aims or logical convenience. Indeed, the majority of concepts are of this sort, and nothing could well be more absurd than the notion of an existing essence corresponding to them.

Nominalism, on the other hand, looks upon classes as only subjective conceptions without objective correspondence. We might illustrate by the parallels and meridians of geography. These are pure impositions of the mind. So with our dates and anniversaries in time. No one day is the beginning of a new year more than any other in respect to the unbroken continuum of the temporal flow. We are all nominalists, so far as any objective significance of these things is concerned. In the same way, nominalism holds that all classes are mental impositions, and not transcripts of facts.

In this extreme form the view cannot be held; for then all classification would be arbitrary, just as fixing the zero meridian is arbitrary. But all scientific classification proceeds on the assumption that natural groups exist, and our aim is to discover them. A classification which threw red cows, red horses, ripe strawberries, and raw meat together, on the ground that all were alike red, would be repudiated by every one as overlooking important natural affinities. Into how many degrees we shall divide the circumference of the circle is our own affair, but we have no such liberty in classifying natural objects. Nominalism is right in saying that the concept, as such, has only a mental existence. The reality is always singular and concrete; but the realities, though no accidents of a common or identical essence, still have affinities and likenesses among themselves which our classes aim to reproduce and represent. The question how these groups are produced is a separate one. The realistic notion of the universals as metaphysically real is absurd, and the nominalistic refusal to see anything but the unrelated individual is equally so.

We might illustrate the question and the shortcomings of both views by a mathematical series whose members are deduced each from its antecedent according to some law. The realist would hold that the idea of the series is the reality, and not its actual terms. The nominalist would hold that the terms are the only reality, and would deny the law which connects them. The fact would be the terms related according to law; and if we insisted on knowing how such a series came to be we could find no answer in hypostasizing the idea of the series, but only in going back to intelligence, the only real universal, and the author both of the idea and of the terms in which it is realized.

It is plain that this debate is antiquated in its ancient form. No one would longer maintain the existence of universals as a species of real essence. No one, on the other hand, could maintain in the face of universal scientific procedure that the unrelated individual is all, and that no classification has any objective foundation. With regard to many classes we are all nominalists, but some we are compelled to regard as natural groups. The origin of these groups is a question which leads out into the general question of theism.

So much for the objective significance of the concept, supposing the concept itself possible. But this whole discussion is vacated by an extension of the nominalistic denial to even the subjective existence of the concept. It is alleged that concepts are impossible even as conceptions, and thus at one stroke both realism and conceptualism are declared impossible. This brings us to the second question mentioned: the subjective significance of the concept.

This denial comes chiefly from the empirical school. It has its root in the desire to reduce the activity of the mind to a minimum. Indeed, a consistent empiricism cannot admit anything universal, whether subjective or objective. This fact makes the denial intelligible in its origin; it remains to inquire into its justification.

What, then, has the mind before it in the case of a general notion? Some extreme nominalists have maintained that the name is the only object. But if the name have no meaning, then bare noise or visual sensation is the sole contents of thought. In that case those who use different languages would have no common intelligence whatever, and one who knew two languages would have two distinct minds. Others less extreme, as Berkeley, have held that the mind has only a particular object before it, and that on the ground that a real object always must be particular. Any real triangle must always be acute or oblique or right-angled, and cannot be all of these at once. Hence I cannot form a conception of a triangle which is all of these at once; and hence, again, I cannot form any general notion of a triangle.

Some truth, some error, and much confusion mingle here. It is quite true that I cannot form a general picture of a triangle which shall belong to all three classes at once; but it is also true that I can conceive a general rule for forming triangles without taking these classes into account. It is quite true that I cannot conceive of an actual triangle which does not belong to some one of these classes, to the exclusion of the other two; but it is equally true that I can so deal with the conception of triangularity as to need to take no account of the sizes or ratios of the angles, and so as to get results valid for all triangles whatever. This fact is the foundation of geometry.

Besides, the objection, if good for anything, is good for more. The triangle must be particular not only in its angles, but also in its other elements—its area, its sides, its location, etc. If, now, my conception be particular, I ought to be able to tell the particular values of all the elements of my conceived triangle. The general notion of man has similar difficulties; and as I can conceive only of particular men I ought to be able to name my man, and tell his age, height, nationality, occupation, the color of his eyes and hair. Thus the doctrine perishes of its own absurdity. How a conception which, as an act, is particular and individual can be seen to be universal in its validity, or to be a law for the formation of other conceptions, is certainly beyond all telling. It suffices to see that such is, nevertheless, the fact.

Hence to the question, What has the mind before it in the case of general notions? the answer is, Their meaning; and this meaning is seen to apply indifferently or equally to an indefinite number of special cases. This meaning, however, is so rapidly grasped, and, if need be, dismissed, that it is easy to persuade the uncritical that only the word is before the mind. The rapidity of the mental movement in dealing with written or spoken language defies all attempts of the reflective and analytic consciousness to keep pace with it. Nevertheless, that there is something more than the word in play appears from the fact that the process is informed with meaning, while the word in itself is mere noise or a conventional sign.

The conclusion is that a general notion is no actual or possible metaphysical existence. All real existence is necessarily singular and individual. The only way to give the notion any metaphysical significance is to turn it into a law inherent in reality, and this attempt will fail unless we finally conceive this law as a rule according to which a basal intelligence proceeds in positing individuals. Such a result would recognize the truth in both nominalism and realism.

But, however this may be, the notion has a most important mental existence and logical function. As a conception or law which is valid for many particulars, it is an undeniable fact of our experience and an indispensable condition of our mental development. But this subjectivity has often been misconceived, with the result of turning conceptualism into a barren formalism.

On the one hand, it has been contended that logic has only to do with thoughts and not at all with things. On the other, it has been maintained that logic has to do with things and not with thoughts. There is just ambiguity enough in the terms to give each of these views a semblance of truth. That things can exist for the mind only through the thoughts we form of them is manifest; and, therefore, in a sense, the mind has to do only with thoughts.

But thoughts, again, have none of the properties which the mind attributes to things, and these are the great concern of thought. Hence the mind, in its search for truth, has to do with things and not with thoughts. In this contention we have the reappearance of the dual aspect of the thought process to which reference has so often been made. Considered as existing or becoming, the fact of the mental life is the particular stream of consciousness and its specific contents. But this life in its thought aspect relates itself to an independent order, and thought busies itself not at all with itself as a mental event, but rather with those independent facts and relations. Things cannot appear bodily in consciousness. In this sense the mind can deal only with thoughts. But the contents of these thoughts claim to be independent of the mental act whereby they are conceived. In this sense thought deals with things. Of course things here are not limited to material bodies, for much of our thinking has to do with immaterial objects and relations. These are *thinks* rather than things; at the same time, they are fixed factors in that order of reality which we do not make but find.

This objective reference to a common to all exists even in the case of fictitious objects, as the creations of mythology or the characters of fiction. These are, of course, subjective in the sense that they are no actual existences in physical reality, but they are not subjective in the sense that one is perfectly lawless in dealing with them. They represent fixed conceptions in the world of fancy, and have in this fact a kind of objectivity and independence; and whoever will deal with them must recognize the laws of their existence as established by their creators. The conception of Pegasus or Rosinante may not be applied indifferently to any barnyard animal. Pecksniff and Micawber likewise are fixed types of which the law must always be regarded.

The concept, then, has a double aspect. On the one hand, for thought it expresses a fixed meaning or a rule for dealing with objects, and, on the other hand, it applies to a set of objects. This is recognized in the familiar distinction between the intension and extension of concepts or between their connotation and denotation. The intension or connotation refers to the meaning; the extension or denotation refers to the objects to which the meaning applies.

This distinction, however, though manifestly valid in many cases, is not easily made universal. To begin with, it is easy to fix the denotation, even formally, only in the case of objects which have substantial existence. When we come to objects which have only conceptual existence, it has an aspect of grotesqueness to speak of the denotation. What, for instance, would be the denotation of liberty, piety, knowledge, reverence, etc.? Possibly some formalistic rigorist would insist in finding a denotation for these terms, but it would not pay expenses.

The connotation is easily determined by formal definition as the meaning of the concept. In practice some uncertainty arises from the fact that the connotation is often changing or enlarging. In such a case it is easy to raise a scruple whether the new elements are a part of the connotation or not. If some new property of the triangle were discovered, it might be claimed that that property was no part of the connotation, since the connotation is what we mean by the term, and the new property does not enter into the meaning.

Two facts make this scruple possible. The first is the implicit assumption of a self-identical and universal system of things and ideas which our actual conceptions represent. Without this reference to an abiding reality there would not be any possibility of a changing connotation; for then every notion would centre in itself, and a changed connotation would be a changed idea; that is, a new idea. We are saved from this conceptual flux only by reference to the world of abiding meanings back of our conceptions.

The second fact underlying the scruple mentioned is the gradual development of our knowledge. We first posit our objects as self-identical and abiding, and then we slowly determine their attributes. In this way the notion which represents these objects acquires a kind of fixity and identity, however much the contents of the notion may change. It is the same notion through all changes of connotation, because the notion throughout applies to the same things; and this sameness of the things is readily mistaken for the sameness of the notion. When, finally, by the connotation we understand only as much as may be necessary to mark off the notion from others, it is then very easy to raise difficulties about the connotation.

In fact, however, this question belongs to psychology and philology rather than to logic. From the logical standpoint the meaning is the connotation, and if anything be added to the marks of a concept it becomes part of the connotation. The fact that many have not heard of it, or that the dictionary-makers have not got wind of it, does not modify the logical fact.

The extension and intension of notions are commonly said to vary inversely. This is another doctrine which has only a limited validity and a still more limited value. It does not apply at all to the relation between individuals and the class next above them. There is no relation between the marks which make up the notion horse and the number of horses. The same is true for all other natural kinds. Neither does it apply to the many cases where two or more marks form a fixed group; for in all such cases the inclusion of one mark would give the same extension as the inclusion of all. The doctrine is valid chiefly for artificial classifications where we may add or subtract marks at pleasure, or for those abstract classes which we have called symbols rather than conceptions.

This consideration of the connotation leads to the subject of definition. On this point also there is a deal of confusion, owing to uncertainty as to the meaning of definition. If knowledge were complete the connotation would be the definition, and the definition would be the connotation. But as knowledge is not thus complete we have to content ourselves with approximations. Definitions vary all the way from conceptions which only serve to mark off a thought content from all others to those which give the essential inner law of the object. Of course our concern is with real definition. Nominal definition is only an accident of language.

The traditional conception of definition is that it consists in giving the genus and differentia. This of course presupposes that a system of classification already exists. Such a definition has its chief value in enabling one to locate the object in our mental system by marking it off from others, but it does not give much further information. When we define man as a rational animal we know that he belongs to the genus animal, and has rationality as his specific mark or difference, whereby he is distinguished from other species within the same genus. This type of definition must always be prominent in practical thought.

But another conception of definition is that it gives the essential nature of the thing. Here the higher speculative tendency of thought is in play. It is not content with surface classifications, but seeks to penetrate to the essence of things. Nor need we adopt the classification of Porphyry in his famous tree to see that there is here a genuine speculative problem. Things may have many properties in relation to ourselves, but, apart from our thinking and apart from us, they have a law or nature which determines what they are and do, and any fundamental knowledge must aim at grasping this essential nature.

This is indeed the ideal conception of definition, but it is an ideal which is very rarely realized. Even in mathematics differing definitions of the same thing, as the ellipse, are possible, and there seems to be no reason for saying that any one more truly represents the essence than any other. The ground for choice lies in the convenience of manipulation or elegance of exposition. Really it seems as if we should come nearer the truth of the matter if we should say the ellipse is the ellipse, and it may be produced in such and such a way, or it has such and such properties. Any inquiry after the essential ellipse which should go beyond this statement would seem to be idle if not meaningless.

In dealing with things, however much we may believe in the abstract possibility of realizing our ideal definition, we have to admit that most of our definitions are purely relative to our own ends or convenience. Such definitions would not exist for one studying the purely objective fact, and hence can lay no claim to express an essence. While, then, a definition may be possible from some absolute standpoint which should express the essential nature, we have to content ourselves with a humbler point of view.

This general conception of definition cancels the distinction between essence, property, and accident, except as relative to ourselves. The most remote and occult property of the triangle is as essential to it as the most familiar and obvious. Any distinction which is made must be relative to the order or measure of our knowledge.

It seems, then, that definition is a rather complex matter. If we are not content to define by genus and difference we must admit that complete definition can never be given. The definition of the triangle becomes the whole science of trigonometry. The definition of anything becomes the complete science of that thing. Such a conception of definition is, of course, practically worthless. Its only value lies in keeping alive the ideal of knowledge, and in maintaining the idea of rational connection among all the various properties and manifestations of our objects. In practice, however, it is always possible to understand ourselves and one another, and if we make sure of this we shall secure all that is practically important in definition. The theory may be left in its uncertainty, or, rather, incompleteness, without any practical loss.

Classes also can be classified, thus producing concepts of greater and greater extension and abstraction. In this activity thought becomes more and more symbolic. The conceptions become more abstract, and have less and less content. The best illustration is found in the natural-history sciences. Here we have a highly complex and interesting series of classes ranging from the lowest species to the highest genus. In such cases the concept, which is a universal for one group, may be an individual for another; and, finally, all classes may be gathered under some one inclusive genus.

This fact has given rise to the fancy that all classes admit of a linear or pyramidal classification, so that by adding or subtracting marks we can pass from any notion to any other, and thus at last embrace all classes in the sphere of some one. But this is a mistake. In a general classification of the contents of thought we come down to notions, none of which can be subsumed under any other without distortion or violence. In fact, we come down to the categories, or to those primal distinctions and classifications on which thought is based. All nouns lead to the notion of thing; all adjectives to the general notion of quality; all variations of a common quality to the notion of quantity; all active verbs to the notion of causation, etc. Of course we might unite all these under the one head of the thinkable, but nothing would be gained. Wherever there is any element of similarity among individuals we may make a class; and wherever there is any unlikeness we may make a division. But the value of a classification is not in itself, but in what it helps us to, and classifications for form's sake are to be avoided.

The logical mechanism of classification is simple, and from the standpoint of abstract theory its working is equally simple. We have only to compare individuals and separate the like from the unlike, and the work is done. In practice, however, the matter is more difficult. It is not always easy to determine either the individual or the common mark. This mark may be of the most varied kinds — sense-quality, form, relation, function, etc. Whatever things have a common factor may be classed together; but it is found that some similarities are more important than others, being inherent and essential, while others are superficial, if not accidental, like the alphabetical classification of catalogues and dictionaries. Even the latter cannot be dispensed with, for we often have nothing to take its place. But if we are not content to form artificial classes only we must look for the natural and essential affinities, and these are not easily found. In every-day classification, where we deal mainly with sense-objects, individuals are marked off from one another by space limits, and fall into easily distinguished groups. But when we seek to make an extended and scientific classification it is not easy to find a common and consistent standard, or even to determine what the individual itself is. Illustration is found in the conflicting uncertainties and complexities of botanical, biological, and mineralogical classification.

Moreover, the things which in some respects are alike are often in other respects different. Minerals which have the same chemical composition may have very different physical properties, as graphite and the diamond. A mineralogical classification according to chemical composition would be very different from one determined by physical characteristics. Again, things are often different in the respect in which they are like. The color scale is a case of this kind. In what we call the same color there is an indefinite variety of shades. Popular language recognizes only a few classes, and treats these shades as modifications of one color or assimilates them to the nearest lying class, as when we speak of a greenish yellow or a yellowish green. There is a double reason for this. One is the feeling that the case in hand does not deserve to be made an independent class. The other is the limitations of language and the confusion which arises from multiplying classes beyond necessity. Of this confusion we get some hint when confronted with the bewildering color terminology of trade.

Of making classes, then, as of making books, there need be no end, so long as any likeness or any difference remains. Both excess and defect in this matter are alike dangerous, and for hitting the golden mean there is no apriori prescription. The survival of the fittest will have to look after the matter.

The ideal of thought, we have said, is to gather our experience under concepts which shall be distinct and clear in themselves, and also adequate to the matter to be expressed. That we are at an indefinite distance from the attainment of this ideal is plain upon inspection. Our concepts, as a whole, exist in all degrees of completeness. We find many notions in a state of growth and without any sharp definition. If there is a central point of light there is also a large border of penumbral haze. Art, life, society, culture, literature, and poetry are examples. Here also belong the vocabulary of superior persons in general and a large part of the terminology of criticism. Many notions are only conceptual forms whose contents remain to be determined. The form may be correct, but the values are all given in unknown or indefinite quantities. With the uneducated most notions beyond those denoting sense objects are in this state, having only a vague intimation of a meaning. None of these are completed conceptions, although they have the place and form of such. Here belongs the "it" of impersonal judgments. In this case an almost formless matter, the bare category of ground, is given the place and function of a conditioning subject. In such cases the naked framework of the categories holds the thought together, but there is no content beyond the form. And what is true of this "it" is equally true of many other terms. The bare form of thought is present with little or no content.

Much of our sensitive and emotional experience also is so fluent as to defy accurate definition or even description, except in the most general way. We may call it feeling, but this term only locates the experience without saying much. The material is fluent and elusive. In the world of the senses we seek to escape from this subjective uncertainty by inventing objective measures which shall enable us to define our objects in objective terms. In the world of feeling this is impossible. Emotions shift as we contemplate them. Feelings fade into their opposites. This fact will long forbid any hard and fast definition and classification in this realm. Here thought only forms and names a content which it cannot produce, and which can be realized only in living experience.

Many of our concepts have to do with the world of reality, and the most important function of the concept is to mediate a knowledge of that world. Hence the doctrine of the concept has been largely constructed along metaphysical lines. This is necessary when dealing with the cosmic reality. But there is a large body of concepts which have to do with the world of custom and convention—that is, with things which have only a notional existence. This world, which embraces a large part of the human world, abounds in arbitrariness and confusion. It represents no fixed nature of things, no abiding rational connections, but rather passing convention, fancy, and caprice. To one fixing his attention upon this world it might well seem that logic has nothing to do with metaphysics, but when we view the whole field of thought this illusion disappears.

Hence our concepts vary all the way from constructive definitions to descriptions, and even to mere names which may denote something but which connote nothing. It would, then, be a great mistake to suppose that the contents of consciousness consist of sharply defined and clearly conceived ideas. These are really the exception rather than the rule, the ideal rather than the actual. They are peaks which lift themselves above the general cloudiness, or islands in the obscure flood.

There is somewhat of vague matter in the current logic which finds such justification as it has in this psychological fact. This appears especially in the attempt to find something between the particular experience and the general notion. Accordingly, we are told much about the "general presentation," the "representative image," the "abstract word," the "phantasm," etc. The little truth in all this is that the concept is not completed at once, but is subject to growth. But the concept in its general representative character is given as soon as articulate intelligence is given. We have abundantly seen that the particular becomes anything for intellect only as it comes under some universal.

Thus far we have treated only of the concept as the thought element, and have taken no notice of its expression in language. As thus expressed the concept becomes the term or the name, with the proviso, however, that the term need not be a single word. In logic the term is the linguistic expression of the conception, and very often it is a single word; but often it consists of a group of words, as in the logical subjects of grammatical analysis. It seems desirable to say here a word about language and its relation to thought.

Thought might conceivably be complete in itself without language, and every practised thinker has experience of thinking without words; but for the communication and preservation of thought, language is of the highest importance. It is the great instrument of mental intercourse and the great storehouse of thought. Without it there could be only such imperfect society and imperfect mental life as exist among deaf-mutes, and even among these the union depends upon the invention of some imperfect substitute for language.

The use of vocal signs is natural to man. The particular signs used have in them something arbitrary and contingent. If it were not for the multiplicity of languages we might be tempted to think that there is some pre-established harmony between sound and sense, but the facts forbid any such notion. The physiological and psychological factors which condition language in general are very obscure, and the historical conditions which have led to the differentiation of the particular languages are even more obscure.

For thought, then, language as a set of vocal signs is something extra-logical. Our interest in language concerns solely its relation to thought.

In the fundamental parts of speech we observe the reappearance of the categories. Noun and adjective reproduce being and quality, or substance and attribute. The active verb rests on the notion of causality. Other parts of speech represent other rational relations.

The root noises of a language may be looked upon as extra-logical, but the root conceptions are a mental product. The development of a language beyond its root forms involves a deal of logical activity. Old terms have to be modified, or combined, or extended to new meanings to fit them for the expression of new ideas, and this involves the detection of analogies and a complex activity of generalization. Particularly is this the case in forming a language for the inner life. From the nature of the case this must be based upon physical images, and the finding of fit images is a task demanding the labor of generations of poets and philosophers.

Language has a double function—the communication and the registration of thought. Its registering value is very greatly increased by the invention of written language. As a register of thought, language very greatly abbreviates the work of thought. Every word expresses the result of a process of abstraction and generalization, and we who inherit a language find a vast amount of mental work done for us. We have simply to understand the language, not to invent or construct it. This convenience of language has often led to the inverted fancy that language is the generator of thought.

This fancy finds a kind of support in a misinterpretation of the following facts: It is often said that no thought is complete until we have found a word for it. Until then it remains a bodiless abstraction with only a shadowy substance. There is, then, no thought without speech.

The mistake here lies in attributing to the naming the

effect of the classifying activity implicit in the naming.
Superficial thought easily confounds the two, and then it
is easy to maintain the inseparability of thought and speech.

The second misinterpreted fact is this: Individuals born
into a community which has a developed language find a
store of words ready made for their use. Thus the word
precedes the thought, and one of the tasks of the educator
is to make sure that the youthful thought shall overtake
and inform its words.

The mistake here lies in mistaking this accidental order
in the history of the individual for the essential order in
the development of thought.

The true order is most clearly seen in the structure of
scientific language. Here an order of conceptions arises
which, for the most part, is foreign to popular thought
altogether, and for which popular language has no adequate means of expression. Then it becomes necessary to
construct a terminology which shall be adequate to the
matter and be free from the indefiniteness of popular
speech. Endless illustration is found in the language of
the classificatory sciences.

But language not only serves thought by storing up its
results and abbreviating its processes; it also often misleads
thought, and thus becomes responsible for much error.
Some of the chief blunders of speculation have been diseases of language. Verbal distinctions and identifications
have been mistaken for real ones. Often the figure involved in the word is mistaken for the thing, and the exegesis of the figure has been mistaken for an analysis of the
thing. In this way psychology, philosophy, and theology
have often been infested with mythological fancies born of
language. Often, too, language is used without any definite thought, and if only the conventions of grammar are
regarded the fact is unnoticed. In this way phrases and

doctrines often acquire currency which are equally sonorous and unsubstantial. Mere words so often usurp the place of thought that, to many, to change the word is to change the thing. In general, in matters of abstract thought, it is much safer to use the same words for very different things than to use different words for the same thing. A political party may change all its principles and remain the same party, but a change of name would be fatal.

The great elementary experiences of humanity are identical among all peoples, and for these all languages of any development furnish adequate equivalent expression. But when we get away from these simple facts there is seldom a complete equivalence between the corresponding terms of any two languages. The underlying metaphor, or the angle of view, differs. The associations also differ. Hence a word, in addition to its logical meaning, acquires a complex suggestiveness. Dire disaster indeed would overtake one who should attempt to use words with regard only to their logical connotation and without considering the company they have kept. This is permissible only with the colorless and objective language of science. The associations of words are the overtones of speech, and they have the same function as overtones in music. They constitute a literary language in distinction from a purely logical one, and form the insuperable barrier to perfect literary translation.

Language is never thought, but only a symbol of thought, or a stimulus to think the thought. When our terms denote sense objects, or simple and elementary conceptions of the intellect, we may be fairly sure of mutual understanding; but when we get beyond these there is no security for agreement. The language itself is figurative and admits of misunderstanding. The hope that the metaphor will be rightly understood, and neither over nor under estimated is by no means always realized. In such cases we can only vary the expression, often availing ourselves even of contradictory expressions, with the aim of shutting up the recipient mind to a form of mental activity which shall put before it the meaning we seek to impart. In this aim we are often defeated by the dulness and irresponsiveness of the party of the second part, and our discomfiture is completed by the discovery that said party generally regards his own failure to understand as a disproof of the matter in question.

Sometimes, also, the subject-matter eludes any articulate thought and expression. This is particularly the case with the emotional life. In setting forth this deeper life of feeling and aspiration we fall back on music, art, worship, and various symbolic activities which alone serve to give voice to the dumb souls of men.

And now, by combining the indefiniteness or equally dangerous overdefiniteness of language with the indefiniteness of thought itself, we see that we have to deal with an indefiniteness of the second order. We have to struggle with the difficulties of the subject itself, and also to guard ourselves against the omnipresent imposture and deceit of language.

The concept is the first and the last in thought. It is the first in form and the last in completion. Meanwhile it represents an ideal which we must follow, however far off.

CHAPTER VI

THE JUDGMENT

DEFINITIONS of the judgment are tautologous, and descriptions serve only for identification. The understanding of the matter must be sought in our immediate experience. Our aim, then, must be not so much to tell what the judgment is as, rather, to tell what we do when we judge.

The judgment is a mental act in which an affirmation or negation is made with the conviction of its validity for the world of fact or the world of reason. It is this conviction of validity and this reference to an independent order which distinguish the judgment in its intention and subjective nature from the groupings of association, and which make it possible to consider judgments as true or false. This fact has been sufficiently dwelt upon in treating of the objectivity of thought. Judgments as associations of ideas in a particular consciousness are neither true nor false, but only mental events. They become true or false only when related to an abiding order beyond them. When expressed in language the judgment becomes the proposition.

With this conception of the judgment it is plain that judging enters even into our most elementary consciousness. Any consciousness which has passed beyond the stage of unqualified, unrelated feeling and become a consciousness of something has already reached the stage of judging. This fact has already appeared in the discussion of the mind's activity in getting objects.

The uncertainty in the traditional treatment of the judgment has a double root. In the first place, the sensationalists, owing to their congenital mental myopia, have always overlooked both the constitutive rational activity underlying all articulate consciousness, and also the objective reference implicit in thought. Aided and abetted by these two oversights, they have found it easy to assume particular units of consciousness as undeniably given, and then to unite these by association into groups and series. When finally we are assured that this is all there is to the judgment, all those who remain on the sense plane are fairly sure to be convinced. The hopeless superficiality of this view is already familiar.

In the next place, and on the other hand, those whose studies in psychology and epistemology have revealed the logical activity in consciousness itself, when they come to study logic are apt to forget the results of their previous study and accept uncritically the old tradition. Thus Sir William Hamilton repeats his uncertainty respecting the concept in his treatment of the judgment. In discussing the conditions of consciousness, he shows very clearly that there can be no consciousness without judgment; but when we come to his doctrine of the judgment, we find the familiar subordination of the judgment to the concept without a trace of insight into their true and essential relations. Such vacillation necessarily results from trying to separate logic, as the science of thought, from that living activity which underlies the whole mental life, from elementary consciousness on to its most abstract speculative constructions.

Mr. Mansel, in his *Prolegomena Logica*, has shown a perception of this inconsistency, and has thought, or at least sought, to mend matters by distinguishing logical from psychological judgments. Those judgments on which consciousness depends are psychological; properly logical judgments are those in which the full-fledged concept plays its well-known part.

This distinction was manifestly made for the sake of saving the conceptualistic logic and keeping the form of thought clear of any compromising alliance with the matter. Beyond this adventitious teleological function, it has no warrant in the nature of the case. The utmost that can be allowed is this: The activity of judging is by no means always attended by a reflective consciousness of the activity itself. In such cases reason has us rather than we have reason. In other cases we may judge with full consciousness of our material and our aims. But any distinction which may be made here must rest upon the measure of reflective consciousness, and not upon any difference of the logical elements in the two cases.

The question whether the concept precedes the judgment, or the judgment the concept, may be variously answered according to our standpoint. Some concepts precede some judgments, and some concepts succeed some judgments. The concept is quite as often the product of the judgment as its antecedent. Here there is large room for one of those sterile debates with which the history of logic has so abounded. On the one hand, it might be contended that an analysis of the judgment shows that the concepts which appear in the subject and predicate are presupposed. On the other hand, we might be challenged to show any concept whatever which does not imply some precedent judgment.

The way out of this deadlock lies in the insight that neither the judgment nor the concept is anything by itself or in abstraction from each other. The judging act has a double aspect. It involves a matter and a reduction of that matter to rational form. But while the act, upon analysis, falls asunder into these two factors, there is no proper precedence or sequence; for neither is anything for thought except through the other. Of course this mutual interpenetration of the two elements finds no proper expression in the conventional symbol for the judgment, A is B. While, then, we must retain such symbols for the sake of exposition, we must be careful to remember that they are only symbols which stand for the judgment rather than represent it.

The difficulty in finding a single satisfactory formula for the judgment is due to the fact that judgments are of all degrees of complexity, and occur under all the categories. Judgments of likeness, of space, of time, of number, of quantity, of identity, of causality, of inherence, of subsumption, of existence, are incommensurable as the respective categories themselves; and when we seek to force them into a common expression we are in danger either of ignoring the peculiarities of some of the judgments, or of making a formula so general as to have no valuable meaning. Attributive judgments, subsumptive judgments, quantitative judgments, existential judgments, judgments of identification and equivalence, are hard to describe by any common formula other than that given—namely, a judgment is a mental act, or the result of a mental act, in which an affirmation or negation is made with the conviction of its validity for the world of fact or the world of reason. Most of what is said in logical treatises about the judgment is false to its logical and psychological nature. The exposition is commonly constructed with reference to syllogistic necessities rather than logical truth. Sometimes, also, the exposition is determined by the exigencies of a partisan doctrine; in which case, of course, truth is a secondary consideration. Both forms of aberration deserve illustration.

For entering into and illustrating syllogistic forms the

subsumptive judgment is best adapted. The judgment A is B, then, means that the subject or the class A is contained in the class B. Oaks are trees means that the class oak is contained in the class tree. Maples are not hickories means that the class maple lies outside of the class hickory. Some trees are chestnuts means that the class tree lies partly within the class chestnut. And this relation is easily demonstrated to sense by the familiar illustration of circles which include or exclude each other, wholly or partially. Besides, this conception of the judgment has the advantage of evading, at least apparently, all metaphysical questions concerning inherence and connection; and thus the judgment is kept clear of all vexatious and irrelevant consideration of the matter of thought, and confined to its own proper subject of the form. On all these accounts there has been a very general tendency among formal logicians to recognize only judgments of the subsumptive type.

How foreign this is to logical and psychological truth is plain upon inspection. In comparatively few judgments is the thought that of subsumption. Quantitative judgments are commonly not subsumptive at all. In attributive judgments the aim is to affirm a predicate, not to subsume one class under another. And subsumption itself commonly depends on connection. This is the case even when classes are affirmed of classes. Here the essential thought is not the inclusion of one class in another class, but rather the attribution to the objects denoted by one class term of the properties connoted by the other class term. Thus pigeons are birds does not mean that pigeons are included in the class birds, but that pigeons have the properties connoted by the term birds. The belonging together of two or more marks is the essential conception. While, then, the subsumptive rendering may be allowed where any practical convenience results, as in syllogistic exposition, we must be on our guard against taking it as other than a superficial or artificial conception of the judgment.

This illustrates what is meant by saying that a large part of the current exposition of the judgment is constructed with reference to the needs of the syllogism, and not with reference to the logical fact. A traditional definition of the judgment illustrates the second form of aberration mentioned, that which results from defining the judgment to fit a theory.

According to this definition the judgment is a declaration of the agreement, or disagreement, of two notions. This view has attractions for philosophers of very different schools. The empiricist is naturally drawn to it, as it seems to reduce thought to such low terms that association by similarity, or dissociation by unlikeness, might well be able to manage the matter. Certain types of idealism, too, find their account in it, as it says nothing of things, and keeps the mind within the realm of ideas. The conceptualist and the logical formalist also are fond of this definition, and for obvious reasons. It carefully excludes all reference to matter-of-fact, and leaves the mind free to contemplate the unstained purity of the thought form.

Whether we are to accept this definition must depend on its meaning, which, unfortunately, is not immediately clear. It may mean that judgment is a declaration of the agreement or disagreement of the ideas as mental states; or it is such a declaration concerning the contents of the ideas; or it is a declaration concerning the things which the ideas represent. The first sense is manifestly absurd. Ideas have none of the properties of their contents. The thought of ice is not cold, and the thought of fire is not hot. The qualities are in the objects, and not in the ideas. And hence it is said, with correct meaning but doubtful expression, not ideas but things are joined in the judgment.

But, on the other hand, it is plain that very many judgments do not concern things at all, as in the subjective sciences. Besides, when they do concern things, things themselves are never in thought, but only ideas. Hence it would seem that we must say that the judgment deals neither with ideas as mental states, nor with things as extramental existences, but only with the logical contents of ideas. This we must allow to a certain extent. Thought has no way of dealing with things except through ideas, and hence the contents of our ideas must necessarily make up the whole sphere of consciousness. But, on the other hand, we must equally allow that the judgment is never complete until these contents are related to a world of fact or reason which these contents apprehend or reproduce. Even in the case of purely fictitious objects, as we have seen, there is the same objective reference, not indeed to the world of cosmic fact, or historic event, or pure reason, but to the world of convention. An artist who would paint a griffin must regard the nature of the beast as certainly as in painting a camel. To be sure, the griffin exists only in the world of mythological and poetic convention, but as an inhabitant of that world it has a fixed character which must be regarded in all our dealings with it.

While, then, the judgment does not connect or disjoin things, it certainly aims to declare the connections or disjunctions of things; or, while the judgment does nothing to things, it nevertheless busies itself with the relations and truth of things. Understanding by things the objective implication of thought, we may say that all judgments have an existential reference in them; not always to substantive existence of course, but to an order of some sort to which the judgment is related as true or false. Without this reference the judgment loses all meaning and sinks to the level of children's formulas of incantation.

Many schemes for classifying judgments have been invented, all of which are rejected by somebody. These often have their source in psychological or epistemological theories, and vary with the sect. Judgments may also be classified by the categories under which they occur, and in many respects this classification is valuable. Judgments in space, or time, or quantity, cannot be understood except from their own standpoint. In the Kantian sense they are intuitions; that is, no analysis of the subject reveals the predicate, but by constructing the problem we see the truth.

There is, then, an element of arbitrariness, or at least of relativity, in the classification of judgments. Fortunately, this fact in no way affects the aim of the judgment, or obscures our insight into its truth. But the fact itself and this saving clause are often overlooked; and strenuous attempts are made, agonistic in the inverse ratio of their importance, to secure an absolute classification. Abandoning such high aims, we point out that the classification which has most logical merit is that which divides judgments into categorical, conditional, and disjunctive; and it has this merit because it is the only one which adequately represents the form of living experience. In the first the predicate is unconditionally affirmed or denied; in the second, conditionally; in the third no predicate is affirmed, but a necessary choice between two or more.

Of course much effort has been made to reduce the two latter forms to the first, but with very imperfect success. After a fashion, indeed, any conditional or disjunctive matter may be put into a categorical form. Thus, If A is B, A is C, may be read, All A B's are C's. If A is B, C is D, may be read, $A B$ and $C D$ come together. In like manner the disjunctive judgment may be thrown into both conditional and categorical form. Thus, A is either B or C may be read, If A is B, it is not C. Or B and C are the divisions of A.

At best, however, this only shows that a conditional or disjunctive matter may be put into an equivalent categorical form; it is very far from dispensing with the conditional and disjunctive ideas. These ideas remain under the alleged identification of form, and modify the predication. The common form does not remove the fact that in some judgments the predicate is unconditionally affirmed; in others it is not so affirmed. It remains to point out that all three forms are alike necessary for the expression of real thought.

Of the categorical judgment nothing need be said. The conditional judgment is necessary for expressing the conditional laws and forces of reality. The categorical form is needed to express simple connection, A is B. The conditional form is needed to express conditional connection, A is B if A is C; that is, A is B under the condition C. In the earlier logic, beginning with Plato, we have an attempt to gather all reality under a rigid and resting classification of ideas, and formal logic has largely held the same view. For this the law of identity and the categorical judgment suffice, but the view reduces thought to the rigid monotony of the Eleatics. In fact, reality is in motion. Nothing has its properties absolutely, but only in relations and under conditions. In place of rigid monotony we have movement and combination according to law. To recognize and express this fact we need the form of the conditional judgment. To be sure, there are metaphysical depths underlying the conditional judgment, the consideration of which logic hands over to metaphysics; but the judgment itself is necessary to the expression of experience. Indeed, if our thought were fully expressed, it would appear that most of our categorical judgments are really conditional. Things have color, but only in the light. Water is fluid, but only within certain limits of temperature. Water boils at 100° C., but only under a certain atmospheric pressure.

The disjunctive judgment is likewise necessary to express the movement of living and concrete thought. Notions, we have seen, may be read in intension or extension. A purely intensive reading would leave thought with a rule, but without objects to which it might be applied. Thus the judgment, Man is mortal, read in intension, says only that the conception humanity involves the conception mortality; that is, it is a rule for dealing with men, if there be any such. The judgment, then, becomes operative only as we pass from the intension to the extension. But when we read a notion in extension, at once it falls into its various divisions or disjunctions. Thus the notion man read in extension breaks up into male and female, or men, women, and children, or Americans, Europeans, Asiatics, etc., or other divisions according to nationality, race, occupation. In such cases the disjunctive judgment is necessary. It is primarily the declaration that a notion taken in extension falls into such and such divisions, and that any particular case of this notion must be found in some one of these divisions to the exclusion of the rest. Thus the disjunctive judgment arises necessarily whenever the notion is read in extension.

We conclude, then, that actual thought cannot dispense with the conditional and disjunctive forms. They necessarily emerge in concrete thinking. To the objection that this is to take account of the matter of thought, while logic confines itself to the pure form, the answer must be that a form so pure that it omits the living principles by which thought proceeds cannot be of much practical importance. Of course, if any one chooses to retreat into a mental vacuum and manipulate meaningless symbols, and call the performance the science of the pure forms of thought, there is no law against it. Such a procedure could hardly fail to be its own exceeding great reward.

We return now to the categorical judgment in its affirmative form. The traditional formula is A is B. This formula fits well into the claim that the judgment is a declaration of the agreement of two notions; but it is a sorry expression for a large body of judgments. In all cases where we posit the subject as real, whether as substantive fact or as historic event, it is not easy to find the B with which A agrees. The distortions of thought and language which have arisen from the determination to crowd the historic tenses and all judgments of existence into the one form of subject, copula, and predicate are instructive illustrations of what steep places of nonsense one may rush down when possessed by the demon of system. The meaning of such judgments is obvious. The subject is posited as belonging to the world of real things or events, and nothing is gained by confusing this transparent clearness for the sake of a barren form.

But a great many categorical judgments are of the form A is B, and these deserve special consideration. Here the fundamental thought is that of connection. The subject A has or implies the predicate B, or A and B belong together in the nature of fact or reason. We have already seen that subsumptive judgments are secondary, and depend upon this basal judgment of connection.

Thus far all is plain sailing; but there are unsuspected complexities in the matter which must be brought to light. At first we might think that the judgment might be possible with two entirely singular conceptions, as, This A is this B; but plainly this will not do. This A and this B presuppose A and B limited to a special case; and if we drop out the universal element, the judgment reduces to,

This is this. The utmost that can be allowed in this direction is that the subject may be singular; the predicate must be a class term.

But whatever the subject and whatever the predicate, a little nominalistic reflection must convince us that, in any concrete case, neither subject nor predicate appears in its generality, but each is limited to special values, and each is modified by the other. This results necessarily from the mutual relations of the universal and the singular. The singular can be thought only in a universal form, and the universal can be realized only in particular cases. It is not the concept A which is B, but the individuals included in the class A. Not the king or the oldest inhabitant dies, but kings and oldest inhabitants die. Again, in concrete cases B is not affirmed in its generality, but only in some special modification, for only thus can it be realized. Thus A and B are both specialized in practice, and they are also limited by each other. The predicate defines the subject, and the subject limits the predicate.

To illustrate the matter. In the judgment, Man is wise, it is plain that the subject is not man the concept, but men, the living realities. It is further plain that all men cannot be the subject, for a great many men are not wise. Only the wise men are the real subjects when we think the matter out. Again, the wisdom is not to be taken absolutely, but only in relation to the human subjects. It is not, then, angelic or superhuman wisdom of any kind that can be affirmed, but only human wisdom; and, indeed, in any special case, only the wisdom of the particular subject. Newton's wisdom could not be affirmed of one learning the multiplication table. When these considerations are duly reflected upon, it would seem as if the judgment A is B must become $A\ B$ is $A\ B$, and thus vanish into an identical judgment.

And now it would seem that, as is most meet, we have

fallen a prey to overdone acuteness, and have landed ourselves in a blind alley, where we can neither go on nor back out. For an empirical theory of thought this is probably the end. It can find no subjects which last long enough to be subjects, and no connection to serve as a basis of predication. Its excessive nominalism also leaves it without any law-giving universal, and the judgment vanishes into tautology or contradiction. And for any theory of thought the only way out of the puzzle lies in the general assumption of connection and in the subordination of individuals to the universal. The former fact makes it possible to form groups of elements, AB, CD, etc. The meaning of these groups is that their elements belong together, and this fact we express by saying A is B, C is D, etc. These judgments are entirely in intension, and are simply rules of procedure for dealing with particular cases. In this respect they are closely allied with the concept, which, we have seen, is not a conception of any particular thing, but a rule for forming conceptions of any number of particular things. The intensive judgment A is B finds concrete application only as we pass to the extension of the terms and consider the individuals included under them, and subordinate those individuals to the general law, A is B; that is, in practice, if anything is A it is also B.

If, then, we ask for the implications of the actual working judgment we find the following: It must first be possible to form general groups of elements, as AB, which admit of being expressed in the form A is B. This possibility depends on the primal assumption that some things belong together in the order of fact or reason. But this form remains only a general rule without application, unless A and B become universals comprehending an indefinite number of individuals for which they are law-giving. Of course it is not meant that these implications lie on the surface of the judgment, so that he that runs may read, but only that when the judgment is criticised these implications appear as the condition of saving it from collapse.

In the fundamental judgment of connection, A is B, there is no reference to extension; but as the judgment becomes concrete and operative only as we pass to the extension of the terms, the quantity of judgments has to be considered. In the fundamental judgment, also, the quantity is universal. A is B declares that A and B belong together, and hence if anything is A it is B, or All A's are B. It is easily conceivable that the material of thought should have been of such a kind that only universal judgments should be possible. All A's are B, or No A is B. Particular judgments arise from the possibility of cross classification. The same objects may be classified according to different standards, thus producing overlapping classes. This relation is expressed in the particular judgment, Some A's are B; Some A's are not B.

From the standpoint of formal logic the negative judgment is entirely simple. It denies the connection of A and B, or declares that they belong apart. Attempts have been made to turn it into an affirmative judgment by attaching the negative to B. Thus, A is non-B; so that, instead of denying B, we affirm non-B. But this is mainly misplaced sharpness. Non-B is no notion at all, but only a chaotic heap of all things and thoughts which are not B. The terms of this kind, which abound in language, are negative only in form, or their negation is limited to the class in question; for instance, immortal, inhuman, unjust, indecent, etc.

The traditional logic gives us a table of judgments as follows:

All A is B, No A is B,
Some A is B, Some A is not B,

or universal affirmative and negative, and particular affirmative and negative. This scheme rests on reading A in extension, and says nothing of the essential judgment A is B, which alone brings out the idea of law or connection. Thus the most essential factor of thought is missed entirely.

In this table also no account is taken of the quantity of the predicate; that is, it is not stated whether All A is All B, or only Some B, etc. This addition has been made to logical doctrine under the name of the quantification of the predicate. It is a mere formalism of no practical or theoretical importance.

A final step in this mechanical formalism is the equational and symbolic logic. In this the attempt is made to express judgments in the form of equations; and thus, it is thought, a notable advance in logical theory is secured. But of this also it must be said that it has neither practical nor theoretical importance. It might have some practical value if the solution of artificial verbal puzzles were the whole duty of logic. As it is, it is little more than a study of verbal permutations and combinations without any valuable result. Resting, as it does, on the view that the judgment expresses merely the mutual inclusion or exclusion of classes, it misses the nature of living thought altogether. As in the case of nostrums in general, the testimonials to its value are to be found chiefly in the advertisement. To be sure, it will be said that logic is under obligation to exhibit all possible forms of judgment for the sake of systematic completeness, and if one has time and taste for that sort of thing there is no objection. But it has as little significance for the knowledge or progress of real thought as a study of the possible permutations and combinations of the words in the dictionary would have for literature.

Thus we have sought to show the leading forms of the

judgment, and the thought principles on which they rest. The modifications of these forms as expressed in language are inexhaustible, and must be dealt with as they arise. An insight into the principles involved is all that is needed or even desirable.

CHAPTER VII

INFERENCE

By far the larger part of our judgments are not given as true in immediate experience or in direct insight. We reach them by analyzing or combining other judgments which are given or assumed. This process is called inference. It is another phase of the complex movement by which we attain knowledge. From the nature of the case, inference implies imperfect knowledge, and must be limited to beings of finite range. This fact is often overlooked in the criticisms passed upon the forms of inference.

Inference consists in drawing from one or more judgments, called premises, some others, called conclusions, which shall always be true if the premises are true. The validity of the inference does not depend on the truth either of the premises or of the conclusion, but upon their mutual relations. From untrue or purely fictitious premises conclusions may be logically drawn. They do not, of course, become true thereby, but their necessary connection with the premises is shown; and this connection, as in the reduction to absurdity, may be used for overthrowing the premises themselves.

The falsehood of both premises and conclusion, then, is quite compatible with the validity of the inference. On the other hand, the truth of both is no security for the validity of the inference. A conclusion, true as to its matter, may be drawn in connection with either true or false premises without being implied in them. Finally, a true conclusion may be validly drawn from fictitious and even from meaningless premises, provided we are allowed arbitrarily to construct the premises with reference to the conclusion. The doctrine of inference, however, does not concern itself with the truth or falsehood of premises or conclusion, but only with the conditions of valid inference from admitted or assumed premises. And here, as elsewhere, we confine our attention to the general principles, leaving details to technical treatises.

Inferences are divided into mediate and immediate. In the latter the conclusion is drawn from the analysis of a single judgment; in the former from the combination of two or more. It is by no means easy to draw the line between these two classes at their adjacent frontiers; but our previous study has taught us that few logical distinctions exist in any such hard and fast form as they assume in the text-books. We may allow this distinction also in a general way, without feeling any obligation to waste time in mapping out the territory of the respective realms. It is much more important to see that the inference is valid than to decide what to call it. We consider first the immediate inferences.

In conversion we interchange subject and predicate, so that AB becomes BA; and this second judgment is said to be an immediate inference from the first. Thus from Squares are rectangles we conclude that Some rectangles are squares.

Whether conversion involves any inference is a point which has been very warmly debated, some contending that there is real inference, while others maintain that we have simply the old matter in a changed verbal form.

The latter claim is certainly true for all judgments of pure quantity. $7+5=12$ and $12=7+5$ are not two equations, but one; that is, when considered as derived from one another. In like manner $x=y$ and $y=x$ are the same equation; there is no inference or progress in passing from one to the other. The same is true for all equipollent judgments, as in definitions. There is no inference or change of thought in conversion in such cases.

With attributive judgments no conversion is possible until the judgment is given an artificial form. Thus, The rose is red remains unconvertible until we take it to mean that the rose is a red thing, or is contained in the class of red things; and then we may convert it into Some red things are roses. But here again there is no proper inference; for when we say that roses are red things we do not mean that they are all sorts of red things, as strawberries or flamingoes, but only rose-red things; and when we say that some red things are roses, again we do not mean any red things indifferently, but only the red things which are roses. Whichever way we work the matter, therefore, if we know what we mean in the primal judgment we have no new matter in the converted one. Similar considerations apply to the conversion of negative judgments.

The importance of the doctrine of conversion, then, is not positive, but negative. It secures no new knowledge, but wards off a familiar fallacy, and even this function is limited to the universal affirmative judgment. From the fact that All A is B it is easy to conclude that All B is A; and hence it is pedagogically important to remind the unwary that A may be included in the class B without exhausting B. That all men are animals does not imply that all animals are men.

Other forms of immediate inference arise from what is called the **opposition of judgments**. This involves no new principle beyond that of consistency in affirmation, and leads to nothing positive. It merely states the relation of affirmative and negative judgments of different quantity and quality when the subjects and predicates are the same.

Immediate inference by added determinants is more significant. This finds its chief field in quantitative reasoning. Its typical form would be

$$A = B.$$
Hence
$$F(A) = F(B).$$

That is, if any two quantities are equal, then equivalent operations performed on both will give equivalent results. In dealing with class terms the same principle applies so long as we do not change the quality of the judgment by our added determinants.

In this class of immediate inferences, and also in those which may be obtained by analyzing the implications of the predicate, a little ingenuity might find some ground for claiming that they are really mediate, as depending on some back-lying principle which is the major premise of the inference. Thus, it might be contended that if A is B, NA is NB, is really a mediate inference depending on the principle that equal operations on equal quantities give equal results; but it would hardly pay expenses. Without doubt the inference would not be true if the principle were not true; and equally without doubt the principle would not be true if the inference were not true. No rational principle is in dispute at all, but only the barren psychological question whether we can see rational necessity in particular cases without having first consciously generalized the problem.

In any case, the great bulk of inference is mediate. Its principles we now pass to consider.

There are two general forms of deductive reasoning, subsumptive and substitutive; and corresponding to these there are two general principles of inference. In subsumptive reasoning we deal with class notions, or the relation of individuals to the universal. The law for this type of reasoning is found in Aristotle's dictum *de omni et nullo*. If I am able to affirm a class mark or law, then I may affirm that mark or law of any or all of the individuals subsumed under the class. Negatively, when I am able to deny any mark or law of a class, I may deny it of the individuals which compose the class. The gist of this reasoning is the subordination of individuals to the universal, and a determination of them in accordance with the law of the universal.

In substitutional reasoning we do not proceed by the subsumption of individuals under a class, but rather by the substitution of equivalents. In any judgment whatever assumed to be true I may substitute equivalent values for either subject or predicate, and the resulting judgment will be equally true. This law appears especially in the quantitative reasoning of mathematics.

All deductive reasoning proceeds by one or the other of these principles, or by both together, and there can be no reasoning without them. Subsumptive reasoning disappears unless we can subordinate the individual to the universal. Quantitative reasoning disappears unless we are allowed to substitute equivalent values. Inference consists essentially in such subsumptions and substitutions, and in drawing the appropriate conclusions. In affirmative reasoning either we subsume a thing under a class, and then affirm the class mark or law of the thing, or we identify or equate a given thing with some other thing, and infer that what is true of one is true of the other. False inference in such cases is due to a false subsumption, or to a false identification and substitution. The negative application of the laws suggests itself.

The earlier traditional logic recognized only subsumptive reasoning, and of course was much puzzled what to do with the quantitative reasoning of mathematics. In much of the latter there is no subsumption, and it pays little, and often no, attention to syllogistic form. On this account some logical rigorists were inclined to deny that logic has anything to do with mathematics. This ancient one-sidedness has been paralleled by a modern one-sidedness which seeks to reduce subsumption to substitution. Such attempts do not tend to edification. They have interest only for those ill-starred beings who see in verbal unifications the ideal goal of thought and knowledge. Living thought is content to see the reality and importance of both types of inference.

The simplest form of mediate reasoning involves (1) a statement of the mark or law, positive or negative, of a class; (2) a ranging of some individual or individuals under that class; and (3) the affirmation of the class mark or law of the subsumed individuals. Or we affirm or deny something of something, substitute some equivalent for that something, and affirm or deny the original something of the substituted equivalent. Such an argument is the simplest unit of mediate reasoning, and into such units any complex argument may be broken up. This unit we call a syllogism, and its sufficient law is given in the general rules of inference already laid down. Wherever these are regarded the inference is valid.

The traditional doctrine of the syllogism is somewhat artificial. The truth therein lies in the rules just mentioned; the artificiality is due to a mechanical interpretation of the rules. An instance is found in the doctrine of three terms. Commonly, where there are more than three terms there is no proper subsumption or substitution, and hence the doctrine of three terms is laid down as fundamental. But this inverts the true order. The subsumption or substitution is the thing, and if we have this the inference will be valid with three terms or thirty. It is well known what distortions of thought and language the defenders of the doctrine of three terms have had to resort to in order to save it. This results necessarily from a mechanical externalism which misses the living movement of thought. Because of the complexity of human speech we often come upon forms of argument which are perfectly clear and valid from the side of the fundamental rules of inference, but which only violence can bring under the artificial rules of the syllogism. Hence we regard the special rules of the syllogism as given in the traditional logic as secondary, and by no means always valid. And when an argument is invalid, it is not because the artificial rules of the syllogism have been violated, but because there has been a false subsumption or exclusion, or a false substitution. Even the fallacies of the undistributed middle and the illicit process of the terms fall under this condemnation. And our criticism of an argument must always direct itself to considering the validity of our subsumption or substitution, and not to a mechanical counting of terms or other unprofitable externalisms. In this way we shall relieve the syllogism from the artificialities which have brought upon it just reproach.

Aristotle's dictum has been subjected to a deal of criticism, much of it irrelevant and much of it directed against loose or careless formulations of it. Illustrations of the latter are found in such statements as that what is true of all is true of each, or what is true of the class is true of the members. Of course it is easy to point out that what is true of all is not true of each, unless the all be taken distributively, and then it is a tautology—what is true of each is true of each. In like manner, what is true of the class is true of the members only when by the class we mean the members; and thus we fall into tautology again.

Other criticism is directed against the dictum as resting

upon a realistic conception of the class as a metaphysical essence. Mr. Mill visits some condign chastisement upon the doctrine for having formerly kept company with scholastic realists, and insists that it must go, along with the metaphysics from which it sprang.

On all of these accounts the dictum is often represented as something which progressive logicians have outgrown. Reflection, however, upon the manifest fact that the real principle of reasoning, whatever it may be, must be the same, yesterday, to-day, and forever, leads to the surmise that this criticism does not get to the root of the matter. In fact, the real meaning of the dictum has always been the subordination of the individual to the universal, and the judgment of the individual in accordance with the law of the universal to which it is subordinated. Hence the law of the class—that is, the universal—applies to the members of the class. This is the affirmative meaning of the dictum. Conversely, nothing may be affirmed of the members which conflicts with the law of the class. This is the negative side of the dictum.

How this subordination of the individual to the universal is secured has no doubt been variously conceived, and the metaphysicians are by no means yet agreed about it; but the subordination itself cannot be questioned as the principle of all subsumptive reasoning. Whenever any substitute is proposed, if valid at all, it always turns out to be a new, if not an inferior, formulation of the old principle. This is manifestly the case with Mr. Mill's supposed improvement. According to him the true principle of reasoning is this: Attribute A is a mark of attribute B, and hence wherever we find A we may affirm B. This is identical in meaning with the dictum, and inferior in expression; for it is by no means clear that attributes may be affirmed of attributes. Up to date, human speech declines to say yellow is sour, or white is cold, as an equivalent for lemons are sour, or snow is cold. It would seem, then, that logicians would do well to distinguish between the metaphysical question of how the subordination of the individual to the universal is secured, and the logical doctrine which affirms such subordination as the principle of reasoning.

The division of syllogisms into moods and figures is something of neither theoretical nor practical value. In its best estate the doctrine of figure is rather an accident of language than a peculiarity of thought. Language admits of the varying position of the middle term and of the resulting permutations. The end of the cumbrous special rules is better attained by remembering the meaning and extension of our terms. When this is done the reasoning will take care of itself; and when this is done we can draw valid conclusions in every figure, though violating all the special rules of the syllogism.

The first figure admits of universal and particular, positive and negative conclusions, and thus embraces the whole table of judgments. Hence it has been called the perfect figure. A better reason for calling it perfect lies in the fact that the subordination of the individual to the universal appears more clearly in this figure than in the others. And as, by implication, the other figures were imperfect, a desire arose for translating them into equivalent values in the first figure. The mechanism for reduction thus resulting belongs entirely to the barren and artificial formalism which has been such a reproach to logic. It is a monumental illustration of misdirected and fruitless ingenuity.

Mathematical reasoning shows some peculiarities beyond those mentioned above. In geometry both subsumption and substitution enter to some extent; but, in addition, the argument generally depends not upon an analysis of notions, but upon a construction of the problem and of the relations expressed. No analysis of the notion of the triangle as a three-sided plane figure reveals the equality of its angles to two right angles. This is found not by reflecting on a definition, but by auxiliary constructions. That a straight line is shorter than any curved or broken line between the same points is not known by analyzing the notions, but by constructing the problem. Then the proposition is not deduced, but seen.

The same fact appears also in numerical reasoning. Here, too, thought proceeds not merely by substitution and analysis, but also and more essentially by synthetic processes based on an insight into the nature of number. Furthermore, in most mathematical reasoning no attention is paid to syllogistic form. The manipulation of equations, the construction of proportions, the formation and summation of series, and all the complex reasonings which attend this work go on in supreme indifference to syllogistic forms, but also in entire certainty, so far as the reasoning goes, if due care be paid to the subsumptions and substitutions. Syllogistic form would add nothing to the cogency of the reasoning, and would be almost fatal to its facility.

Conditional and disjunctive syllogisms contain nothing which calls for special criticism.

The formal logician should look more to the living principles of inference and less to its mechanical forms. The latter should be seen in their secondary character in their best estate, and in their artificiality and even invalidity in many cases. But the syllogism in any form has long been rejected as worthless or as begging the question, and hence as useless in real reasoning. These objections have become traditional, and a word must be devoted to them.

And first, it is said, the syllogism begs the question. If M is P and S is M, of course S is P; but the M is P already contains the S is P, and thus begs the question. Here the difficulty is with the major premise. It contains the conclusion, and there is no valid argument.

This objection rests on taking some natural-history notion, as man. Thus, All men are rational; Cæsar is a man, and hence Cæsar is rational. Now it is said the major premise contains the conclusion, for we could not know it to be true unless we had already examined Cæsar's case. But even then the objection is badly put, for the major premise does not beg the conclusion in any case. From the fact that all men are rational, nothing follows as to Cæsar until the minor premise declares him to be a man. If Cæsar were a horse, or the house-dog, the major premise could never beg him into rationality. The correct objection, if there be any, should be, not that the syllogism begs the question, but that it is barren and leads to no new knowledge.

But this objection also would be short-sighted. It has significance only for one who looks away from the living movement of concrete thought. Such force as it has rests on the assumption that we get our major premises only by summing up individual cases, and that whoever thinks the universal thinks also the individuals subsumed under it. If the former part of the assumption were correct, of course the statement of a universal would presuppose an examination of all the particular cases. Any deduction of particulars from the universal would then be simply retracing our steps, and there would be no progress. The second part of the assumption would make the syllogism equally futile, for in thinking the major premise we should think the conclusion without any deduction.

In fact, however, logical universals are not reached in that way. A universal reached by simple summation would not be any rule for thought, but merely a dead register of experience. Even in the physical sciences general propositions are not won by merely summing up particular cases, but certain cases are taken as specimens, and from them a law is inferred for the whole class. For a general proposition about hydrogen it is not necessary to examine all cases of hydrogen, and it is also possible to infer much about a given element when we are able to identify it as hydrogen. Neither is it true that whoever thinks the universal thinks all the particulars under it. In general the universal is a rule for dealing with particular cases as they arise, and can be very conveniently thought without reference to individuals.

In the rational sciences our universal propositions are the expression of immediate insight or are reached by general reasoning, which takes no account of particular cases. In such cases the syllogism contains advance. Thus, if I know that $s = \frac{1}{2} gt^2$ and $v = gt$, I have the whole science of uniformly accelerated motion, and a law for all possible cases. And in any particular application of this law it would be about equally absurd to claim either that the question is begged or that no new knowledge is gained. The same is true for mathematics in general. We reach and comprehend the general propositions without the slightest consideration of particular cases, and we combine and apply these propositions in a way which leads to real and important advances in knowledge. The higher mathematics may be latent in the elementary intuitions and principles, and yet there is real progress in making the latent patent. It would be highly humorous to claim that every one is a master of mathematics because he has all the elementary intuitions from which mathematics is developed.

But the charge of begging the question may be directed against the minor premise as well as the major. For if we say, All men are rational; Cæsar is man, hence Cæsar is rational, it is plain that we cannot call Cæsar a man unless we know him to be rational, and thus again we beg the question. If we say he might be a man without being rational, that might well be true as a matter of fact, but it would not be true in the sense demanded by the argument. For if Cæsar is a man in some sense which does not imply rationality we make no connection with the major premise, and the argument fails entirely. So, then, the minor begs the question.

The truth of this claim depends on what is necessary to classification. If in order to classify an object we must consider all its attributes there would certainly be no gain in reasoning. In the previous case the objection was that the knowledge of the universal involves a knowledge of all the individuals; here the objection is that the classification of the individual involves a complete comparison of the individual with the connotation of the universal. Before, then, we can say that a given being is a man we must know him thoroughly, and of course reasoning is fruitless.

But this is a formal rather than a real objection, and has only an academic significance. It is not valid at all in the rational sciences. We might argue, The area of the triangle is equal to one-half its base by its altitude. This is a triangle, and therefore its area is equal to one-half its base by its altitude. No one would think of saying that the minor premise begs the question, because we cannot tell whether the figure really is a triangle until we have discovered that its area is equal to one-half its base by its altitude. The practical absurdity would be manifest. We can indeed feign a world of objects where classification should be thus difficult and uncertain, and in such a world reasoning would not be of any value. But in the real world the order of things is more manageable, and we do contrive to add to knowledge in spite of the shortcomings of both the major and the minor premise.

As was said at the beginning of this chapter, reasoning is a device for helping beings of imperfect insight to knowledge. Reasoning might be vacated or made valueless by either of two facts. Perfect insight would make reasoning needless. Or reasoning might be made impossible by the intractibility of our objects, such that they could not be subordinated to any law-giving universal. But we can decide whether reasoning is possible or valuable for us only by consulting experience. When we adopt this method these academic spectres will cease to haunt us.

Thus far of inference as if its premises could always be adequately expressed. This, however, is rarely possible, except in the formal sciences. But a great deal of valid reasoning may be done which does not admit of adequate formal statement. The grounds of the inference are too subtle, delicate, complex for verbal expression. For instance, how do we recognize a face or discern the trustworthiness of a friend? There is here an action of the whole mind, with its furniture of experience and tendency, which would only be caricatured by syllogistic formulation. Much of our practical reasoning is of this sort. It may be perfectly valid, but it cannot be formulated. Hence the wisdom of the rule, in such cases, to give our decision, but never to give our reasons. The real reasons cannot be given, and the reasons we do give only expose us to further quibble or objection.

When definite concepts are given and can be united into definite premises the reasoning may go on in perfect certainty. But in concrete matter this is by no means always the case. As the definite concept is an ideal which is only rarely reached, so the demonstrative inference is an ideal which is only rarely reached. Hence some provision must be made for the recognition of probability, which is proverbially the guide of life. In mathematics our objects are our own creation, and there is no question of a parallax between the thought and the thing; but as soon as we come to concrete matter this possibility has to be reckoned with. Here, of course, we can shuffle our symbols at will, and say M is P, S is M, and hence S is P; but it is not easy in reality to be sure that M is so certainly P and S so certainly M that S is necessarily P. The trouble is that real individuals are often not exhausted in the universal, or that they come under many universals, and finally have their own incommunicable difference besides. For instance, I wish to get some idea of a given person's character, and I enumerate a list of universals. Thus: Man has a conscience; man is rational; man is religious; man is sympathetic and sociable; but all of this is no surety for my man. In spite of these universals he may be a knave, an imbecile, an infidel, a hard-hearted law-breaker. To know him I must know his own equation, and this I shall never get from formal universals.

To all of this the professional logician will reply that logic has nothing to do with such cases, and will betake himself to his symbols again, and with much emotion will recite M is P, S is M, S is P. But the answer must be that, while logic may have nothing to do with such cases, living thought has a great deal to do with them. It is indeed desirable, from a logical standpoint, that all our conceptions could be reduced to definite M's, P's, and S's; but where it is not possible we are still allowed to do the best we can, even if we do not always observe strict logical form.

In the physical and chemical laboratory, and in dealing with some natural species, we are generally sure enough that our A's are really A. We have here the whole accumulated tradition of experience and scientific work; but as soon as we come to life and man, and to truths which take hold on life, the matter is very different. Thus, take any case of circumstantial evidence. How shall we estimate the bearing of the testimony, the character of the witnesses, the previous character of the accused, the facts themselves, supposing them true? There is here a complex action of the living mind with its stores of experience which the syllogism could never reproduce. The reasoning is not indeed demonstrative, but it is of the kind on which life mainly depends.

Reasoning gets still further away from the possibility of formulation and becomes more questionable when it deals with subjects which admit only of subjective estimate, or when the possible premises are many. The personal equation of the investigator is apt to color the estimate or to affect the choice of the premises. No logic could compel an Irish Catholic and an Irish Protestant to draw the same conclusion from the facts of Oliver Cromwell's life. In the inferences we draw from life and history the personal factor gives direction to the logic. In such cases formal reasoning only gives an air of reason. We analyze and express our feelings and desires, and if we succeed in impressing them upon others the reasoning is held to be good; if not, it is bad. The real conflict is between different ideas and ideals, and these have to fight it out on the field of personal experience and the larger field of history. In the meantime we make the motions of reasoning, but the real argument goes on in the hidden depths of the spirit.

It is important to bear this general line of thought in mind, as some uninstructed people often fancy that veritable syllogistic argument must be given for all that is to be believed; whereas the fact is that such argument is but a small factor in living experience. Commonly no one shows such inability to appreciate the living movement of thought as the formal logician in his pathetic devotion to the formal syllogism.

CHAPTER VIII

PROOF

A PROPOSITION may be given of whose truth we are not sure; then we seek for proof or disproof. In general this consists in bringing the proposition into relation to something known, so that we may see the proposition to be a necessary implication or incompatibility. This process is proof or disproof. Logic can give no rule for the process; it can only criticise it and determine its validity. The discovery of the argument itself is left to individual sagacity and invention.

Thus, proof appears to be a kind of reversion of the process of inference. There we had the premises to draw the conclusion; here we have the conclusion to find the premises.

Proof may be direct or indirect. In the former case we directly deduce the proposition as a consequence of other propositions; in the latter case we disprove its contradictory and then infer the truth. The reduction to absurdity is the leading form of indirect proof. Some have affected to find direct proof more cogent than indirect, but this is mere pedantry, or an undue estimate of logical form.

From the nature of the case, proof is limited. It presupposes some propositions back of itself as its own condition. If these also are to be proved, proof will never come to an end, and thus nothing will be proved. We must, then, have certain propositions indisputably given, or standing secure in their own right, if proof is ever to begin or end. Not everything can be proved.

Here again some pedants have confused themselves into thinking that this is a dire disaster for knowledge, but this is due to overlooking the true nature of proof. For the essence of proof is insight into the necessity of admitting the proposition in question, and this is reached by so combining the insights we have as to reach the new insight. But the insight is the gist of the matter, and if we have this at the start it is a waste of time to ask for more. By a certain operation in the calculus of maxima and minima a straight line may be shown to be the shortest distance between two points, but it is no clearer or surer than when directly seen.

Further, proof does not make a proposition true, but only enables us to see it. It is the ground of our knowing the truth, not the ground of its being true. Oversight here has led to various absurdities in philosophy. Thus the argument for the First Cause has been rejected on the ground that anything deduced must be inferred from premises superior to it, and hence must be second and not first. This conclusion might be valid, if our premises were the ground of being, instead of the ground of our knowing. Otherwise it hardly rises to the dignity of a sophism.

In general it is very common with beginners to think that their arguments make the thing true, and to mistake the order of their learning for the true order of existence. The distinction, however, is palpable. The grounds of our knowing or believing are commonly incommensurable with the grounds of existence. The grounds of knowing are relative to our standpoint and grade of development. Hence many valid arguments are possible for the same thing. Our geometry is made up of propositions and arguments. In different works the arguments are often different. The doctrine of the ellipse may be developed from different standpoints. The ellipse may be considered as a conic section or as a curve of the second degree, or it may be defined with reference to two fixed points. Yet the same properties of the curve may be reached by these very different roads. Truth is known to be true only when it is proved; but truth is true, whether we can prove it or not.

Proof, too, is limited by the nature of the knowing mind. It is only a stimulus to see, and a stupid mind cannot see. There is no such thing as an objective proof which proves in the absence of intelligence, something as a Buddhist prayer-mill prays in the absence of the suppliant. It is very common with the dull to mistake their own dulness for a lack of proof. But since proof is really only a stimulus to think in a certain way it is necessarily conditioned by the nature of the mind addressed. Hence, when the subject lies beyond our ordinary range, especially when it rises into the realm of abstract thought, we are apt to view our own limitation as a shortcoming of the argument. In such cases the swaggering announcement, I don't see that, is properly met by the question, Well, what of it?

In general the need of proof is a mark of limitation. The self-evident is what we see without a process, and its limit depends on the degree of mental insight. For perfect knowledge everything in the system of reason would be equally self-evident. We, however, not having such insight, have to find our way by combining the little we know so as to advance into the unknown. Reasoning in general would be needless for a perfect mind. It is only the device of a limited intelligence for extending its realm when direct insight fails.

What has been said thus far applies to proof in the strict sense of rational demonstration. But the word is often used with less stringency, and then proof consists in giving reasons which, while not compelling assent, produce conviction. A word must now be said on the general subject of probability.

Probability

In strictness only that is knowledge which is indisputably given, rationally self-evident, or cogently deduced from unquestionable facts. Hence, strict knowledge is limited to the immediate data of consciousness or to the contents of the rational sciences. All other so-called knowledge is properly belief. It could be denied without contradicting any law of thought, though perhaps not without practical absurdity. Belief varies all the way from complete conviction to the lowest probability. The psychology of belief has many peculiarities, owing to the fact that an element of volition enters into it. We have, then, an island of knowledge, a border of belief, and, poured round all, the ocean of the unknown.

The distinction of knowledge and belief is a purely subjective one. Both alike presuppose objective connection; the difference lies only in the subjective certainty with which it is grasped, or in the reasons on which that certainty is founded.

Probability, then, is the guide of life. The degree of this probability admits of no exact determination. In most events we have to judge by practical sagacity rather than any formal rule. He who can successfully discern the signs of the times is the person of good sense. If he should report his reasons they would make a sorry show tested by logical rule, and probably he would hardly know the real reasons himself. In such cases we proceed by instinct or a kind of knack rather than by formal rules. The probability here admits of no exact determination; first, because we know little about the factors at work, and, secondly, because the factors themselves often admit of no numerical statement.

Trust in evidence and in one another, forecasts of social and political movements, are cases of this kind. These subjects, especially the credibility of testimony, have often been elaborately treated, and with the most astonishing mathematical skill; but it is only wasted time. In estimating, say, the credibility of a witness we should have to take many things into account, as the character of the witness, the nature of the story, his interest in the truth, and a variety of complex circumstances besides; and these defy numerical calculation. If we nevertheless insist on figuring we merely delude ourselves with a false show of accuracy, while the facts remain as vague as ever. Sometimes, however, numerical determination is possible, and then the calculus of probabilities comes in.

The calculus of probabilities began in a study of games of chance, and from this unpromising origin it has become a matter of great practical importance. Still, there has been little agreement as to its foundation, or even as to its meaning. Some seek to found it on apriori considerations, and others found it on experience. As to the meaning of probability, some make it subjective only, and declare the aim of the calculus to be to find the quantity of belief. Others insist that this is meaningless, that quantity of belief admits of no intelligible interpretation, and that when we say that our belief is three-fourths in one case and four-fifths in another, we do not find any corresponding subjective difference, but mean that we expect the event to happen three times out of four in one case, and four times out of five in the other. The truth seems to be as follows:

1. Ultimately the probability expresses a ratio, the ratio of the favorable possibilities to the whole number. If, then, m equals the whole number of possibilities, and n equals the favorable ones, then $\frac{n}{m}$ equals the probability of the event

in question. Thus, in throwing a cube, as in the playing of dice, any one of the six sides may turn up. The probability that any one side will turn up is one-sixth.

2. This ratio may be found in many cases by mathematical analysis of the possibilities, as in games of chance—cards, dice, lotteries, etc. In such cases we have primarily only a study of permutations and combinations and a finding of certain ratios. Such study is quite independent of experience, as much so as the calculus of variations; and the results reached are logically valid, even if they are practically worthless. But that these results have any application to experience can be learned only from experience. In practice the important averages are obtained entirely from experience, especially from statistics. This is the case with all the averages on which the various forms of insurance depend, and with social averages in general. We find, as a matter of fact, that certain averages hold in experience, and from these we calculate what we may expect.

3. The probability reached determines only our expectation beforehand, and is no objective quality of the thing. Hence, after the event has declared itself, the previous improbability is no argument against it, and for two reasons: First, the event which was antecedently improbable may be attested by evidence which removes all doubt. The antecedent improbability, according to the life-tables, that a healthy youth will die during the year is not the slightest reason for denying his death when it occurs. Secondly, while any one event is improbable as against some one of all the rest, it may be no more improbable than any other of the same class. If one were about to throw a handful of type on the floor, any definite preannounced order of falling would be very improbable, but no more so than any other of the same complexity. Their falling so as to form an intelligible sentence would be no more improbable than

any other equally complex order agreed on in advance. In general the intelligible order would be vastly more improbable than an unintelligible one, as anything would suffice for unintelligence, while only a complete determination of all the letters to only one position would produce the intelligible order. Delusion at this point is common. When all the other possibilities are many we lump them all into one case, and then feel great surprise that the single event, with so many chances against it, should nevertheless have succeeded in occurring. In all such cases our surprise is not logical but psychological.

4. The probability is not a thing. In itself the thing is fixed, and our expectation has nothing to do with it. In itself the probability is only a ratio, or the fact that the average of events is such or such. We are not, then, to view the probability as a secret something which determines events. This blunder is often made in moral statistics. After finding a certain average in human affairs we conclude that some secret fate is at work. By the aid of a little rhetoric we easily persuade ourselves that an event is fully accounted for when the law of averages demands it. There may be an average in birth and death and crime, but, after all, the average is not responsible for any of them. It takes something more potent than an average to produce typhoid fever or to crack a safe.

5. In a series of mutually exclusive events conceived as equally possible we have no reason for expecting one rather than any other. Conversely, in a series of actual events, if we find one form recurring much oftener than calculation would lead us to expect, we conclude that something favors that form, so that the assumed equal possibility is not true. Continued runs of luck in games of chance are apt to awaken suspicion. It is this principle which underlies inductive logic.

6. The doctrine of probabilities in no way applies to first facts. It assumes a definite set of facts and principles as its starting-point, and is otherwise meaningless. It would be absurd to ask what would be probable if nothing existed. Of course in its application to a mechanical system it is simply an expression of our ignorance. In such a system everything is fixed. The actual is the only possible, and the non-actual is the impossible.

The doctrine is often misused in theistic discussion. If the question were as follows, it would apply: Is it probable that mechanical elements without law or essential relation to intelligible forms would ever attain to them? The answer must be, No; but to make the conclusion applicable it must be shown that such elements ever existed. Why not view law and order as eternal, which we no more explain than theism explains God himself? Atheism, on the other hand, often misuses the doctrine by supposing that in infinite time all conceivable combinations must be hit upon. This confounds conceptual with actual possibility, and breaks with the notion of law upon which all thinking depends.

So much for the theory. Its application is notoriously difficult. The very greatest mathematicians, as Pascal, D'Alembert, and Leibnitz, have stumbled over the simplest principles. Many of the results are questionable in their best estate, not, indeed, in the mathematical analysis, but in the concrete application. Thus the rule of succession given by most writers without suspicion is extremely treacherous. This rule seeks to conclude from the past to the future, or from the known to the unknown. Its form is $\frac{m+1}{m+2}$, where m stands for the total number of occurrences or known facts. Of course if m is large the fraction closely approaches unity or certainty. Suppose the question to be the probability of the sun's rising to-morrow; m is the number of past risings, and the probability is high. But the reasoning here is illusory. In the application of this law we only give the appearance of logic to a conclusion we have otherwise gained. Without consulting experience as to the application of the law, and thus making it superfluous, we should be met by Venn's objection. It has rained for three days; I have given three false alarms of fire; and I have fed my chickens three times with strychnine. What is the probability for the fourth case? By the rule it is four-fifths that it will rain the fourth day, that the neighbors will respond to the next alarm, and that my chickens will die the next time.

Finally, we must remember that the most remarkable coincidences are possible. The calculus does not say what must be, but what we are to expect in advance. In fact, the most improbable things occur every day without surprising us; but when they are at a distance, especially in time, it is possible to show a deal of acumen in contesting their occurrence. It would be easy to gather out of the recent history and diplomacy of the most civilized nations a collection of things so strange that, when tested by their antecedent probability, every one would pronounce them incredible. No more treacherous pitfall besets the steps of the historian than the temptation to construe history on the basis of apriori probability.

Even in matters of pure chance runs of luck occur, and some have even held that in the long-run every bank and insurance company will fail. This is, of course, mistaken, as it rests on the assumption that every conceivable possibility must become actual; but the probability alone will not save a bank from failure. Jevons, in his *Principles of Science*, mentions a case in which three computers were set to calculate the place of a star. All blundered, and in precisely the same way, yet for no apparent reason. In history, also, remarkable coincidences abound which are the chief stock in trade of a species of prophet. By a little manipulation any name or series of names, or numbers, may be made to show the most extraordinary coincidence with the number of the beast, or with any prominent date or striking historical event. Professor Benjamin Pierce claimed that the Neptune discovered by Leverrier and Adams was not the planet they had calculated; that the problem admitted of a double solution, but that at the time of the discovery the two solutions gave a common position for the disturbing planet, and thus by chance the mistake was rectified. The previous improbability of such an event was indefinitely great, but it would count for nothing against direct evidence of its occurrence.

The conclusion is that demonstration is an ideal which is only rarely attained. For the most part we have to content ourselves with probability, and this can seldom be accurately determined. The calculus of probabilities, while beyond question as a specimen of mathematical analysis, has only a limited application in experience. Doubt here attaches not to the mathematics, but to the assumption that the mathematics accurately represents the facts. Without such accuracy the longer we figure the further we go astray.

CHAPTER IX

DEDUCTION AND INDUCTION

SOMETIMES we are able to give an exact definition of our objects, and have such an insight into their nature that we are able, on the mind's own warrant, to make universal statements about them. By combining the definitions and these judgments we may advance to still other judgments indefinitely. In such cases we are said to reason deductively, or to follow the deductive method. This term is not the happiest, as all inference is a deduction of consequences from premises, universal or particular, but the usage is fixed.

The most striking example of this method is found in the mathematical sciences—geometry, algebra, trigonometry, analytics, calculus, mechanics, etc. Here we have certain ideas of space, time, motion, number, etc., which are perfectly clear in the sense in which we use them, and concerning which we are able to affirm some universal principles on our own warrant. Setting out from these principles, perceived by intuition, we travel far and wide, and build up a great and important system of truth.

If it were possible to apply the same method to the study of nature we should in like manner be able to build up an apriori science of nature. Misled by the analogy of mathematics, and also by the native dogmatism of the human mind, the early ages followed this method very largely, with vanity and vexation of spirit for the main result. Verbal definitions were constructed and verbal judgments were formed, and these were united into fantastic or barren systems. This sterility, together with the growth of critical reflection, led men to see that an apriori science of nature is impossible, except to a very slight extent.

In mathematics we have a knowledge of our objects: in physics we have only a knowledge about our objects. In the former we begin with a constructive definition; in the latter we begin with a denotative name. In the former we define our objects from within; in the latter we describe them from without. In the outer world, then, we are kept on the surface of things. We name our objects and recognize them, but we are not able to penetrate into their hidden nature so as to say what it implies. Hence, instead of the deductive procedure which seeks to learn particulars from the universal, we invert the process and seek to gather universals from the particulars. This procedure is called induction.

The same thought may be set forth in a somewhat different manner. The categories of our thought apply to all contingent objects, but they completely express none. In so far as the categories express the objects an apriori science is possible, and only in so far. Thus, in so far as objects have regular form, outline, area, etc., we can determine their properties by means of geometry. In so far as they are countable the category of number applies to them, and they become amenable to the science of arithmetic. In so far as they are events the categories of time and causation apply to them; and whatever these categories imply may be affirmed apriori of events. But these formal relations are far from exhausting the objects. They only tell the general relations which must obtain among objects, without revealing their specific nature. Thus space applies to all external objects, but it does not decide what objects shall be external. Time and causation apply to all events, but they do not decide what the events shall be. Number likewise applies to all objects, but it does not prescribe the nature of the things numbered. Hence the categories which give the general form of experience, or the outlines within which alone experience is possible, are entirely compatible with a great many other systems of specific contents. So far as the abstract categories go, any number of other worlds are as possible as the actual one. Hence, in the mastery of experience, we may proceed deductively for a little way, but for the most part we must fall back on induction.

If induction is to mean anything more than simple experience, its practical problem must be to infer general principles from particular facts. At least that is the sense in which it will be used here. The tedious and sterile disputes over perfect and imperfect induction must be left to those who deal in that sort of thing.

The starting-point of induction in this sense is the world of particular facts, which, however, are already qualified and constituted by the categories; that is, it is the world of experience as it exists for spontaneous and unreflective thought. Objects are already given as abiding things with fixed meanings and in fixed relations, and the work of inductive inquiry can never be to discover and establish these relations, but only to specify them and render them more exact. When a disciple of induction fancies it possible to begin with pure experience unqualified by any work of thought, he forgets, if he ever knew, that Hume and Kant have lived. The constancy and continuity of objects which first produce fixity in the weltering chaos of impressions, and which are the foundation of all articulate experience, are no such matter-of-course as the empiricist thinks, but are a notable contribution of thought.

And even assuming the world of abiding things, the

foundation of inductive inference is commonly misunderstood. It is said to be the uniformity of nature, or that like is true of like, or some such general formula. Much doubt might be raised as to the meaning of these expressions. If we speak of the uniformity of nature as a whole, we exclude change altogether; and when we admit non-uniformity at all, it is not clear what it is that is uniform. If we say the true principle is that like is true of like, it would be easy to define like in such a way as to turn the statement into tautology; and if we allow any difference in the likes, who can tell what effect this difference will have on the outcome? If, finally, we decide that the principle should run that like antecedents have like consequents, or like causes like effects, we are by no means out of the woods yet. For it would seem that the entire universe is the antecedent of every event; and if the universe be the same the event should be the same; but if the universe be different the principle would demand a different effect. We can get nothing out of any of these formulas unless we assume that real likeness exists among things, thus constituting real kinds, and that the cosmic causality proceeds along multitudinous lines, each of which may be traced by itself. Without the latter assumption we inevitably fall into the above dilemma. The entire universe, as antecedent, is either the same or different; and in either case we are grievously tormented.

But whatever the principle of uniformity may mean, it is fruitless in actual research in any case. It is, in a way, a postulate of induction, as the universality of law and connection is a postulate, but it is a presupposition of all research rather than a guide in any. The actual aim in concrete investigation is not to prove that nature is uniform, but to find what the uniformities are. In deciding between competing theories, the uniformity of nature is impartial, and for the manifest reason that we are trying to find which of the theories expresses the uniformity. Again, that like is true of like is equally barren, however true it may be; for the real question is: Are there any real likes or kinds as distinct from superficial resemblance, so that we may affirm of each and all; and supposing such kinds to exist, what are they?

The actual movement of thought is this: We tacitly assume a system of reality with fixed laws of existence and sequence among its elements. These are fixed connections and not chance conjunctions. Without this assumption, there is no order for thought to grasp, and the conditions of truth do not exist. With this assumption, the problem becomes to find what these fixities are, or how we are to distinguish between the chance conjunctions of experience and the essential connections of reality. The notion of connection is contributed by reason. The nature of connection is a metaphysical problem which only reason can solve. The actual connections are mainly to be discovered by experience.

And here the mind proceeds on the principle that uniformity or frequency of coincidence cannot be the effect of chance, but must itself have a reason. Such coincidence becomes a problem which finds a solution only in the assumption that it rests upon one of the uniformities of reality. This is the fruitful principle of inductive reasoning. We observe coincidence, and explain it as the expression of a law. Then we assume that the cases observed are specimen ones, and extend the law to all similar cases. This is, in brief, the logic of induction.

This result may become clearer by some further exposition. It is, first, plain that inductive inference can never get clear of metaphysical assumptions. The objective order of law is assumed, not proved. Particular laws may be discovered, but the general assumption of law and order is essential to any inference whatever.

In the next place, it is plain that this general assumption is only a presupposition of all investigation, and is no guide in any actual study. Inductive science which understands itself confines itself to discovering the uniformities of things and events. These cannot be discovered by metaphysical speculation of any sort, and the nature and place of the ground of these uniformities can never be determined by inductive methods.

Finally, the statement concerning chance and coincidence needs some further explanation. By chance is not meant lack of causation, but the coincidence in an event of mutually independent series of causation. Thus the unpurposed meeting of two persons is spoken of as a chance one when the movement of neither implies that of the other. Here the antithesis of chance is purpose. Effects in nature are ascribed to chance when the elements that co-operate in their production are mutually independent, and when the effects appear simply as resultants of forces which have no essential relation to them. With reference to the forces such effects are by-products. Thus the existence of water in the Atlantic basin might be referred to chance, but the union of oxygen and hydrogen to form water could not be so referred. The former might seem to be an accidental resultant of mutually independent agencies, but the latter is founded in the essential nature of the elements. Here the antithesis of chance is law. Possibly the two antitheses of chance are really one, and purpose is that one.

When we are dealing with single or simple facts it is easy to rest in the reference to chance. That boulder in yonder field, or that ledge of rocks, expresses no purpose and no law. It is the outcome of laws, to be sure, but the laws contain no reference to the boulder in them. The laws would be all that they are if there were no boulder in existence. For such things the reference to chance seems to suffice. But when the facts constantly recur, or when they are complex and many elements converge to a single end, we are no longer able to rest in the notion of chance. As soon as an event which, considered in itself, might seem to be purely accidental, recurs frequently, we begin to demand a ground for the recurrence. Even runs of luck in games of chance cannot become continuous, or even frequent, without exciting inquiry. Regularity or frequency of coincidence constitutes a problem and demands explanation. It is this principle which underlies the logic of induction and gives it all its cogency.

When, then, we find groups of marks constantly recurring in nature, we assume that they not merely occur together, but that they belong together, so that where one member of the group is found the others may be inferred. Or when we see a given kind of event always following or accompanying another, we conclude that we have a fixed order of causal sequence, or a law of nature. Only thus can we explain the coincidence so as to find rest unto our souls.

It is this fact, that repeated coincidence becomes a problem and demands explanation, which gives meaning to the repetition of experiment, or the extension of observation, in induction. Why should many cases prove more than one? The answer lies in the theory of probabilities, which is only an exposition of our principle. The probability that we have a fixed law grows with the number of cases in which it is found to hold. This is the fruitful principle of inductive reasoning, and it underlies all the inductive methods.

The logic of induction has been much confused by the not over-intelligent strife of the empirical and apriori schools of philosophy. This has led to a failure properly to analyze the problem. The empiricist has claimed that induction may proceed on a purely empirical basis, without any metaphysical assumptions whatever. In so doing he has overlooked the metaphysics immanent in experience, and the objectivity of thought. The apriorist, on the other hand, has insisted on the metaphysics, but has failed to see that the practical problem of discovering the actual uniformities of coexistence and sequence is in no way solved thereby. The debate between the two schools must be carried on at another point—the possibility of experience in general. The discovery of uniformity ought not to be complicated with metaphysical questions concerning its nature and ground.

The inductive problem is manifold, but has three leading directions. First, since our conceptions of concrete things cannot be built up by apriori definition, we have to learn from experience what marks belong together. Finding in many cases a coincidence of marks a, b, c, we conclude that they form a fixed group in the subject S. Of course all we can observe is that they come together; the affirmation that they belong together is a surplus by which the mind seeks to transform the mere conjunctions of experience into a rational connection. This phase of induction consists in forming the notion.

Or, in the next place, we may assume a subject, and seek to determine its properties and law. In rational science we are able to infer the properties of a subject by reflection upon its definition. In the world of things this is not possible. Thus, oxygen, magnetism, electricity are not conceptions from which we can deduce properties, but only names for the subject of certain properties or for groups of phenomena.

The third leading inductive problem is the search for causal connection, as it is called. This is so important that many, following Mill, have made it the whole of induction. The truth is that the real practical question here does not concern itself at all with the idea of causation, but only with the uniformities of sequence. The mind brings the idea of causation into temporal sequences for its speculative satisfaction, but is practically no wiser on that account.

If all phenomena were perfectly simple and easily distinguishable it would be easy to trace the order of connection. Putting C and E for the factors whose connection it is proposed to establish, experience might show us the following cases:

First, C and E are found together or come together, and they are not found apart. When C is given E is given, and when C is lacking E is lacking. We conclude that they belong together.

Secondly, C and E are found to vary together. It is inferred that they belong together.

These two cases involve the gist of experience and the sum of inductive logic. All else is device for discovering whether C and E do really thus come together or not. The conclusion from coming together to belonging together rests on the mental necessity of seeking a ground for regularity or frequency of coincidence.

Mr. Mill has expanded the matter into his five inductive methods of agreement, difference, agreement and difference, concomitant variations, and residues; but these contain no new principle. So far as they transcend the general cases mentioned, they are only practical devices for making the subject-matter amenable to logic. The result of all the methods is only to show that C and E are found together, or come together, or vary together.

All of this is very simple and very conclusive when abstractly considered. We have only to regard attentively our symbols to see how clear the matter is. In practice, however, it is not such plain sailing. Phenomena are not simple or easily distinguishable, and thus it is difficult to reduce them to the simplicity demanded by our logical formulas. In the case of causal connection we may have the following cases:

1. C is followed by E; but C may admit of analysis into $a+b+d$; and possibly not C as a whole, but some one of its factors, as b, is the real cause. Thus, the cause of the coagulation of the blood can be easily named in a general way, but when we seek to trace the exact order it turns out to be a highly involved affair. Then we hear of paraglobulin and fibrinogen and fibrin ferment, with a suggestion of one or two outstanding mysteries. It is also possible that C and E are effects of a common cause, and have only a temporal relation, like day and night.

2. E may be lacking when C is given. We cannot conclude that C is not the cause, for there may have been a hinderance which prevented C from having its appropriate effect.

3. E may be given without C, but we may not conclude that C is not a cause of E, but that it is not the only cause.

4. Remove C, and E remains. Here we can only conclude that C is not the preserving cause. Bad air may cause disease which will not vanish with the bad air.

In practice, then, the plurality of causes and the complexity of phenomena make it difficult to reach certain conclusions. E may be due not only to C, but to C, or C'_2 or C_3. And C itself may be complex and contain unsuspected elements, or may work under unnoticed conditions, which determine the effect. Hence we need to reduce our problem to simplicity so as to know all the factors at work if we would reach any valid conclusion.

This is far from easy even with simple physical experiments. In the laboratory, defective instruments, personal equations, impure materials, and unsuspected conditions, as well as the imperfect analysis of the problem itself, are to be guarded against. The alchemists doubtless were led on and led astray by finding traces of silver in the lead with which they worked. In the complex questions of physiology, hygiene, and society we cannot be too circumspect. Here the facts are always more complicated than we suspect, and the causes are many. The facts take on an unreal and misleading simplicity in our statements, and only the practised thinker discerns the illusion.

For instance: There are more arrests at one time than another, and the conclusion is drawn that there is an increase of crime. But before assenting we should need to inquire whether there has been any change in the laws; whether crime has the same meaning; whether there has been any change in the vigilance of the police; what the nature of the crimes is, etc. Or it is said that there are more divorces in the United States than in Europe; and the conclusion is drawn that the relation of the sexes is looser, or that the marriage vow is held as less sacred. But here again we should first need to look at the nature of the divorce laws in the two countries; and then it might appear that the difference in the laws fully explains the difference in question, and it might also appear that there are worse things than easy divorce. Except when critically collected, so as to reproduce the significant facts, and critically interpreted, statistics are so treacherous that it is not without ground that the proposition has been made to view statistics as the superlative of lies.

In this whole matter of induction logic has an important critical function, in the way of restraining the hasty dogmatism of the human mind. From a few cases we conclude to all. Negative cases are overlooked; positive ones strike the imagination. The relation of positive to negative is ignored. In this way nostrums, amulets, charms, unlucky days, spells, mind-cures, etc., get credit. In such cases we must resort to statistics, experiment, accurate observation, and a careful analysis of the problem. With minds amenable to reason this treatment will commonly prove effectual if continued.

In matters less suggestive of superstition and mental pathology it is common to overlook the complexity of the case and pick out that antecedent which falls in with our fancy, or interest, as the sole cause. This is common in politics and jeremiads. The perennial discovery that the church or the state is in danger is of this sort. The enormous complexity of the social order and the multitudinous factors which work together in society always make this sort of thing possible. The partisan politician can see no other source of public weal or woe than the political administration. If any one chooses he can find the great cause of our social ills in the higher education of women, or in the failure to keep the seventh day instead of Sunday, or in the refusal to put the name of God into the Constitution, or in the distrust of Providence involved in lightning-rods and life-insurance. Such barren mockery and pretence of reasoning are too familiar to need illustration. The only remedy lies in improving the mental type by forming the logical habit, and broadening the outlook upon the facts of nature, life, and history.

The all-sufficient logical rule for induction is to analyze our fact or experiment into all its factors if possible, and note what each contributes to the result. When many things are in play which forbid such analysis only the most general conclusions can be reached, and they should be loosely held. In a great many things it is a mark of wisdom, and often also a mark of conscience, not to have an opinion.

General logic can lay down only this general rule. The practical methods of dealing with various classes of facts so as to bring them under the rule must be learned from the special sciences. In this sense every science may be said to have its own method and its own logic. The value of the general study consists in getting some idea of what proof means, and some conception of the general rational principles involved.

Some traditional quibbles concerning inductive logic remain to be considered. The pure formalist objects that the inductive conclusion is from the particular to the universal, and is therefore illogical. If nothing but logical form is regarded, or if absolute demonstration be demanded, this is correct. Some does not prove all, and inductive conclusions are never demonstrated. But the objection is more sweeping than the objector imagines, for it denies the possibility of any reasoning on objective reality at all. Our experience of most classes of things is limited to a comparatively few specimens; indeed, we have not experienced the class at all. Certain things with a measure of similarity have been found in experience; the passage to the notion of a class which is law-giving for all is a venture of our own. And even of the few things we have found we have had only particular experiences in time; the passage from these particular experiences to the conception of an abiding and continuous law for the things is a very special venture of our own. Hence, if the objection is valid we are shut up to recital of our subjective experiences, and thought vanishes. This puzzle is solved by the facts before mentioned. First, the mind constitutes its objects, and assumes that fixities of coexistence and sequence exist in reality. Secondly, the mind assumes that a continued coincidence of certain marks in many cases proves that they are the sign of a class or law and belong together. It is this notion of a class or law which enables the mind to pass from some to all; and it is the doctrine of probabilities which allows us to infer that a given group of marks, or a given order of sequence, is a true universal. Hence the inductive argument unfolded runs as follows: A is P, B is P, C is P, D is P. These are particular observations. But A, B, C, D are specimens of a class S; hence S is P and all S's are P.

It is idle to quibble over this logic. The necessary particularity of experience is manifest. The impossibility of resting in a recital of particular experiences is equally manifest. Not merely our theoretical but our practical life would be impossible without generalizing particular experience into universal rules. There could be no dependence on anything, and nothing would teach anything. It is hardly worth while to secure formal accuracy at this cost. The regret which the living thinker, in distinction from the closet logician, feels at this point is, that logic has no rule for deciding when coincidence becomes frequent enough to warrant the conclusion to a law. Some coincidences mean more than others. Some facts lie nearer the constants of the system than others. Such differences, however, must be learned from the subject-matter and the general drift of experience.

A second objection proceeds from the empiricists, especially Mr. Mill. He insists that induction proceeds from particulars to particulars directly, and not through the notion of a class or law. For if the fact that some die proves that all will die, it certainly proves that A or B or C will die. This plea is short-sighted. It may be true psychologically, but it is not true logically. The only thing that warrants us in passing from one case to another is the assumption that both are under a common law, or are cases of a common kind. Without this, thought cannot logically move at all; and we can draw no inference, whether from some to all, or from some to some.

A third scruple concerning the logic of induction concerns the plurality of causes. A given event, it is said, can have only one cause; and hence there is no plurality of causes. This scruple arises from confounding the metaphysical and the inductive problem. A pure empiricism is indeed open to this objection, but it does not lie against induction as we have defined it.

It was stoutly contended by the earlier disciples of induction that deduction is useless in research. This was due to the historical barrenness of the purely deductive method. But in time it became apparent that induction alone is helpless, or at best can only crawl. Induction may help us to premises, but deduction must draw the conclusions. The great method of research is this: First, we observe the facts and form a provisional theory or hypothesis. Secondly, we deduce the conclusions from the hypothesis; and, thirdly, we compare the inferred facts with the observed ones. Disagreement disproves the theory. Agreement strengthens our faith, and, when extended, confirms it. Thus, in the case of gravitation, Newton formed the hypothesis that the earth draws the moon according to the law of the inverse square. He then calculated the moon's motion on that supposition; and this, after much mistake and uncertainty, was found to agree with the observed motion. Of course in all such work our experiments and calculations only reveal coincidence, and this the mind, on its own warrant, transforms into law.

After our faith in a theory has once been established, then by deduction we may often advance beyond any possible induction. Thus, in astronomy we reach results deductively which no direct observation could ever discover.

In physics, too, we get formulas from which we draw conclusions impossible to induction. In this way we get a hint of how long the sun can emit heat, or a limit beyond which the fluidity of the earth cannot be placed. Or we get an insight into molecular phenomena which lie beyond inspection, or we conclude to the future of the physical system.

What has been said of inductive inference applies equally to the formation and verification of hypotheses, which, indeed, is only one phase of induction, and cannot be sharply marked off from induction in general. There is no accurate definition or consistent use of the term hypothesis; but, in general, we may define an hypothesis as an ideal conception whereby the mind seeks to reduce a set of facts to rational order and make them intelligible to itself. Such are the atomic, the nebular, the evolution hypotheses. In this sense hypothesis is synonymous with theory. Hypotheses vary all the way from well-established theories to random guesses. There is enough of the latter element still in the notion to make it possible to use the term somewhat disparagingly.

As in the case of proof, logic cannot teach invention. This must be left to individual insight. Success in forming hypotheses demands a familiarity with the laws of the facts in question; but given this knowledge, there is needed an act of intuition for which no rule can be given. Nevertheless, logic can give advice which is negatively valuable. If it does not lead to the true theory it will at least tend to exclude the false ones, and that is no small gain. The demands which logic makes are as follows:

1. The primal duty of an hypothesis is to be intelligible. Many speculative theories sin against this law.

2. The hypothesis must be deduced from the facts, and must in turn explain the facts. An hypothesis which when

granted throws no light on the facts, or which leaves us as badly off as before, is a waste of time—an elephant or tortoise under the earth.

3. Hypotheses must admit of something like proof or disproof, otherwise there is no limit to the vagaries of the imagination.

4. An hypothesis must fit into others so as to be harmonious with our total system of knowledge. The warrant for this demand lies in the assumption that things constitute a harmonious system. An hypothesis constructed purely *ad hoc* without harmony with known laws would be purely arbitrary, a fiction rather than an hypothesis.

Hypotheses are of two kinds. Some are simply offered as explanations of the facts, and give us no new control over the facts. They are necessary to satisfy the demand for a sufficient reason; and when no competing hypothesis satisfies the mind as well, we hold it for the mental peace it brings, although we cannot use it to advance knowledge. Such are the atomic theory, most of the doctrines of geology, many of the theories of physics, the theistic view of the world, etc. None of these are fruitful in practical research; they are simply theories which are necessary to explain the actual order of facts. Their proof or verification consists in showing that the facts shut us up to such a view.

The other order of hypotheses admits of deduction, and puts us in control of phenomena. The proof of these consists not merely in their adequacy to the observed facts, but in the agreement of their implications with other facts not originally contemplated or observed. The law of gravitation, the ether theory of light, are examples. These can be used to advance knowledge, and are generally mathematical. Once in a while a speculator of positivist leanings decides that only the latter class of hypotheses is to be allowed.

The former he rejects as unverifiable figments of fancy. Unfortunately, he does not always have the clearest notion as to what verification means; and, besides, he has the human mind against him.

When the facts are such that we are not shut up to one hypothesis, but any one of many is possible, then it is our duty to hold to the facts and leave the hypotheses to those unhappy beings who must have an opinion, whether they have any right to one or not.

With regard to these uniformities which thought postulates and induction aims to discover, a word of caution must be uttered. They are commonly called laws, a term in the use of which there is very great looseness. The laws of motion, of force, of heredity, of variation, of wages, of probability, etc., are all huddled together under one class, and the force of the term serves to sanctify the mere rough averages of statistics and vague generalizations from experience, as well as the laws of gravitation and chemical combination. In this way it often happens that the problem itself is put forward as its own solution. This misuse of the term law is a large part of the stock in trade of the hearsay scientist and philosopher. It is important to recognize that there are laws and laws, and that some laws are only consequences of others. The laws of phenomena in general are of this sort. The motions of the planets might be called laws, but in truth they are only facts resulting from some back-lying laws. They are not, therefore, original constants of the system, but secondary results, and they might be indefinitely modified without changing the system of constants. The freezing of water in a flame is a departure from the phenomenal order, but the deeper laws of physics find illustration in such a fact. For the fixity of the phenomenal order, which is practically the most important of all fixities, we have no theoretical security whatever.

It is also important to form some idea of what law is to mean in any case. In this matter the connections of reason are the only laws perfectly clear to us. Where these can be discovered there can be no doubt. But most of the conjunctions of nature are no implications of reason, and as such are contingent. Of them we may hold three views:

1. They are mere coincidences in our experience and express no order of reality. They are not laws of nature, but accidents of our experience.

2. They are laws founded in some opaque necessity in things of which no more can be said.

3. They are uniformities of phenomena which represent no necessity but the orderly forms of procedure on the part of some being back of them.

It is impossible to rest in the first view, and between the second and third metaphysics must decide. It is important to note, however, that the necessity posited in nature is not found but assumed, and many considerations make it probable that it is not there. The choice, we have seen, is not between chance and necessity, but between necessity and purpose. But it is well to keep the inductive question concerning the actual order of things distinct from the metaphysical question concerning the nature and ground of that order. Only through this division of labor, or partition of territory, can there be any progress towards the solution of either the inductive or the metaphysical problem.

CHAPTER X

EXPLANATION

THE things and events of experience are such that the mind is unable to rest in them, but seeks to unite them in ways which shall satisfy its own nature by accounting for them. This is explanation.

Explanation, then, is only a special phase of the general mental demand for systematic connection. The driving force in it is the desire for connection and totality, or the desire for a rounded and finished system. It has, however, special forms which make it desirable to devote special attention to it. Some of the chief interests of thought centre in this subject, and some of our worst aberrations have their source in misunderstandings of the same. And here too logic has an important function in analyzing this notion, so as to understand its implications and prevent the mind from losing its way. We approach the subject in a roundabout manner.

Our so-called knowledge is often said to be made up of facts and theories. Whether we shall allow this statement depends on what we mean by a fact. Many a notion might represent either a fact or a theory, according to our standpoint. For instance, is the Copernican doctrine a fact or a theory? Is the law of gravitation a fact or a theory? Is not any proved hypothesis a fact rather than a theory? A better statement would be that knowledge is made up of the data of experience and their interpretation. Of course a scruple might be raised concerning the data themselves, on the ground that they are not free from subjective modification, but it would be a fruitless refinement at this point. It is sufficiently accurate to say that knowledge is made up of the data of articulate experience, and in this sense of facts and their interpretation. That the distinction is purely subjective is manifest.

In estimating the value of any system of knowledge—say, of physical science—we need to keep this fact in mind, and distinguish between science as fact and science as interpretation. The former alone abides. The phenomena and their known laws are the abiding and valuable part of science. They are the valuable part; for when we have the laws of phenomena we can read the past, previse the future, and, by arranging the antecedents, we can determine the consequents. Given a knowledge of the laws of chemical change and combination, we have all that is practically valuable in chemistry. The atomic theory as a metaphysical fact has no practical value. Given the laws of heat or electricity, it is practically indifferent what theory we adopt. Even in gravitation the law is everything, the theory is nothing. The practical astronomer applies the law, and his calculations are valid so long as the law holds, no matter how the planetary motions are produced.

The fact side too contains the abiding element of science. There have been rival theories of light, but optical phenomena are ever the same. Chemical theory has changed again and again, and can hardly be said to have reached a final form even yet. The text-books do indeed give us the most elaborate representations of the inner structure of the molecules, but except as convenient practical fictions only the uncritical dogmatist believes in them. Meanwhile the laws and facts of chemical change remain what they always have been; no fact has been overturned or in any way set aside. Geology has abounded and still abounds in differing opinions: but the strata and their contents are still there, and they would remain there if we repudiated every dogma of theoretical geology. The estimates of time required for certain geological changes vary all the way from a few million years to something like eternity, but the changes themselves are undoubted. No more are the general theories of light, heat, magnetism, and electricity rescued from all doubt and obscurity. In all these fields many useful facts and phenomenal laws are known, but the explanation, the rational comprehension, is lacking. Phenomena occur in certain ways or under certain conditions, but we know not how nor why. The present state of scientific theory, even in the inorganic sciences, is one of fermentation with no signs of a speedy settling.

Of all this, however, the quack and the hearsay scientist have no suspicion. With them facts, theories, and surmises mingle in one inextricable chaos, and all alike appear as invincible science. This pathetic devotion, born of ignorance, has made science and scientific the great question-begging epithets of our time. In truth, however, a large part of what is called science is not a fact, but a theory about facts—a set of theoretical conceptions whereby the mind seeks to make the facts intelligible to itself, and to meet its demand for a sufficient reason. But these theories have changed again and again. Very little scientific theory is now what it was a generation ago, but for the ignorant and the dogmatic the current theory is science now as the current theory was science then.

If now we ask for a theory which shall be final we must admit that we have very little that is secure from overthrow. Of course all such theorizing rests on the assumption that the normal processes of our thinking are valid for reality, so that what the mind infers from facts must also be a fact, and what we need to explain the facts is necessary to their existence. This in itself is an enormous assumption, but even on the basis of this assumption it is hard to reach finality. The trouble is that the facts are rarely so unambiguous as to exclude competing interpretations. In reading the past we can only say, If we know all the significant facts, and if there has been no change in the ways of working, such or such was the case. But in truth all such reading is simply a declaration of what we should expect to find in the past on the basis of our present knowledge. Whether the fact was really so is quite another affair. If we should discover new facts, or should get positive testimony in place of the present circumstantial evidence, we might change our thought of the past very profoundly. In that case, again, no scientific fact would be disturbed, but an inference would be rectified which was based on imperfect knowledge. The old conclusion would still be valid from the old standpoint, but it would be modified, or set aside, by the larger knowledge. To take an extreme illustration, if any one should persuade himself that a divine record sets forth that the earth was really fitted up in six ordinary days there would be nothing in that to modify any geologic fact, however much it might affect geologic theories. We should never reach such a view, indeed, from a study of the rocks; but this study does not tell us what was, but only what we should judge to have been on the basis of geologic appearance.

This matter of reading the past is further complicated by a doubt whether any system of law can give any account of its origin and history. An order of law in a moving world would necessarily have a virtual past. Thus, if we should suppose the solar system created outright, the equations which expressed the positions and motions of the planets at the moment of creation could be read backward as well as forward; but the backward reading would refer to a virtual past, not a real one. The same is true for any order of law in a changing world. It admits of being read backward, and there is no sure test whereby we can distinguish the virtual from the real past. Our analytic thought naturally thinks that the simple elements preceded compounds, but this is only a logical precedence. We find no warrant for turning it into a temporal relation. If there have always been chemical elements, for all we can say they may always have been chemically active and chemically united in any order of complexity.

If we occupy a religious standpoint, and think of the world as created, we are no more successful in demonstrating what the beginning must have been. That everything must have looked brand-new is a thesis for which astonishingly little proof can be advanced. If, finally, we call in the divine veracity we soon find that veracity is a very slippery notion when we get away from the familiar relations of daily life; and, besides, it is very doubtful if that veracity is under bonds to save us from the necessity of looking well to our logical goings. Dogmatizing on origins is logically a very perilous business. It generally ends in mistaking the simplifications of analysis for the original forms of existence.

If we are in such a plight in the physical field, where the facts are relatively simple, and where we seem to be near to the constants of the system, matters are far worse when we reach the human field of history. Here the range of possibility is so great, and the facts are so ambiguous, or so imperfectly known, that little trust may be placed in any theory which does not rest on positive evidence. Plausible suggestions are possible in explanation of any historical fact. Plausible constructions of human origins are always possible in terms of the reigning speculation. Showy philosophies of history are easily constructed by the aid of a little judicious selecting and ignoring. Improvising ancient history is an easy and pleasing task. But in all these matters the trained thinker remains a doubting Thomas until some positive evidence is adduced.

Historical explanations are uncertain enough when dealing with objective facts. When it comes to psychological motives and intentions the difficulty is indefinitely increased. This is a great boon to literary commentators, who find in this fact a chance to market their imaginary wares. The same fact makes possible the whitewashing of almost any historical infamy which lies at a distance. Some facts are so purely objective as to call for no deep scrutiny of motives. That A bought a piece of land from B is a transaction which is easily comprehended; but that Henry VIII. divorced his wives is a fact of another sort, and one which admits of much explaining.

It is this uncertainty and unfruitfulness of most theories which leads both to the positivist restriction of thought and knowledge to the observation and registration of phenomena, and also to the periodical outbreaks of scepticism. The mind, finding itself foiled, or losing itself in inconsistency, for a time despairs until nature reasserts itself, and once more Sisyphus upheaves his stone.

These rather general remarks illustrate the mental desire for explanation, and also suggest the need of caution in its gratification. We must beware of getting through too soon, and of resting in plausible but fictitious theories. We have now to treat the matter more in detail.

First of all, a purely formal type of explanation must be noticed in which the mind makes motions but no progress. It merely gives the form of ground or reason to the fact itself. The qualities and activities of a thing are referred to its nature, which is posited as their hidden ground. This is often derided by amateur critics, who are not too dull to see its unprogressive nature, but are too dull to see its rational necessity. There is certainly no progress in explaining chemical action by affinity or gravitation by gravity, but there is a formal satisfaction of the mental demand for a reason. Without it the idea of connection vanishes, and the events float loose and groundless.

Explanation which deals with real existence, in distinction from pedagogical explanation, has several stages which deserve to be distinguished. The lowest consists in referring the fact to a class or law. We explain the fall or floating of bodies by reference to gravitation. Chemical changes are referred to affinity, magnetic phenomena to magnetism. In this way we gather our facts into classes or refer them to laws, and when this is done we count the facts explained.

It is plain that this explanation gives no insight into the nature of the fact. Its sole value is its logical convenience. It rescues the facts from their isolation, so that they are no longer separate and lonely in our mental system, but are recognized as cases of a kind or law. At the same time the facts remain as separate and distinct as ever, for classification makes no identity and abolishes no difference. They also remain as mysterious as ever; for the nature of a given fact is in no way revealed by the discovery that there are many other facts of the same kind.

Both of these truths are often overlooked, and classification is supposed to reproduce some actual process in reality. The plurality and difference of the facts disappear in the unity and simplicity of the class term, and hence there often arises the fancy that the universal or law represents the original from which the particular realities or events proceed. Still, it is plain that classification in no way changes the facts or reveals their concrete source. If we unite all cows, sheep, goats, etc., under the common term animal we manifestly do nothing to the cattle themselves; least of all do we identify them. It is equally plain that from the general term no actual case can be deduced. The term applies to all cases, but implies none. The individuals are subordinated to the class, but they are not produced by the class. The relation is logical, not ontological; and whenever we wish to think the facts as they are we have to recall all the qualitative and contextual differences which have disappeared from the class term, but which are necessary to constitute the individual. Very much of our thinking, as we have seen, is symbolic, and we have no occasion to go beyond the generalities of the class. Hence we easily mistake the symbol for the thing, and logical relations for real relations. When to this fact we add the element of necessity, which for crude thought lurks in the notion of law, it is easy to think that classification is a complete explanation.

In fact, the mental value of such explanation lies entirely in its convenience, and in reducing many cases to one symbolic expression. And as the mind seldom has occasion to go beyond the symbol, or to think it out into concrete detail, such a reduction to unity or simplicity, or such assimilation to familiar matter, is commonly all-sufficient. When we hear of some unfamiliar mental fact and are able to see it as a modification of some familiar principle, it loses its mystery, and we ask no more. Or when the various energies of the physical system are reduced to some form of movement we fancy that we have effected a great simplification of the system, and have gone far towards explaining it. In fact, we only simplify our ideas and not the system. When we come to deal with the realities themselves we find all the complexity coming back again, if not in the idea, then in its specification and application. The concrete problem cannot be reduced to lower terms by classification.

Thus, in the case of physical energies we say they are all modes of motion. But why should these modes be many, and in what do they consist? Or how does the passage from one form of motion to another cause the qualitative change involved, say, in passing from electricity to chemical affinity? The energies are all one in the catalogue, but in reality they remain as distinct as ever, except that in certain cases one energy may be displaced by another qualitatively unlike but quantitatively equivalent.

Or suppose we say that all the problems of physics are cases of the redistribution of matter and motion. Here we have a generalization much admired but not over-fruitful. Ideas are simplified to the last degree, but the facts remain as complex as ever. The complexity eliminated from the ideas must be brought back in the collocation of the matter and direction of the motion, and there we are as much in the dark as before. That collocation and direction now become the problem. The simple existence and mobility of matter imply no specific grouping or movement. One seeking to invent a machine for a specific purpose would not be much advanced by learning that his problem involved only a redistribution of matter and motion.

When we are further told that all evolution proceeds by differentiation and integration, from the like to the unlike, from the simple to the complex, from the homogeneous to the heterogeneous, we may possibly have a valid description of the appearance and of the general form of the movement; but we have no explanation of the concrete process. We should need to know how the simple can ever become complex, or the homogeneous heterogeneous, unless complexity or heterogeneity were already at least implicitly there. Moreover, such vague formulas, when they claim to be more than superficial descriptions, just because they apply to everything, account for the peculiarities of nothing. If everything had been different they would have applied equally well. They contain no account of direction and no ground of motion. As the laws of motion are valid for all motions, supposing them to arise, while they account for none, so these formulas may apply in a general way to many things; but the true ground of things must be sought elsewhere. In short, in a necessary system any all-explaining principle law or cause really explains nothing unless all the specific conditions are brought in, and by that time the simplicity vanishes. The explaining cause must become as complex as the explained effect, or there can be no explanation.

If, finally, natural selection is offered as an explanation of living forms we have no difficulty in admitting the principle as soon as we understand it. For when the anthropomorphism is climated from selection the principle reduces to the survival of the fittest; and when the ambiguity is eliminated from the latter principle it in turn reduces to the statement that the able to survive survive, and that the unable to survive do not survive; or that things survive in the measure of their ability to survive. One must be dull indeed not to see that this is undeniable; but unless we are able to point out in particular cases what the element of fitness is which leads to survival, or the element of unfitness which leads to non-survival, we make no progress. We know that a thing is fit or unfit because it survives or fails to survive, and then we use this hypothetical fitness or unfitness to explain the survival or non-survival. Such a deep draught at the well of truth could hardly prevent a fairly critical mind from speedily thirsting again.

And if we could point out the specific fitness or unfitness in specific cases we should still be far from any real insight. We should not see how the fitness or unfitness arises, nor how the survivals and non-survivals so fall out that an orderly system of organic existence emerges, nor why the biological movement should take the actual direction. Yet this is what we need to know if we are to get any real insight into the world of organic forms. The arrival of the fit is a greater problem than its survival; and the non-survival of the unfit is a matter of course, but is irrelevant to the real issue.

Explanation by classification is very important as a first step in the mastery of experience, but only as a first step. A second stage of explanation consists in connecting a fact with its antecedents as the result of a law or laws. In the previous stage a fact is viewed as a case of a law; here it is exhibited as the outcome of a law. This, however, is impossible except in cases where the law can be so definitely conceived in its meaning and the form of its application and variation as to admit of deduction from it. In other cases we have merely an example of a law without being able to deduce it. But when we can deduce an effect from a given condition according to a known law, or can trace the co-operation of several laws in a given effect, we have a sense of insight peculiarly satisfying, as when we trace the formation of dew on a clear cool night to several laws concerning the radiation of heat, specific heat, the condensation of water-vapor, etc. When we can thus trace a fact to known laws, so that it is seen to be their outcome under the circumstances, we view the fact as explained.

This form of explanation is an advance on the preceding one. There the event was simply a case of a kind of which no more could be said. Here the event is understood, at least in its proximate origin. Given the antecedents we trace the consequences, or conversely. In the former case we ask what consequents must result from the antecedents according to known laws. In the latter we ask what the antecedents must have been to produce the actual consequents. But whether we trace the antecedents to their consequents, or the consequents to their antecedents, the essence of the explanation consists in connecting a fact or state of things with other facts or states of things according to known laws. Then we see how one state of things arises out of another state of things, and how a present state of things at once points to a past state of things and foretells a future state of things. Of course such explanation is hypothetical, and supposes that we know all the significant laws, and that they are valid for both past and future.

This kind of explanation is relatively independent of metaphysics. It deals simply with the world of experience. Among the coexistences and sequences of this world we find an order of law, and by means of it we seek to unite the various states and factors of the system into a connected whole. Whatever our metaphysics, the phenomena and their laws remain the same, and so long as these remain it will be desirable to trace the phenomenal order in both space and time.

This might be called pre-eminently scientific explanation. It need not concern itself about metaphysics or causation, except in the sense of empirical conditions. It is possible to use causation in an empirical sense; that is, to name the empirical condition which under the assumed circumstances led to the fact, and this condition we may call the cause. Thus, the cause of the gun's bursting was a flaw in the metal or an overcharge of powder. The cause of the man's death was a fever or pneumonia. The cause of the shipwreck was a gale, or a fog, or a snow-storm, or an unsuspected current, or a hidden reef. But in such cases we are not dealing with metaphysical causes, but only with empirical conditions which in the actual order of experience are connected with the event in question. This is the conception of causation which should rule in inductive science, as it is the conception which is most prominent in daily life. With this conception, as we have pointed out, we escape the labyrinths of the metaphysical problem, and we also mark out a definite field of practical inquiry.

In this type of explanation, then, we seek to connect things and events according to rule, so that we see how one state of things grows out of another state of things, or how one state of things is required by other states of things. The rule of procedure would be this: Decompose the fact into its simplest elements and seek for the elementary laws which govern their combination. Then the fact may be exhibited as the result of its components if it coexist with them, or of its antecedents if it succeeds them. All wholes must be understood from their parts, all compounds from their components, all complexes from the simple factors. The atom explains the molecule, the molecule explains the mass. The complex states of consciousness are to be understood in their elementary components. The social order finds its explanation in the many factors which enter into it and combine according to law.

That our study of reality must largely follow this method is manifest. It is the gist of what is called scientific method. At the same time it does less than is supposed. The connections which it discovers are phenomenal only, and are generally matters of fact into which we have no further insight. For all we can see, they might be anything else whatever. Hence we connect one state of things with another state of things indeed, but only in a phenomenal order, and not by any insight into their essential connection. We name and describe the antecedents in the reproduction of living things, but we gain thereby no insight into the forces at work, and we have no knowledge of the antecedents which enables us to see that they can have only such consequents. We also trace the order of chemical change, and the resulting knowledge is of the utmost practical value; but we remain on the surface so far as any insight into that order is concerned. It would be a very great error, then, to suppose that the connections of things, even within the phenomenal field, are transparent to intelligence. On the contrary, they are for the most part pure opacity. The insight we think we possess is entirely fictitious, and is mainly due to the unconscious working of the category of necessity which makes everything clear by hypothesis.

Again, if the connections of phenomena were perfectly transparent, there are some deep-lying difficulties in this form of explanation which must always restrict it to secondary significance. First, in any case, it reaches nothing final. It presupposes the system of phenomena and their laws, and then aims to show how within the system things hang together. But it gives no insight into the system which implies all these things. Given a mechanism, we may trace connection among its parts and movements, but only because the mechanism is originally given. We see how the parts are connected and how the movements follow from one another, but only because the mechanism which implies them is given as a whole from the start. In such an order it is indeed desirable to trace the interconnection of things, but we should greatly deceive ourselves if we fancied that any ultimate explanation can be reached in this way. The mechanism we assume implies the parts, and all our explanation within the mechanism runs back to the mechanism as its presupposition.

The application to the system of phenomena is evident. Here, too, we may trace connection among the coexistences and sequences of the system, but we remain on the surface and within the system. Hence, finally, when we have explained all the particular facts—that is, have connected them with other facts according to rule—the system itself which implies them is found to contain the problem over again, only in a general form.

The study, then, of the connections of phenomena, while practically of the utmost importance, leads to no speculative insight, and reaches nothing in which thought may rest. Its explanations only carry the problem one step backward and leave us as badly off as ever. This is overlooked by crude thought for two reasons: First, it is satisfied if the motions of explanation are made, and does not care to inquire if the solution of the problem is really advanced. Secondly, it tacitly hypostasizes the system into "Nature," or the "Universe," or the "Cosmos," which is self-sufficient and self-administering, and of which no account need be given.

Again, the attempt to explain a whole by the interaction of its parts, or as the resultant of its parts, while a necessity of scientific method, either fails or moves in a circle when it claims to reach anything final or anything more than a partial view. If the parts are not subject to the law of the whole there is properly no whole, and what we call such is only an accident or chance product—a fortuitous coincidence of manifold activities without any unifying law. But if, on the other hand, the parts are subject to the law of the whole, then the whole is deduced from parts which presuppose the whole, and our thought moves in a circle. It is only when we are dealing with numerical and inorganic wholes that we get much insight from our analysis and synthesis. In organic and rational wholes the elements do not explain the wholes, but are explained by them.

The matter may be briefly summed up as follows:

First, the analytic procedure is necessary to any comprehension. If a given fact cannot be analyzed we must stop with it. Only as we break it up by analysis and recombine it in synthesis is there any motion. Thus we decompose the mass into its chemical elements. Thus we isolate the parts of the organism and study their various functions. Thus we reduce the mental life to its components and look for the law of their synthesis.

Secondly, when we allow our analysis to carry us to parts unrelated to the whole all hope of insight fails. Thus, suppose we seek to explain a molecule by atoms whose nature does not imply that form of combination, the molecule is a matter of chance. Or if we explain an organism by elements unrelated thereto, the combination is chance again. It is like explaining a page of composition by plain type, or like finding all literature accounted for by the discovery of a dictionary.

Thirdly, as soon as we exclude the law of the whole from the components the composition becomes a problem, and when we carry the law into the components the data include the problem.

Fourthly, our analysis by no means always gives us the components of the thing, but only partial views and abstractions—aspects of the thing rather than its components. These have their value in what they help us to, but they are not the truth of the thing. Our analysis and synthesis are often relative to ourselves, and represent no real process. In the case of the organism we may abstract parts and functions and study them separately, but they exist only as phases of the one organic whole. The same is true for most psychological analyses. It is only a very crude speculator who fancies that these give the components of mind instead of its various aspects. Sometimes our analysis, instead of giving the components of the thing, may only give its possible transformations, as in chemistry, where the composition of a substance means only its possible chemical transformations.

These considerations serve to show that scientific explanation has only a limited field and application. As soon as it is made all-embracing it becomes empty or self-stultifying.

The previous type of explanation often claims to confine itself to phenomena without saying anything of their causes. This claim is seldom literally correct. The formal renunciation of metaphysics and all its works by no means always secures their exorcism. Hence the scientific explanation has seldom freed itself from the attempt to give a theory of the causal realities which underlie phenomena. Thus, the advanced psychologist talks freely of empirical causation as the only one with which science deals; but when it is suggested that nothing can show a better claim to be regarded as causal, in the empirical sense, than states of consciousness, he soon lets it appear that he has not mastered his own doctrine, and has something metaphysical in mind. States of consciousness are undeniably conditions of certain forms of physical movement; yet he is unwilling to speak of them as causes, although causes, in the inductive sense, are nothing but conditions. This uncertainty shows a mastery of phrases rather than of ideas.

Scientific explanation, then, has commonly been allied with a theory of the causal realities which underlie phenomena. This leads us to the third form of explanation. Here the aim is to infer from phenomena, not only their phenomenal antecedents, but also their ontological grounds. We infer the causes which are supposed to produce the effects. In this way we build theories about atoms, molecules, forces, ethers, etc. These are viewed as the ontological constants in cosmic change, or as the realities by whose interaction and combination the phenomenal world is produced or explained. In such views the metaphysical tendencies of the mind are revealed. The categories of being and causation are imported into phenomena, and an air of solid reality is imparted to the whole.

Concerning the aim of this work criticism has no objection to offer, but doubt may be raised as to its product. This metaphysical work has generally been done under the influence of our natural realism, and with imperfect insight into the nature of thought. Space and matter are viewed as the supreme realities, and our ontology is shaped by and to them. In this way the atom and the void become the great factors in physical metaphysics, and nothing more is needed except a clumsy addition of causation in the form of moving forces.

The fundamental importance of the categories of being and causation has been insisted upon, but whether they can be thought in the form just mentioned must be left to metaphysics to decide. This scheme of physical metaphysics, however, is so prominent in both popular and scientific thought that something must be said about it, both as to the form in which it must be conceived and as to its value as an explanation.

With bare lumps we can explain only heaps. Unless we assume a mover without, we must posit moving forces within; and unless these forces are under some structural law, they will explain only amorphous masses. Simple pulling and pushing in a straight line makes no provision for organization. Assuming, then, the existence of such forces, we have a double order of facts, one of spatial change and combination, and one of a metaphysical nature. The former is a change among things; the latter is a change in things. The former depends upon the latter. All spatial changes among things must be viewed as translations into phenomenal form of dynamic relations in things. And the spatial system can be understood only through the metaphysical system. No spatial change explains itself or anything else until it is referred to a hidden dynamism. If we subtract a chemical element from a given molecule, no one can see the slightest reason in that fact for the resulting chemical change, unless we assume a system of dynamic relations within the elements themselves which determines the form of their manifestation and interaction; and this system must be as complex and various as the phenomena themselves.

This invisible dynamic system is overlooked altogether by superficial thought. Such thought has only the atoms and the void as data, and it can easily conceive the atoms as variously grouped within this void. The spatial imagination serves for this insight, and nothing more is demanded. But when thought is clarified to the point of seeing the necessity of affirming an unpicturable dynamism behind the system of spatial changes, then the dark impenetrability of our physical metaphysics begins to appear. Spatial combination we can picture. Volitional causality we experience. But what that is which is less than the latter and more than the former is an exceedingly difficult problem. Accordingly it is common to hear the leaders of science, and indeed all who have got beyond the naïve dogmatism of the senses, proclaiming the deep mystery, if not the unknowability, of the dynamics of the cosmos. The following words are attributed to Lord Kelvin (Sir William Thomson), on the occasion of the fiftieth anniversary of his connection with the University of Glascow:

"One word characterizes the most strenuous of the efforts for the advancement of science that I have made perseveringly through fifty-five years—that word is failure. I know no more of electric and magnetic force, or of the relations between ether, electricity, and ponderable matter, or of chemical affinity, than I knew and tried to teach my students of natural philosophy fifty years ago, in my first session as professor."

The knowledge of causes in the empirical sense is daily growing. The knowledge of causes in a dynamic sense, at least from the physical standpoint, is more mysterious than ever. We next point out some logical difficulties in any explanation by inferred causes.

In general we infer the causes from the effects, and then we explain the effects by the causes. This seems like movement in a circle. There is real progress in such explanation only in the following cases:

First, the mind may have such insight into the possibilities of the case as to form an exhaustive disjunctive judgment. Then we may show by analysis of the fact that we are shut up to one conception of the cause.

Secondly, the conclusion reached may admit of independent verification, or the theory may be found to embrace many new facts which were not considered in its formation. But when the inferred causes do not admit of being presented in experience, or lie beyond the analogy of experience and cannot be used to extend knowledge, the whole matter floats in the air. We mark time only without getting ahead.

Indeed, this unprogressive character attaches to every system of explanation of a mechanical or necessary nature. We infer A from B and explain B by A. We know that A was because B is, and we know that B must be because A was. Moreover, the A we infer is not A in general, but a definite and specific A which in principle includes B. If we fail to provide for B in A we cannot deduce B from A, and if we do make such provision we only draw out what we put in. In all inference from effect to cause we are bound to determine the thought of the cause by the effect, and we can infer neither more nor less than the cause of just that effect. If we infer more we are guilty of illicit process; if we infer less the effect is unprovided for. The explanation consists in making the effects potential in their causes, and the deduction consists in conceiving these potentialities as passing into realization. As thought goes backward it potentializes the actual; as it comes forward it actualizes the potential. We read the present into assumed past conditions which implied it, and we read the hypothetical past conditions into their assumed implications. In a necessary system we can never escape this barren oscillation.

Our eyes are holden in this matter because of certain easy oversights which have already been referred to in treating of the first form of explanation. The leading one is the mistaking of verbal simplifications for simplifications of things. The complexity, plurality, and differences of things disappear in the simplicity and identity of the class term, and then we fancy that the things themselves have been simplified and unified. We increase the illusion by the further fancy that the class term implies all to which it applies, and that the corresponding reality implies all its subordinated forms. Thus the last terms of abstraction are mistaken for the first and essential forms of real existence, and logical subordination is mistaken for ontological implication. The illusion is completed by our failure to recognize the shorthand character of language in general. We think in symbols, and only fill out the thought as far as may be necessary. Hence the causes to which we refer effects are thought only in a general way, and thus we overlook the fact that in concrete and complete thinking, in distinction from shorthand and symbolic thinking, we can never escape from complexity into simplicity, or pass from simplicity to complexity, as long as we remain on the plane of mechanism and necessity. The perennial attempts to deduce the world from some original state of simplicity and insignificance all rest at bottom on these oversights. The indefinite, incoherent, undifferentiated homogeneity with which they begin is something which can be neither reached nor used without bad logic.

There is a fundamental uncertainty, springing out of this same confusion, which runs through popular explanations of the evolution type. By dint of repetition it has come to be taken for granted that nothing is to be accepted as it is, but everything is to be understood through its history. On this line of thought we are brought down to the indefinite, incoherent homogeneity as the beginning of things. But logic soon shows the emptiness of this notion. Then we begin again. We assume some original datum or data with definite laws and tendencies, and forthwith logic shows that the original assumption must imply and determine all future outcomes. From one point of view something that long ago was explains all that is; from the other, something that forever is is the only explanation of all that was, is, or will be. Popular speculation in this field oscillates confusedly and helplessly between these contradictory opposites. The confusion is especially prominent in the field of biology and psychology. In the study of origins, also, it sometimes appears in the set determination to trace all resemblances of thought and custom and art and rite to a common source, without inquiring whether a common humanity in a common environment might not well have a similar manifestation, apart from any historic connection. At present the historian of religions or institutions feels compelled, at any price and through all manner of logical bushes and briers, to feign a common source whether he can find it or not.

None of these forms of explanation, nor all of them together, give final satisfaction to the mind. Single facts may be shown to be implications of other facts, but the system of facts and laws is left opaque and meaningless. The mechanical explanation with which we have just been dealing comes to no end. It merely gives the form of causality and substantiality to the facts without leading to anything more simple. To escape this collapse the mind has recourse to a fourth and final form of explanation—that of purpose or final cause.

This is the explanation by intelligence which is supposed to be moving towards preconceived ends, so that the activity is not merely driven from behind, but looks before to some end to be reached, and with reference to which the whole is determined. And this explanation takes up all lower forms into itself. From the orderly nature of mind we should expect an order of law, not as a dumb fact, but as expressing at once the orderly nature of intelligence and the way in which it realizes its aims. From the mental demand for unity and continuity we should also expect to find all things and events forming a system in which everything conditions every other thing, and in which each new state of things grows out of a past state of things, and in turn forms the ground of a future state of things. Explanation by intelligence, too, is the only one which ever comes to an end. In any mechanical system we not only reach no simpler state of things, but are shut up to an infinite regress in which thought itself perishes. An ultimate ground of things in which to rest can be found only in free intelligence. This is the only simplicity which can orignate complexity; the only unity which can produce plurality; the only universal which can specify itself into particulars; the only real explanation of anything.

To know what things are for, how they are brought about, how they are bound together, and what the agent or agents concerned in their production—this is the aim the mind sets itself. This aim is a mental ideal only imperfectly realized. But by keeping its several factors distinct, by recognizing their mutual compatibility, or, rather, the necessity of all if thought is to complete itself, and by persistent labor and patient thought in the service of cognition, we may hope gradually to transform the opaque data of experience into the transparent order of reason.

And now possibly it may occur to some reader to ask if the explanation by intelligence be not open to all the objections we have urged against mechanism. And is not intelligence itself the mystery of mysteries, so that we have simply pooled all lesser mysteries in this comprehensive one?

In reply we recall what was said in treating of volitional causality. We there pointed out that any ultimate fact must be mysterious, in the sense that it is something to be recognized and admitted rather than something to be deduced and comprehended. In this sense, no doubt, intellect is a great mystery. We cannot build it out of anything else. We cannot tell how intellect is, or can be, a fact. We can only recognize it as something actually existent.

But we also pointed out that there is a choice in mysteries. Some mysteries make other things clear, and some leave things as dark and impenetrable as ever. The former is the case with the mystery of intelligence. It makes possible the comprehension of everything but itself. In the mechanical scheme we are compelled to use the formal categories of possibility, potentiality, necessity, and causation, of which the concrete significance absolutely eludes all conception. It was to escape this difficulty that Kant invented his schematism of the categories, an invention of which the aim was more manifest than the success. In truth, we can find concrete illustration of these categories only in our inner experience. They remain elusive abstractions until they are interpreted in forms of the inner life.

Again, in the mechanical scheme, thought can never complete itself or satisfy any of its tendencies. We can find no unity, and if we could we could never use it. From the many we cannot reach the one, and from the one we cannot reach the many. We can find no explanation, for the problem ever retreats into the proposed solution. If along the line of a necessary movement we make anywhere a cross-section, logic compels us to find potentially or actually present everything that will ever emerge. Thus we toil along the line of the infinite regress, seeking rest and finding none. Intelligence may be a mystery, but it helps us out of this deadlock by assimilating the cosmic causation to itself. And when there is a little critical enlightenment it is plain that the choice is between this and words which end in nothing.

Much groundless but mischievous misunderstanding has arisen in the history of thought concerning the relation of scientific explanation and the explanation by intelligence. Gradually we are coming to see that they represent two different points of view, and can never conflict except through confusion. However much we may believe that there is a purpose in things, we cannot dispense with the study of the laws of things and events, and no study of the way in which things are done has any logical bearing on the conviction that there is purpose in the doing. The opposition which has actually existed is due to the superficial metaphysics of uncritical thought, which erects law into necessity and makes nature into a self-running mechanical system. This spectre needs no exorcism, but vanishes of itself as soon as thought attains to clear self-knowledge.

In looking over these types of explanation we see that

they form a series, and that we could not rest fully satisfied until the series and all its members are complete. But it is plain that this represents an ideal which is not yet attained in any type of explanation. The simple classification of things and events is far from complete. To be sure, a certain general classification under the categories is always possible, and is indeed necessary to give us any objects whatever; but this is so general as to give little insight. The classification which shall give the natural and essential affinities of things is still far from completion.

It is equally impossible to trace the systematic connection of all events, however firmly we may believe in it. We may be sure that there is a point of view from which we could see how the present state of things arises from a past state of things and produces a future state of things; but here too we walk by faith, not by sight. We are not even sure how this implication and production are to be understood: whether it be ontological and dynamic, or only logical, arising from the plan of the whole. Likewise we are sure that there must be an adequate causal explanation, but we are far from being able to trace it everywhere, even from an empirical standpoint. When we pass to proper efficiency there is great uncertainty as to the form under which causation is to be conceived, whether under a mechanical and necessary form, or under a spiritual and volitional one. Finally, we may be sure that all explanation at last roots in purpose and intelligence, but we are very far from being able to trace this purpose in detail. It remains, for the most part, inscrutable.

We must be careful, therefore, not to confound the legitimacy of the formal demand for explanation with the proof of any particular concrete explanation. Reflection justifies the formal demand, but specific evidence must accompany every particular case.

Oversight of this fact is one of the besetting sins of the uncritical mind. Because it is making motions which are formally justified, it finds it easy to rest in any alleged explanation without inquiring whether it really explains or is demanded by the facts. This is especially the case with all matters that lie at a distance, especially in time, as in ancient life and history. Here the speculator is not confronted with the immediate contradiction of facts, and any plausible or pompous theory is sure to find acceptance with minds in which the sense of logical obligation is weak.

The great majority of the things which pass for explanations in popular thought explain nothing. Often they have only a fictitious connection with the problem; sometimes they repeat the problem; very frequently they float in the air. Our generalizations are often so vague as to have no valuable meaning, as when we explain things by differentiation and integration. Again, in our causal explanation we often fail to reduce the fact to anything simpler, and thus produce elephants and tortoises under the earth. Or we fail to remark the complexity of the facts, and produce explanations without observing that many other explanations are equally possible, or that the facts are so uncertain that any explanation is only a dream. In all such cases the critical mind holds fast to the facts so far as they can be ascertained, and leaves theorizing and system-building to those unhappy beings who cannot live without a theory. The development of a critical habit of thought in this matter is apt to increase wisdom by diminishing knowledge.

In explanation, as in other forms of logical activity, there is needed a certain good sense which, unfortunately, logic cannot produce or furnish. Everything has a great many antecedents and concomitants. In a way the whole universe is antecedent and concomitant of everything. Abstractly considered, the number of possible combinations is indefinite, and life is too short to deal with such a problem. It becomes manageable only as the experience of the community and of past investigators has determined the general outlines within which our thought must move. When this is disregarded there is no barrier against numberless whimsies. So far as abstract logic goes, the direction of the wind, the position of the planets and stars, the phases of the moon, the lines of the hand, the "criminal hand," and even the "criminal thumb," may have deep and far-reaching significance for human affairs. A great many professors from the academy at Laputa are among us, and all make a great show of logic. It is only the slowly consolidated good sense of the community which keeps down this nonsense by persistently ignoring it, and by producing a mental soil on which such crops will not flourish. One must meet a believer in this sort of thing in order to realize how logically helpless we are when there is no common ground of good sense. Then one finds that in very truth this kind goeth not readily out.

CHAPTER XI

SOME STRUCTURAL FALLACIES

It is not my purpose here to deal with the familiar fallacies of logical treatises. These are self-evident in their fallacious character, and no discussion could make it clearer. But there are certain other fallacies which are far more subtle, and which are revealed only to critical inspection. These fallacies are so inevitable to untrained thought that they may be called structural, or at least constitutional. But before treating of them it seems desirable to say a word about error in general.

Error itself is so familiar a fact as commonly to excite no surprise or even notice. Nevertheless, it is theoretically a most portentous fact, being for philosophy something like sin for theology and ethics. The problem of error constitutes a kind of touchstone for philosophical systems. Any system which makes error necessary and cosmic destroys itself.

In the first place, it is clear that all investigation must assume the essential truth of our faculties. If we allow that these in their normal working may lead us astray, there is an end of all faith in reason and knowledge. But since, as a matter of fact, we often do go astray, the problem arises how to combine the assumption of the trustworthiness of our faculties with the recognition of actual and abundant error. Freedom, we shall see, is the only solution of the problem which does not wreck reason itself.

We may get an introduction to the problem, and also a good illustration of the ease with which men overlook it, by considering a passage from Mr. Herbert Spencer's *First Principles*. In the last paragraphs of Part I. of that work the question is raised why an advanced and progressive thinker should oppose traditional and conventional beliefs after he has outgrown them, seeing that those beliefs may well be better adapted to those who hold them than his own broader views. Mr. Spencer gives this answer:

"He [that is, the advanced thinker] must remember that, while he is a descendant of the past, he is a parent of the future, and that his thoughts are as children born to him, which he may not carelessly let die. He, like every other man, may properly consider himself as one of the myriad agencies through whom works the Unknown Cause; and when the Unknown Cause produces in him a certain belief he is thereby authorized to profess and act out that belief."

There is something edifying and inspiring in this utterance so long as we gaze upon the well-behaved and enlightened apostle of advanced thought who thus nobly represents the future and the Unknown Cause. The rights of free thought are vindicated once for all, and are set on high above all bigoted cavil. But when we remember that Mr. Spencer expressly includes all other men and all other beliefs in the same relation, and gives to them all the same sanction and authorization of the Unknown Cause, forthwith we begin to grope. For it is not the advanced thinker only who stands in this august relation, and has this supreme sanction, but "every other man" also "may properly consider himself as one of the myriad agencies through whom works the Unknown Cause"; and when the Unknown Cause produces in every other man a certain belief he too is "thereby authorized to profess and act out that belief."

But it is plain that " every other man " is a somewhat numerous personage, and his beliefs and acts, produced and authorized by the Unknown Cause, are a rather heterogeneous and unsavory collection, for it includes all the superstitions, absurdities, and imbecilities which have ever been believed, and all the horrors and atrocities which have ever been perpetrated. All of these are the products of the Unknown Cause, and the believers are, of course, " authorized to profess and act out" their beliefs, for all these are "as children born to them which they may not carelessly let die."

But what is truth in such a system? The Unknown Cause seems to have not one opinion but many, and it does not abide in any one for long. For a disciple of this view it must be a very grave circumstance that the Unknown Cause has produced a great many false opinions for one true one; that, along with a little truth, there has been an almost overwhelming production of error. The Unknown Cause has shown a grotesque tendency to revel in low and unseemly views, fetishisms, anthropomorphisms, theologies, whims, infatuations, obstinacies, instead of attaining to the sun-clear truths of the synthetic philosophy. This fact has so impressed many critics of a pessimistic turn that they have not hesitated to think meanly of the Unknown Cause and all its works. In any case it is clear that, up to date, the Unknown Cause has not advanced beyond an indefinite, incoherent heterogeneity of opinions, any one of which has the same source and sanction as any other.

This illustrates the position in which every system of necessity finds itself in dealing with the problem of error. For in such a system every thought, belief, conviction, whether truth or superstition, arises with equal necessity with every other. The belief in freedom is as necessary as the belief in necessity. Theism and atheism, spiritualism and materialism, freedom and necessity, consistency and caprice are alike necessary. Thoughts and beliefs become effects, and to speak of true and false thoughts seems like speaking of true and false chemical action. On this plane of necessary effect the actual is all, and the ideal distinctions of true and false have as little meaning as they would have on the plane of mechanical forces.

But possibly we may say that there is nothing in the notion of necessity to forbid that some thoughts correspond to reality while others do not, and thus the distinction of true and false is saved. Allowing this, we are still no better off. For if of these multitudinous thoughts which are necessarily produced some are true and some are false, we need to have some standard for distinguishing them from one another. And this standard cannot consist in the necessity of the true thoughts and the contingency of the false ones, for all are alike necessary. The belief in necessity is no more necessary than the belief in freedom. It would not help matters to declare that true thoughts are the product of normal thinking, for the same puzzle would arise in finding a standard of normality. Just as little would it avail to take a vote on the subject, for there seems to be no logical connection between the notion of a majority and the notion of truth. The necessitarian, moreover, would be in a specially sorry plight, as the necessity which produces beliefs has produced the belief in freedom much more profusely than the belief in necessity. If he should bethink himself that there is no one necessity which produces these many and contradictory beliefs, but that there are many necessities for the many beliefs, the question of a standard would at once emerge among the necessities themselves.

Besides, if we found a standard, how could we use it? The thought of a standard implies a power to control our thoughts, to compare them with the standard, to reserve our decision, to think twice, to go over the ground again and again, until the transparent order of reason has been reached. But on this theory there is no such power. Thoughts come and thoughts go. Some are displaced by others, not because of any superior rationality, but because the new conditions have produced new conceptions.

Thought as thought counts for nothing. The underlying dynamic conditions determine the rational movement without being determined by it. When, in a chemical molecule, one element displaces another the new combination is not truer but stronger than the old. So when a mental grouping is broken up and displaced by another it is not a question of truth or rationality, but of change in the underlying dynamic relations. There is, then, not only no standard of truth, but no power to use it if we had it. Thus all beliefs sink into effects, and one is as good as another so long as it lasts.

These considerations make it clear that the question of freedom enters intimately into the structure of reason itself. It concerns not merely our executive activities in the outer world, but also our inner rational activity. The only escape from the overthrow of reason involved in the fact of error lies in the assumption of freedom. Our faculties are made for truth, but this alone does not secure truth. We must use those faculties carefully, critically, persistently if any valuable knowledge is to be gained. Our faculties are made for truth, but they may be carelessly used, or wilfully misused, and thus error is born.

Of course this freedom is not a power to make things true or false at will. The rational connection of ideas and the cosmic uniformities we can neither make nor unmake. If we have the premises we cannot change the conclusion. The laws of thought are secure from all tampering and overthrow. Yet, though thus imperative, they do not of themselves secure obedience. If they did error would be impossible. Hence, in addition to the laws of thought founded in the nature of rationality, there is needed an act of ratification and self-control in accordance with those laws. Only thus does reason become regnant in our thinking, and only thus do we become properly rational beings. The laws and relations of numbers are inviolable, but they do not insure us against blunders in calculation. For this we need a somewhat intense attention and a careful scrutiny of our mental operations. Again, the truths of reason and of physical science are quite independent of our volition; but this fact does not provide for our knowledge of them. They do not get themselves known, but we come to know them only through slow, painful, and persistent research. Science itself is one of the great achievements of human freedom. We do not drift into it, neither is it let down ready-made from the skies; but by the patient toil and devotion of free men the temple of science and knowledge is built up.

Freedom, then, has great speculative significance. In discussing causation we saw that this notion vanishes in the infinite regress unless we elevate it to the volitional form. In the previous chapter we have seen that freedom is the condition of any real explanation. Here we find that every system of philosophy must invoke freedom for the solution of the problem of error or make shipwreck of reason itself.

Returning now to the fallacies, the first to be mentioned may be called the fallacy of the universal. It consists in mistaking class terms for things, and in identifying the processes of our classifying thought with the processes of reality. For its understanding we must recall a few considerations from our previous study.

That nothing happens to things when we classify them is familiar to us. Even if we should succeed in reducing all objects to a common class we should only unify our conceptions without in any way modifying the facts, and our gain would be not a deeper insight but a more convenient or extensive symbolization. That many classes are relative to our own purposes and have no essential significance for the objects is equally known. That our thinking is mainly symbolic, dealing not with the full conception of the reality but only with shorthand expressions of it is also undoubted. That concrete thinking—that is, thinking which is adequate to reality—must be as complex as reality itself is likewise beyond question. Our class terms in their generality may represent reality, but they never adequately express it. They have value as logical symbols, but they are as little to be mistaken for the reality as man in general is to be mistaken for my next-door neighbor.

Now of all this, which is clear enough when stated, our spontaneous dogmatism never even dreams. The order of thought is identified with the order of things as a matter of course. The plurality and differences of the facts disappear in the unity and simplicity of the class term, and a double fancy arises. The first is that the facts themselves have been identified, and the second is that we have come upon the true essence of the facts or the original from which they proceed. This is the fallacy of the universal, and this is how it arises. We must now proceed to illustrate the ravages it has wrought.

A very large part of popular speculation, both cosmological and psychological, is but a case of this fallacy. Physical objects are all classified as material, and their various activities are said to be manifestations of force. Thus we reach a pair of abstractions, matter and force, from which all the peculiarities and differences of material things and their energies have disappeared. This gives us a species of unity and simplicity of conception which is forthwith mistaken for a unity and simplicity of real existence. Then we are all ready for evolution. As in the system of conceptions, the species may be looked upon as modifications and specifications of the genus, and as being in that sense derived from the genus, so in the world of things the species may be looked upon as specifications of the supreme genera, matter and force, or as derived from them. Matter and force, then, simple and homogeneous, are the basal fact, and from their simplicity and homogeneity have proceeded all the complex forms of physical existence. And as the basal realities have no contents beyond bare being and causality, there is nothing about them to start questions or awaken surprise; and as they are also manifestly the source of the higher forms, there is no assignable limit to their efficiency. In this reasoning we have the fallacy of the universal in its most striking form— the form in which it has been the prolific and perennial source of atheistic and evolutionary speculation. When set forth in imposing terminology, in which homogeneity and heterogeneity, differentiation and integration play their familiar parts, it rarely fails to pass for the last profundity.

The fictitious and verbal nature of this reasoning is manifest. As soon as we think concretely and critically it is plain that this is simply a shuffling of logical abstractions and relations which have been mistaken for real existence. These abstractions have only a formal existence and a logical function. They are indispensable to us in mastering the manifold of experience, but when mistaken for reality they become absurd. We have seen in the preceding chapter that free thought is the only real principle either of simplification or differentiation. Without it logic can find its way neither from the many to the one, nor from the one to the many; and if we seem to do so we merely fall a prey to the fallacy of the universal.

If one should say, given a multitude of elements of various powers and in complex relations, and in general such that they imply to the minutest detail all that they will ever do, we can explain whatever they do, no one would think it a very edifying or progressive performance; and yet that is the exact value of all mechanical explanation which does not appeal to mind. But when the complexity is hidden by the simplicity of our terms, and the implicit implications of our data are overlooked through the deceit of the universal, we advance with the utmost ease from an indefinite, incoherent homogeneity to any desirable definite, coherent heterogeneity, as per contract or schedule. So great are the imposture and deceit of the universal.

This fallacy underlies the system of Spinoza, so far as it is reasoned. It vitiates a large part of Hegel's work, and is the gist of Mr Spencer's philosophy. The bulk of pantheistic speculation roots in it, and it is the perennial source of atheistic reasoning. In the former case the individual is merged in the class term, and this soon passes for the universal and all-embracing being. Thus a harmless logical subordination becomes a fatal ontological implication. In the case of atheism the complexity and plurality of real existence are reduced to simple abstractions, which are so low as apparently to demand no explanation, and thus the world-problem is triumphantly and most luminously solved.

In psychology also this fallacy has been rampant, reducing a good part of psychological discussion to irrelevance and barrenness. Psychologists have been greatly exercised as to what faculty is concerned in a given experience, and also as to how many faculties are to be assumed or allowed. There has been a general aim to reduce mental principles to the fewest possible, and there has been a very general fancy on the part of the operators that they were dealing with the nature of the mind itself rather than classifying the mental facts. Hence each new simplification has been viewed as a triumph of analysis, and as pointing to a corresponding simplicity of the mental nature.

Here too the illusion is patent. The classification of mental states contains no doctrine of the soul and no hint of the genetic relations of the facts as occurring. Neither does it in any way identify or even modify the facts. These remain what they are, to whatever faculty or class we may refer them. If we should reduce all the faculties to one the facts would remain as distinct as ever. Light, heat, and sound are all sensations, but they are incommensurable, nevertheless. If we say, with Condillac, to think is to feel, we have to confess that to think is not to feel in the same sense that to have a pain is to feel; and if the matter were pushed it would turn out that the feeling which is also thinking is not any and every feeling, but only a thinking feeling, and indeed we should finally see that even the thinking feelings vary among themselves. The thinking feeling which is geometry would not be the thinking feeling which is economics. Thus the things which we identify in the noun or verb we have to distinguish in the adjective or adverb, and we have our work for nothing. The identifications and constructions are mainly verbal. At this verbal mill the associational psychologists have been grinding with sad patience but dreary monotony for generations. In comparison the blind leading the blind would present a hopeful and inspiring spectacle.

The general discussion of evolution in the biological realm has been greatly confused by this fallacy of the universal. The very phrase, the transformation or transmutation of species, betrays its presence. It suggests an essence which is transformed and which abides. Because it is transformed, the lower forms are made over into the higher; because it abides, the higher are really identical with the lower. But when we remember that a species is really only a group of more or less similar individuals and is nothing in itself this notion vanishes. The transformation of a species could only mean the production of dissimilar individuals along lines of descent, thus forming a new group. If in tracing the history of organic forms along genealogical lines we find a growing complexity and a continued progress, the simple fact is that the power which produces individuals, instead of producing them all on a level, produces them on a varied and rising scale, a scale of greater complexity and heterogeneity, and one of growing adaptation to larger and fuller life. There is nothing whatever in the fact of such connection which identifies individuals, or which identifies higher and lower forms. We may indeed class them together for logical convenience, and may speak of later forms as modifications of earlier forms, but both the identification and the modification are purely subjective, and have no significance for the real things. Apart from our subjective manipulation, the fact is the individuals and the power which produces individuals through the processes of generation in such a way that they admit of being classed according to an ascending scale. All else is the shadow of our own minds. To keep this steadily in view would reduce the doctrine in question to a subordinate significance, and would empty it entirely of those fearful implications which it has for popular thought.

The discussion of the relation of the human mind to the brute mind has been largely vitiated by the same fallacy. Assuming the truth of evolution, the fact would be that minds of a lower grade preceded those of a higher grade; that these successive minds appeared in connection with organisms genealogically connected; and, finally, that if we should classify these minds we should find them constituting an ascending order. This fact would leave entirely untouched the question, What are these individual minds, and what is the power or powers concerned in their production? Our classifications decide nothing as to the reality, and when we transcend our subjective manipulation we see that the objective problem is not to gather things into a common class, but to produce a series of existing minds, each of which is a distinct individual, and no one of which, except in a figurative sense, inherits anything from any other. Given one or more minds to produce new minds of higher kind or degree, or indeed of any kind or degree, is the real problem. But this fact is obscured by constructing a pair of abstractions, the human mind and the brute mind, and by making the most agonistic and even agonizing efforts to identify their contents. Yet this debate does not touch reality at all, but only the contents of two logical abstractions.

A further illustration of this fallacy is found in a current doctrine concerning the origin and progress of religion. This theory looks for the earliest form of religious conception and views all later forms as developed from it, so that they may be regarded as but sublimations of the initial conception. But as the earliest notions were crude, some form of animism or fetishism, and as all later notions are but developments of the earlier, we can only look upon them as being involved in the condemnation visited upon their beginnings. This kind of thing has been thought to be immensely significant, but in truth it is only the full-blown fallacy of the universal. The objective fact in the case is that men, in different stages of development, have formed varying and competing conceptions concerning the invisible world and its hidden agencies. Animism, ghostism, fetishism, polytheism, monotheism, pantheism, deism, Christianity, are illustrations. These are one in the sense that astronomy and astrology, or chemistry and alchemy, are one. But this fact of a plurality of competing conceptions is easily hidden by verbal thinking. For all of these conceptions may be looked upon as phases of religious belief, and thus they are verbally identified or unified. Then we have only to look for the earliest form of this belief to find its true original and abiding essence, and then we turn on the terminology of evolution and exhibit the higher forms of religious faith as only sublimations of an earlier belief in ghosts. That all this is only verbal manipulation is plain upon inspection. With equal cogency we might maintain that astronomy is only sublimated astrology and that chemistry is only sublimated alchemy, and with equal relevance we might suggest that no one can have much faith in these sciences who duly considers their low and unseemly origin.

These illustrations give only a faint hint of the ravages of the fallacy of the universal. And, in general, if we should eliminate from speculation and discussion the various forms of this fallacy their volume would be surprisingly diminished.

This fallacy as applied to concepts I call the fallacy of the universal. As applied to principles it may be called the fallacy of abstraction. It is essentially the same fallacy in both cases, but the manifestation in the two fields is sufficiently different to make it permissible to have a double name, especially as thereby we secure a pretext for another lot of illustrations.

Thought cannot get on without the universal, but it must be critical in its use. In like manner thought cannot get on without abstract principles, but it must be equally critical in their use. As the concept may be valid for things without being the thing, so principles may be valid for things without being the thing. And as the concept must be specified into particular values when applied to any real thing, so principles must undergo specification and even modification when applied to actual cases.

Through oversight of this fact men often lose themselves in theories which may be abstractly true and even theoretically important, but whose practical application is uncertain. In many cases, too, the modifications in practice are so great as to leave the theory as true as ever but worthless.

Theoretical mechanics illustrates all of these cases. The science is valuable only as it finds the abstract law, and to do this it must abstract from all the concrete circumstances. It feigns a lot of abstractions as a material point, a flexible and frictionless cord, a homogeneous and regular body, and then formulates their law. But this law is strictly true only for the abstractions; when applied to reality, allowance has to be made for all the actual circumstances eliminated from the abstractions. And sometimes, as in the case of the wedge, the theory is correct but worthless, for in practice the use of the wedge depends upon the friction which is omitted in the theory.

There can be no science without abstract principles, but there can be no sane and safe thinking without carefully inquiring into the form which they assume in application, or without inquiring whether the conditions assumed in the theory are realized or realizable in practice. Failure here has resulted in a vast amount of closet theory and academic debate, productive of nothing but confusion and mischief.

This fallacy of abstraction is almost as pervasive as the fallacy of the universal. It leads to a great many unreal simplifications and illusory solutions of practical problems. Thus in ethics the theory of responsibility is very simple. We form the abstraction of a "moral agent," or a "sinner," and have no difficulty in laying down the law for him. And this law may be abstractly correct and express the essential judgment of our moral nature. But when it comes to applying this law we begin to grope. For we have not a moral agent ready-made from the start, and endowed with all necessary knowledge and sensibility. The actual moral agent has to be developed. The knowledge, the moral sensitiveness, the volitional control—all have to be developed or acquired. And the process is a slow one, and is never completed. The morality of the actual man is potential, partial, relative. This fact complicates the concrete problem to an unknown extent. But the ethical and theological theorist often overlooks all this, and contents himself with theorizing about the " moral agent" and the "sinner." The result is something either purely academic or practically atrocious.

Indeed, even the virtues themselves depend to some extent upon the context. As abstract principles they may be abstractly affirmed, but in application they must be adjusted to circumstances. Thus, justice ranks high among the eternal principles, and is of inalienable obligation; but it is not always easy to see what justice demands in a given case, or how far it is practically attainable. In fact, the abstract principle may be insisted upon in a way to make society impossible. A fanatical theorist may easily persuade himself that all social arrangements and all laws are unjust, and a great many facts might be offered in evidence. No perfectly just system of taxation is possible. Every law is unjust to some one. The order of life itself seems unjustly partial. To him that hath is given, and from him that hath not is taken away even that which he hath. What could be more unjust than a world of heredity and social solidarity? With such facts abounding it is easy for the ideologist to heat his own and other weak heads, and then we become aware that there is a certain truth in Hobbes's claim that right and justice depend on the law;

they are what the law allows or commands. It would be impossible to maintain social order if there were not a power to end the wrangles which could arise out of the notions of abstract rights when abstractly interpreted. There is no more potent and destructive solvent of civilization than these same notions when held without regard to the concrete conditions of human existence. The kind of justice that brings down the heavens is of a piece with the malignant philanthropy of some historical reformers.

The same fallacy runs through a great deal of moral teaching and moral reform. A set of abstract moral principles is set forth, but the mode of application is overlooked. Then with a few such phrases as "loyalty to principle," "loyalty to conscience," "no compromise with sin," it is easy to make a great show of lofty purpose. Such phrases readily lend themselves to effective rhetorical display, and commonly aggravate the evil in question. For with persons of this type it is not a question of doing the best possible when the ideally best cannot be attained, but of "keeping their own skirts clear of blood," or of making no "league with death or covenant with hell." The more fanatical had rather see evil flourish than "compromise their conscience," which is often a most singular organ; and the weaker minded are afraid to do anything for fear of doing wrong. This fallacy of the abstract has always been a great weakness of moral reform.

Philanthropy suffers in the same way. It tends to remain abstract and academic, dealing with man, or the laborer, or the criminal in general, instead of studying the concrete case. To be sure, the concrete case can never be effectually studied except in the light of some principle, and this is the justification of the abstract view; but with equal certainty the abstract principle leads to nothing until it is studied in its concrete application. Human equality is a great ideal, but how to secure it among men who are profoundly unequal is not always evident. That we are all children of a common Father should always be borne in mind; but this does not remove the fact that some of the children are lazy, or filthy, or turbulent, or ignorant, or vicious; and this fact must also be taken into account.

When we have the abstract principle the concrete problem is only half solved. The mode of application remains, and this is often the question of chief difficulty. Here is where the ethical casuist, the religious disciplinarian, and the social reformer all come short. They fall back on the abstract. The amateur sociologist falls back on some glittering generalities about man and the golden rule, and possibly even some theological doctrine. But these are rarely in dispute. The practical question is, How shall these generalities be applied in the actual social condition? Moses on the mountain holding up his hands is doubtless an important factor, but nothing will ever be done until Joshua goes down into the valley and brings things to pass.

We also need to bear in mind that a great many practical problems alike in ethics and sociology, in economics and politics, are theoretically indeterminate. Good men may differ, and only life and experience can finally point out the way. In a great many things we must feel our way, and in such cases the flourishing of generalities at best leads to nothing better than fine writing or showy speeches, which in no way advance the matter. The high moral stand often taken by politicians in dealing with their opponents, when it is not plain hypocrisy, illustrates this wretched mockery of reasoning. The religious casuist especially needs to remember this indeterminateness of practice, as he is peculiarly liable to mistake his own conviction or habit for a universal law, if not for a divine command.

We find the same devotion to the abstract in a great

deal of economic discussion. The "economic man" of the economists is an abstract fiction like the "moral agent" of ethics, and is in equal need of watching. For this man, when he appears in reality, is more complicated in his nature and relations than he is in the speculation. But his makers and managers commonly overlook this, and when they have formulated some principle, which may be abstractly true, they think that nothing more is to be done. But here again it may be that the theoretical postulates have a parallax with reality, and that the abstract principle must be greatly modified in the application. Thus, free trade may be an ideal both morally and economically from the academic standpoint, but it by no means follows that it is always the best for every people without regard to their economic conditions. Such a question cannot be academically settled. The argument may still be sound as an abstraction, but it is important to inquire whether the conditions assumed by the argument actually exist. That one hundred men can do one hundred times as much as one man is self-evident when abstractly taken; in practice, however, there might be conditions such that they could not do as much as one man, and there might be conditions where they could do many more than a hundred times as much as one man. For instance, one hundred men could never dig up a plot of ground six feet square on the condition that they all stand on it, while one man could manage it very comfortably. On the other hand, a hundred men in co-operation might do something which singly they could not accomplish at all. So simple a case of co-operation as pulling on a rope may illustrate the matter. Of course the abstract hundred men must always do just one hundred times as much as the abstract single man. The mathematics is perfect, but the concrete problem remains unsolved. The straight line is always the shortest distance between two points in pure space, and yet in a world like ours the longest way round may sometimes be the shortest way home. A guide who had landed his followers in a bog would excuse himself in vain by falling back on the mathematics of the line, but he would not be much more absurd than some of our theoretical economists.

So much for abstract free trade. That abstract protection hangs equally in the air is too evident to need illustration.

The root of these two fallacies, or of this one fallacy in both of its forms, is the failure to think concretely in concrete matter. A great many social disputes also are confused if not produced by this same failure. Thus, a dispute between a debtor and a creditor, or an employer and his employees, is always something specific, and can be understood only in its special circumstances. If thus dealt with there would be some hope of understanding, and, possibly, of settling the difficulty. But the rule is to generalize, and then the abstract debtor and creditor, labor and capital, play their familiar part. The lurid rhetoric which is kept in stock for such occasions is turned on. Octopi and polypi, boa-constrictors and hydra-headed monsters crawl all over the subject. Vultures and cormorants flock in, and the whole region swarms with anarchists, Shylocks, and barons. This performance, which, in principle, is the gist of so much popular discussion in this field, is always exceedingly humorous, although at times it may, in addition, become dangerous. How to conduct a political campaign without it is quite beyond the heart of the natural man to conceive.

The fallacy of abstraction is especially the scientific fallacy; that is, science, by its aim and form, is apt to fall into this fallacy unless duly chastened by criticism. Science as such exists in abstract form, and we are prone to forget that any science is never the reality, but only a partial and abstract view of reality. The same thing, as man. may fall under a great many sciences. His being has physical, chemical, physiological, biological, psychological, economical, ethical, and religious aspects, and he belongs to all of these sciences. But no one of them alone can fully express him. We have to be on our guard against science itself; for these abstractions are very apt to set up for the true reality, and to seek to exclude one another from existence. The mind which has produced them must remain their master by remembering their abstract and partial character, and by persistently returning to the realities from which they have been abstracted.

The science of man himself furnishes the most striking illustration of this usurping tendency on the part of the abstract sciences. The physicist and chemist, left to themselves, tend to regard man as a physical and chemical combination. Physical changes due to human volition are fairly familiar facts of experience; but as they lie in a field outside of physics and chemistry the mere physicist or chemist is perpetually sliding into their denial. In like manner the biologist, when he has classified man in the natural-history series, tends to think that he has adequately grasped humanity. The economist mistakes his partial view for a complete one. The mere physician does the same, and, for the sake of life, is sometimes ready to ignore life's true significance. The moralist goes and does likewise; and, finally, the theologian tends to ignore all the phases of human life except the abstractly spiritual. The currier with his high estimate of the defensive value of leather is a figure of perennial significance.

And now it will doubtless seem to some readers that this nominalism is a recantation of our earlier insistence upon the necessity of the universal. But this too is a mistake. We still insist that without the *validity* of some universals there can be no knowledge. But this does not imply their thinghood in any case, nor remove the fact that a great many universals are relative to ourselves. The mind needs watching in all its elements and functions. The particular needs watching, lest the mind lose itself in a meaningless chaos of details. The universal needs watching, lest the mind lose reality altogether in its devotion to abstractions. For finding the golden mean there is no rule which can be mechanically applied. The mind itself, alert and critical, in contact with the facts, is the only standard.

A third great source of error is language itself. This has already been referred to in treating of the notion, but some elaboration may be permitted here. Such errors may be called fallacies of language. In some respects they are closely related to the preceding fallacies, but they have some features peculiar to themselves.

Words, from their structure and associations, come to have a force of their own which is quite distinct from their logical connotation. In this way they often have a parallax with our real meaning. Popular thought, also, when it is not busied with sense objects, is so dependent on the word that it soon identifies it with the thing; so that to change the word is to change the thing, and whatever the word implies is true of the thing. It is this fact that gives nicknames and epithets their power. In a rational world they would have no significance; for every one would pass behind the word to the object, and would see that this is the same, whatever we call it. In the actual world, which is not rational, we have constant illustration of what Dr. South calls "the fatal imposture and force of words." Popular discussion is largely vitiated by them. Things are displaced by question-begging epithets, often of odious association and connotation. "Trenchant arraignments" are made; insults are exchanged; "replies" abound; but the matter itself is left untouched.

The fallacy of language in this form is simply a movement of human pugnacity and passion made articulate by speech; it has no rational character. The fallacy is a little higher in the familiar argument from the word rather than the thing. Often the word is more definite than the thought, and shows no trace of the necessary limitations. In such cases we trust to the good sense or knowledge of others to supply the limitations. Or we use various expressions, and approach the subject from different standpoints, in order to show that we must not stop in the expression, but must go on to the thing. Such expressions always suffer when they fall into the hands of persons who interpret them by the dictionary, or who are without fairness or good sense. Instances of dictionary interpretation occur when literary men wander into some scientific field, and begin to interpret doctrines by the literary or every-day uses of the terms. Then some astounding nonsense is pretty sure to be evolved. Physical, biological, economical doctrines often undergo the most grotesque distortions in this way.

But the greatest man at this fallacy is the maker of "logical consequences," who is generally a "practised debater." These are, as a rule, only verbal consequences, but with the uninitiated they are often very effective. The godlessness of the Constitution and the schools, the potential, if not probable, treason of those who believe in a higher law, or who hold that it is better to obey God than man, are illustrations of this sort of thing. The right of revolution, the word of God, the supremacy of the church or of the state, are phrases well adapted to this kind of treatment, and they have suffered from it accordingly. The terrible consequences sure to result from this or that social change, or doctrinal modification, are reached in the same way. The common mark of such persons, when they are honest, is that they are totally destitute of the sense of reality. They seem to have no idea of how living men think, or of how language is used. It is well known that about everything worth having is logically impossible or self-destructive. Our federal government is logically self-destructive; for it is logically possible for Congress, or the Executive, or the Judiciary to block the governmental administration. Whatever they can do they will do, of course, and the government must perish. The English Constitution is logically non-existent, for Parliament may do what it pleases. Universal suffrage has the most fearsome possibilities. The admission of the laity, and especially of women, to a voice in ecclesiastical administration is logically nothing less than the abomination of desolation standing where it ought not. There is nothing that is not open to quibble or cavil if, from dulness or other causes, any one inclines to it. The answer to all such scarecrow reasoning is that back of all logic, and conditioning its use, is the mental and moral sanity of the individual and the community. While this lasts the logical consequences will remain the nightmares of weak minds, and if this should vanish no theory could save us.

Another form of the fallacy of language consists in arguing from the metaphor involved in the word. Heredity and natural selection owe a good part of their efficacy in solving biological problems to the metaphor implicit in them. The explanations of current psychology are mainly figures of speech, and a good part of traditional theology is an exegesis of misunderstood metaphors. In both of the latter fields speech must be metaphorical in the nature of the case, and thus the mind is put upon the special task of using metaphorical language, and, at the same time, of guarding against mistaking the metaphor for the thing. This can be done only by the cultivation of a critical habit and by varying the expression, so that the mutual incompatibility of the metaphors shall force us to the insight that they are not the truth but only its adumbration. Psychology, theology, and the religious life in general would be vastly helped by a determined effort to reduce their metaphors to their net significance. We should still use them thereafter, for there is nothing else to use; but we should be freed from bondage to them. It might also appear that there is a choice in metaphors. In the slow development of humanity we grow away from the customs and modes of thought which once made forms of speech intelligible and expressive, and we need new forms for the best expression of the growing thought and life. But of this the traditionalist, ignorant of the nature of language and unsuspicious of its imperfection as an instrument of expression, never dreams, and devotes himself with pathetic blindness to the letter which killeth, while grievously missing the spirit which giveth life.

Finally, we may mention the fancy that a new name means a new thing. This form of the fallacy is by no means without potency. By means of it a deal of shop-worn material has been worked off at a profit under such titles as the " New Education," the " New Psychology," the " New Philosophy," the " New Pedagogy." Enterprising conductors of teachers' institutes and publishers of educational works have found no small advantage in this form of verbal illusion. In this way matter which scarcely goes beyond the wisdom of the nursery is made to look like a new discovery. In such cases the passivity of the disciples' judgment is often as striking as that shown in the absolute credulity of dreams. To this fancy may be added the allied notion that a name implies some corresponding thing. This makes it possible to constitute a new science to order by simply constructing a well-sounding name of classical origin.

These fallacies of the universal, of abstraction and of language, I have called structural fallacies of the human mind. They lie very much deeper than the familiar fallacies of logical treatises, and only a careful critical procedure can guard us against them. They have wrought, and still work, the greatest ravage and devastation in human thinking, reducing a very large part of speculation and discussion to tedious and sterile formalisms and verbal disputes —sterile, that is, of good, but sadly prolific of evil.

Herewith we close the discussion of thought and pass to the problem of knowledge. We have learned something of the nature and ideal aims of thought, and we have seen how far those aims are from being realized.

Part II

THEORY OF KNOWLEDGE

CHAPTER I

PHILOSOPHIC SCEPTICISM

Our study thus far has been mainly of thought as a subjective activity with various forms and laws. Its relation to knowledge has been only implicitly considered. Thought as leading to knowledge is the next subject for consideration.

It is quite conceivable that one should allow the main results of our previous study as a description of the thought process, and should at the same time doubt or deny that thought mediates for us any valid knowledge of reality. Thought may exist as fact, and may even have laws peculiar to itself; but this does not secure the validity of knowledge. In the form of philosophic scepticism this doubt has been an important factor in the history of thought.

Our present purpose is to expound this problem of scepticism, with the aim not of refuting, but rather of understanding it. This will enable us to estimate the logical standing of scepticism, and will free us from bondage to names and authorities. We do not seek, then, to convince the sceptic, but to understand scepticism. Conviction itself is a matter into which the personal equation enters too largely to be wholly amenable to argument and logic.

Knowledge as a form of subjective conviction is familiar to all, and admits of no definition. It also admits of no question. What we experience we experience. But knowing claims to be more than a subjective experience. As a mental event it is, of course, only an occurrence in the consciousness of some one; but in addition to being a particular mental event it claims also to be an apprehension of independent fact or truth. This is what we have before referred to as the objectivity of thought. It is this aspect of thought which constitutes the philosophical problem. There is no doubt, indeed, that thought spontaneously takes on the form and conviction of knowing; but whether the apparent knowledge is valid, or the extent to which it is valid, remains an open question.

Chronologically, this question is second and not first in our mental development. We have repeatedly pointed out that thought goes straight to its objects in complete unconsciousness of its own complex processes. Objective validity is implicit in all thinking. Our objects, too, all seem to be so immediately and manifestly given that to question their reality appears wanton and absurd. This primal trust of the mind in knowledge is shaken only as difficulties, inconsistencies, and contradictions are discovered among our apparent cognitions. These prove the fact of error and make doubt possible. Having once begun, this doubt may spread over the entire intellectual life until the validity of all cognition is called in question. Such is the genesis of philosophic scepticism.

Very little of concrete belief or unbelief is the outcome of rational reflection on the part of the disciples. There is vehement partisanship, but no understanding. This is a necessary consequence of the hearsay form in which the mental life of the individual always begins and largely continues. We believe and disbelieve alike on authority rather than on reason. In this way it often happens that, instead of a knowledge of our own faith or unfaith, we have only a repetition of its phrases. Such is especially the case at present with the subject of scepticism in its various forms of agnosticism, relativity, phenomenalism, etc. Opponents shudder rhetorically, and disciples proudly profess; but neither party seem to have any settled notions of the problem itself, or of the method of its solution. Such a mental condition is not favorable to understanding or progress; for, as Locke says, it is all one to go about to draw those men out of their mistakes who have no settled notions as to dispossess a vagrant of his habitation who has no settled abode. In order to bring the problem out of this amorphous state we note several conditions which scepticism must fulfil if it is to have any rational standing whatever.

First, if scepticism is not to be pure arbitrariness and ipsedixitism, it must be supported by reasons. Belief and unbelief alike, as subjective facts, have no rational significance. They become rational only through the grounds by which they are justified. The mere fact that the sceptic doubts means no more than the opposite fact that the believer believes, and neither fact means anything apart from the reasons that may be rendered. The sceptic acquires importance, not through the doubts he utters, but through those which he rationally justifies. The judicial critic, therefore, must compel the sceptic to take his place along with other theorists, and give reasons for the unfaith that is in him. Until he does this his position is arbitrary, capricious, and irrational.

Strangely enough, this manifest dictate of logic has often been overlooked in the history of speculation, and dogmatic denial, especially if it be of some important practical interest, has been judged to have high speculative significance. The ease with which good people have been stampeded by unsupported denial is one of the humorous features of the history of philosophy.

Secondly, the attempt to give reasons presupposes valid

laws of thinking and reasoning, whereby the consistent and consequent may be distinguished from the inconsistent and inconsequent. Without such laws there can be no thought whatever, and of course no inference. Hence the sceptic must fall back on arbitrary and unsupported assertion, and must refrain from all criticism of opposing views, or he must admit the laws and principles of logic as binding upon all thought as at least negative conditions of truth.

Thirdly, if the sceptic expects his doctrine to be more than an individual whim of his own he must assume the community and identity of intelligence, so that truth for one ought to be truth for all. Otherwise his faith or unfaith would be his private possession, and nothing about which others need in any way trouble themselves. Without the assumption of a common truth and a common reason speech itself would be impertinence.

Fourthly, in addition to the community of intelligence the sceptic must also assume the identity of the object in experience. Whatever view we may take of the nature of the object, we must assume that we all have the same object in experience. Without this assumption we have no common ground and no possibility of mutual understanding. All diversity of intelligence and experience must be interpreted in accordance with this fundamental community. It must be referred to difference of development or of standpoint, and not to any essential difference of intellect or of objects.

Fifthly, something must be known. Where nothing is known nothing can be inferred or doubted. Hence the question finally becomes one of more or less, and not of knowledge or no knowledge. Scepticism must know something in order to exist at all as a rational theory. Absolute scepticism is a contradiction, and exists only as an academic abstraction.

Now these assumptions are far-reaching, and carry the matter pretty deep. They in no wise admit of demonstration, and yet they are manifestly necessary as the conditions of a rational life. They carry with them some profound mysteries, but they cannot be rejected without rejecting reason itself. Whatever system claims to have rational standing can have it only on these conditions. When they are not fulfilled nothing remains but volition, obstinacy, conceit, and caprice. A scepticism of this kind is indeed always possible, but criticism must ignore it as belonging to mental or moral pathology. The problems of thought must be solved within thought by thought itself, and in accordance with its own laws; and any theory which does not recognize those laws must be treated as non-existent. Thought must accept itself, and rational scepticism can arise only from the discovery of insoluble contradictions within our thought system. Only as we insist on this rule can we escape from random babblers and tedious airers of small conceits.

The beginnings of sceptical doctrine with the Greek sophists owed their form largely to the crude and undeveloped condition of logical and metaphysical theory at that time. Their theories of perception and their metaphysical doctrines made it possible, as a play of logic, to deny (1) the existence of truth; (2) its knowability, supposing it to exist; and (3) its communicability, supposing it to be known. The purely verbal character of such denial, and its self-contradiction, are manifest. The only question about such scepticism is not whether it be rational, but how did it arise.

Scepticism, we have said, must know something. Accordingly we find that, historically, scepticism has commonly been an inference from a doctrine held as true. As just said, ancient philosophy explains ancient scepticism.

Both the Eleatic and the Heraclitic metaphysics lend themselves readily to sceptical conclusions. In modern times also scepticism has generally been derived from antecedent theories. This was the case with the scepticism of Hume and Mill. They regarded the sensational theory of knowledge as established, and their sceptical conclusions resulted as a consequence. Scepticism of the Kantian type has the same derivative character. It is the outcome of a theory of knowledge which is believed to be true, and which rests upon a special conception of the relation of the mind to the world. Plainly all of these derived scepticisms stop short of absolute scepticism, since they would lose all rational warrant if their theoretical foundation were disputed. To reject their basal assumptions would discharge the resulting scepticism. Scepticism not only must know something, but it actually has a large supply of knowledge on hand. It may not appear among the published assets, but it is a very important part of its stock in trade.

In further exposition of the general problem we first inquire what is meant by the doubt or denial of truth.

Every judgment, we have seen, presupposes or relates itself to a fixed order which exists independently of the knowledge and volition of the individual. This order we do not make, but discover. We do not produce it; we reproduce it. This order may be one of fact or one of reason. In the order of fact there are certain things in certain relations and with certain laws. In the order of reason there are certain ideas which belong together and others which are mutually repugnant. Judgments are true which agree with this order; those are false which depart from it. Important truths are those which relate to the abiding facts and relations of this independent order. They may be called general truths. They are not limited by time or place, and are expressed in universal form. The laws of physics and the truths of mathematics are examples. They are not accidents of the individual, but express abiding relations among cosmic facts or rational ideas. Besides these there are truths which express simple facts of consciousness, or items of individual experience, or particular historical events. Thus, I feel cold; or, John was here yesterday; or, Cæsar crossed the Rubicon. Such particular facts have no such abiding and theoretical significance as truths of the former class.

Of course the sceptical doubt may be extended to everything, but it has theoretical importance only in the case of general truth. A scepticism which should dispute the present fact of consciousness, or the general trustworthiness of memory, or the reality of all historical facts, would soon break down from the weight of its own dulness and tedium. The doubt of truth has commonly been a doubt whether in the nature of things there are any fixed relations, or whether all things and laws may not be comprised in a process of change which shall, sooner or later, break up all those conjunctions which to us seem fixed. In that case, what we call truths would represent no fixed rational connection, but only an accidental and shifting conjunction; and this would be equivalent to a denial of truth altogether.

When abstractly stated, with careful abstinence from concrete application, such a view meets with little protest from the passive intellect. Indeed, it may even seem attractive, as it readily lends itself to sentimental treatment. By making the rate of change very slow we can easily secure "a reasonable degree of extension" of apparent truth "to adjacent cases," and thus escape the practical absurdity; and by vaguely dreaming of some ineffable æonian evolution we can to our own satisfaction persuade anything to dissolve into anything, and even into nothing. But the critic remembers that when a theory has been stated the next thing is to prove it. Hence, before despairing of knowledge he asks the sceptic for his argument.

The objects of thought fall into two great classes: truths of reason and truths of objective fact. Corresponding to these, the sceptical doubt divides into two: first, a doubt whether there be any truth in reason; and, secondly, a doubt concerning what seems to be objective knowledge. Besides these leading doubts there is a cloud of minor ones which call for no consideration.

The first doubt often takes the form of denying that reason has any laws of its own, or that it is anything more than a copy of experience made coherent by association. This is the claim of sensationalism. Reason is product. As such it is purely passive, and quite unable to say what may or may not be in the nature of things. Reason being only a shadow of sense, it can report nothing which cannot be presented in sense; and if it seems to report more, the surplus must be reckoned an illusion. Hence the various unpicturable relations and categories which seem to be in the understanding are illusory, and, for aught we know, two and two may make five in some other part of space and time. The mind, being passive, can never prescribe what its experience shall be, but must wait and see.

This doubt of reason can be justified only by proving the psychology on which it is based. Unfortunately, more attention has been devoted to drawing conclusions from that psychology than to proving it. It has been too handy a polemical weapon not to be appreciated by the voluble, and the labor of investigation is tedious and exacting. Moreover, since the time of Kant sensationalism has been kept alive only by ignorance of the fact that it is dead. He showed, once for all, that experience itself is possible only through formative and constructive principles inherent and immanent in the nature of reason.

But scepticism is tenacious of life. The doubt arising from sensationalism was discharged by showing the formative principles which make experience possible. But this very result gives birth to the old doubt again in a more subtle form. Let us admit that there are laws of thought which, as expressions of our mental make, must govern our thinking; it does not follow from this that they must be universal, and must lead to true knowledge. These very laws may themselves belong to error, and thus may shut us up to hopeless illusion. What they give us is not a knowledge of universal truth, but a shadow of the human mind. Hence even the truths of reason have no universal validity, but, as transcripts of our mental nature, are true only for us.

Concerning this claim, it is to be admitted that every thinking being must think as determined by his mental constitution. In this sense all our knowledge is necessarily relative to our cognitive faculties. We cheerfully make the sceptic a present of this admission. If mind were otherwise it would be otherwise. If there were anything essentially unrelated to our faculties we could never know that thing. But from this abstract relativity it does not follow that there is not a universal element in our intelligence, so that what is true for one may be true for all. At the utmost, all that follows is the abstract possibility that our intelligence may be particular and individual; and then the question of fact remains open, and must be decided by evidence or argument. The claim that we think as we do because our intellect is constituted as it is is as true and as barren as the equally important proposition that the properties of the circle are relative to the constitution of the circle.

Turning now to the question of fact, it is plain, first of all, that every one spontaneously assumes intelligence to have universal elements. There is one truth for all, and the individual does not own it, but shares in it. One logic, one arithmetic, one geometry suffice for all. Variations of opinion are explained as resulting, not from essential differences of mental nature, but from difference of standpoint or grade of development. Even the relativist assumes this community of mental nature. Truth is relative, not to me, but to us; not to a human mind, but to the **human** mind. In all of this it is tacitly assumed that the individual can transcend the limits of his own personality and discern the truth for other minds as well. Finally, even the thoroughgoing individualist who, with Protagoras, holds that each man is the measure of his own truth, implicitly assumes the community and identity of intelligence, for he holds that whoever will listen to him and candidly weigh his arguments must come to his conclusion.

In this state of affairs, then, knowledge, or the appearance of knowledge, has the field, and it is incumbent on the sceptic to justify his demurrer; until he does this his position depends on caprice rather than reason. How this community of individual intelligences is possible is a question by itself, and one well worthy of study. Reflection might show it to be possible only through an all-embracing intelligence, the source and creator of finite minds. But the fact of such community is the necessary condition of social existence, and can never be denied in good faith. That it is necessary in order to give scepticism itself any rational character we have already seen. The limitation of community to human minds removes the practical absurdity, but only at the expense of a logical inconsistency. It allows the individual to transcend the limits of his own personality, which is the point of metaphysical difficulty, and fails to give any reason for limiting him to the human sphere. For as the individual transcends himself by virtue of the intelligence common to all he can be limited only by the sphere of intelligence as such. If by intelligence other than human something is meant which is not intelligence there is nothing to argue about, for the terms have no longer any meaning.

In the formal and metaphysical laws of thought, and especially in mathematics, we have a great body of what reports itself as true and is accepted as such. Some of these truths are self-evident, and the others are deduced from them by cogent logic. They have, then, all the marks by which truth can be known, and all the evidence which truth itself could offer. Hence, in order to maintain his denial of truths of reason, the sceptic must overturn, or at least throw doubt upon, these apparent truths, and that not by assertion, but by valid argument.

This doubt also must be brought out of its abstraction and put into concrete form, so that its meaning may be understood. If the sceptic will not allow that every event must have a cause, then he holds that events may happen without a cause, and he should be called upon to support his position. If he will not allow that two and two make four everywhere and always, then he holds that two and two make something else—say, three or five, or fifty or nothing—and he should be asked to prove his paradox. By ignoring blank assertion, and by putting the burden of proof upon the sceptic, where it belongs, the matter may be brought to an issue. This plain dictate of logic, we repeat, has been too much neglected in the past, and the sceptic has won undue importance accordingly. There has been so little understanding of the logic of the case, and so little mental balance also, that the mere utterance of conceits has served to scare whole bodies of supposed thinkers. In logic, however, there is no occasion for alarm until the sceptic has given reasons for his doubts or denials. In the meantime, propositions which are self-evident and consistent, or which are deduced from such, may be accepted as true.

A formal justification of the general doubt may be attempted as follows: Our determination of rational truth necessarily depends upon reason itself. We identify the true with the rational, and to the question, What is true? we respond by showing what is rational. And when we come to pass upon the competency of reason itself we can only fall back upon reason, whereas for perfect assurance we ought to have an objective standard, independent of reason, whereby reason might be tested. Indeed, to invoke reason to settle its own claims can hardly seem other than a begging of the question.

This is verbal rather than real. It is evident that the demand here made could not be met by any intelligence whatever. The notion of an official speculative standard apart from mind, a kind of philosophical standard metre, is absurd. Mind is necessarily its own standard and judge. At bottom the system of knowledge must rest upon self-evident principles, or principles which the mind takes on its own warrant. It is mere pedantry to demand proof for these, for if the proof were possible it could give us no more than the insight we had at the start. We can test our mental dicta only by comparing them with some more ultimate dictum, and the final standard can be known as such only by the self-evidence with which it appeals to the mind, or by the necessity with which it forces itself upon our recognition. Every rational being must at last trust his rational insight. The only way of shaking this trust would be to show fundamental inconsistency in the nature of reason itself. Until this is done the mind will insist that the self-evident, with whatever may be deduced therefrom, is true.

But we may still say, This does not carry us beyond the rational, whereas we are after the true. May not these laws of thought themselves belong to error? May not our constitution be such as to cause the false to appear true to us? This doubt is forever irrefutable and forever baseless. Rational it is not, as it expressly disputes the authority of reason, and appeals from it. It will always be possible for the sceptic to suggest that truth is altogether other than we think it; that two and two are anything but four; that events may happen without a cause; that things may not be equal to themselves; and that a broken line is the shortest distance between two points in space. But these utterances are not born of reason, but of unreason, and must be left to their own irrationality. They are not supported by any rational grounds, but depend on the bare possibility of constructing the phrases. In fact, they are only conjunctions of words to which no positive thought corresponds. Such doubting can go on forever, but it ought not to be exalted as a profound or brilliant performance.

The sum is this: There is a large body of apparent truths of reason which have all the marks of truth possible in the nature of intelligence. They are self-evident, or are founded on self-evidence, and they are consistent and harmonious. The sceptic who disputes them must overturn this self-evidence and this harmony. In default of disproof, scepticism must be reckoned as only verbal and volitional, and as containing no ground for alarm and panic. When the sceptic suggests that rational truth is relative to us, and hence may not be valid for other orders of being, it will be in place for him to show (1) that these hypothetical beings exist; (2) that their truth contradicts ours; and (3) that, in case of contradiction, they are in the right and we are in the wrong. When all these points are established the subject will deserve consideration.

If from the truths of reason we could deduce the forms

and details of cosmic existence the field of scepticism would be confined to rational truth. For us, however, no analysis of reason will give the world of perception. We reach this by the perceptive process, and this fact gives another occasion for scepticism. The validity of our knowledge of objective reality is disputed. This doubt, too, is an old one; but both its form and the reasons offered have been various. The arguments of the early Greek sceptics were largely drawn from their antiquated theories of sense-perception. These have long been obsolete. In general the ancient sceptic did not doubt that reality was knowable in itself; he held only that the evidence leaves us in balance and uncertainty. Reality was unknowable because our data give no unambiguous results. In this sense we say it is unknowable whether the stars are inhabited or not. In modern times the doctrine has generally taken the form of denying that we can know things in themselves. The mind by its very nature masks reality, and makes it inaccessible to us. Our knowledge, then, is limited to appearances or phenomena, and never grasps the thing as it truly is. This form of the doctrine we are now to consider.

This view depends on the Kantian theory of knowledge. Kant overturned once for all the naïve theories of perception and experience which had ruled before his time. He showed that perception is no passive reception of ready-made knowledge, but involves a complex constructive activity on the part of the mind, whereby the object is put before consciousness. The object we perceive is really the object we mentally construct. This fact makes it possible to hold that our apparent objects are not independently existing realities, but only projections of our own conceptions. The laws and forms of thought have only a subjective validity, and instead of revealing reality to us they mask it by covering it with their own image.

In further exposition of this view it is well first to note what it assumes. Some of the earliest sceptics maintained that each man makes his own truth, so that truth and reality are purely relative to each. Even they, however, admitted the coexistence of persons as a fact beyond question. For the rest, their view rested largely upon a misunderstanding of the function of the senses in knowledge. The senses are individual, and do not of themselves contain the warrant for a universal affirmation. My sweet may be your bitter, my agreeable your disagreeable. But the view in question equally assumes the coexistence of real persons, though not with the clearest theoretical right, and then provides for the identity of objective experience through the work of the understanding. This faculty, which is supposed to be common to all human beings, transforms the raw material of the sensibility into the rationalized forms of experience. In this way a common world is produced. The theory, then, assumes a world of coexistent persons, and also a common world of experience for them. But here, as in the case of rational truth, no good reason is given why the world common to the human understanding may not be common to all understanding, in so far as it is understanding. To find a middle way between the universal object which is common to all and the private dream which is confined to the individual has always been a task of exceeding difficulty.

The admitted coexistence of persons also, as just suggested, is a point of much obscurity in the theory. It has never been made clear how persons, who are never phenomenal, can be reached in a theory of purely phenomenal knowledge. The method seems to be to lump them under the one term, mind, or subject, and then mistake the abstract subject for a plurality of ontologically distinct subjects.

In the next place, this scepticism assumes the reality of things, and doubts only whether our knowledge can reach them. This assumption is implicit in all its leading terms and phrases. Phenomena, appearances, things in themselves alike imply the reality of things. If behind phenomena or appearances there were nothing as their reality the phenomena would be all, and in knowing these we should know all there is to know. And, on the other hand, it is hard to say in what sense a phenomenon can be such unless it really manifests the thing. A manifestation in which nothing is manifested, or an appearance in which nothing appears, would be a somewhat obscure notion. The utmost that could be made of it would be an event in an individual consciousness which pointed indeed to an external cause, but which revealed no existing fact.

Further, there is a tacit assumption that the real things are external and antithetical to all thought whatever. Spontaneous realism easily mistakes the existence of things apart from our thought for their existence apart from any and all thought, and the doctrine in question follows it in this fancy. Only thus can it maintain the unknowability of things; for if they were the product and expression of some creative thought they might well be commensurate with our intelligence. In that case there would be as little reason for thinking of an unknowable thing in itself behind the apparent thing we perceive as there is for thinking of an unknowable thought in itself in our neighbor's mind behind the thought we comprehend. This theistic suggestion in this connection deserves more consideration than it has ever received. If things originated in thought and express thought there is no difficulty in principle in their reappearing in thought. Such difficulty as exists is simply the mystery of personal communion and mutual understanding.

But this point is ignored in the discussion, and things in themselves are set up as external to intellect and beyond its grasp. These things, however, are only a transformation of the crude realism of the senses. The uncritical mind projects its objects, not merely beyond its own consciousness, but in lumpish externality to all consciousness; at the same time it assumes that it has immediate knowledge of them. Then, when a little reflection has shown that the mind can grasp objects only through ideas, the sceptic, instead of doubting those extra-mental objects of uncritical thought, retains them as things in themselves, and laments our inability to reach them. But in so doing he proceeds most uncritically, and falls a prey to one of the spontaneous prejudices of common-sense. There is a debate of long standing in philosophy as to the nature of the external world, and as to the place and mode of its existence. No one has ever doubted that there is something not ourselves, but the idealist has offered a good many weighty reasons for thinking that the objects of perception exist in no such brute lumpishness and externality to intelligence as is commonly assumed. The scepticism with which we are dealing ignores this dispute, and, taking the things for granted, doubts our power to know them. It is, then, based upon the assumption that the thing is external and unrelated to thought.

And here again the sceptic proceeds uncritically. He assumes that things are the first and undoubted fact, and that thought has the function of copying them. In truth, however, in the order of knowledge experience is first and basal, and things are only the assumptions we make in order to explain and express experience. But they do this only as they have an intelligible content. When they have not this they are not only the unknowable, they are the unaffirmable. Phenomena and things inferred from them are amenable to our thought; beyond these we have no warrant for saying anything. The sceptic, instead of assuming things and proclaiming that they cannot be known, should rather consider whether he has any right to affirm any other than those known things which our thought posits. That things, external to all thought and essentially unrelated to thought, are unknowable is self-evident; but before we despair of knowledge the sceptic must prove that such things exist. Unfortunately, he has never bethought himself to furnish this proof. The unsophisticated disciple of the senses finds himself in the presence of a system which he did not make and which in no way depends on him. This independence of his thought he mistakes for an independence of all thought, and this existence apart from his consciousness he identifies with existence apart from all consciousness. This rather crude ontology is unhesitatingly accepted by the sceptic, and when it is united with the theory of perception we have relativity and the rest.

These considerations show that the theory in question is by no means presuppositionless. On the contrary, it rests upon a definite theory of knowing and being; and its theory of being, so far from being established, admits of no establishment.

Returning now to the claim that objective knowledge arises only through a subjective activity determined by principles within the mind itself, it is plain that this fact alone does not warrant a sceptical conclusion. In the first place, modern psychology has made it clear that knowledge must arise in this way in any case. If we suppose the world to be as real as the most unsophisticated rustic assumes, the knowledge of the same is not provided for. The world cannot know itself, neither can it pass in its reality into the knowing mind. The former can only awaken conceptions in the latter, and these conceptions can only be a mental reaction against external action. But this is as true for our knowledge of persons as for our knowledge of things; and if a sceptical conclusion is to be based upon the process of knowledge alone, it cannot be restricted to things, but must also be extended to persons. If this be done, scepticism becomes farcical; if not done, it is convicted of arbitrary inconsistency.

In the next place, the fact at best would only prove a possibility; the question of fact would still remain open. The knowledge arising within the mind according to mental laws might still lie parallel to things, existing according to their laws. My conceptions of my neighbors reproduce a real existence; it is equally possible, at least so far as the knowing is concerned, that my conceptions of things reproduce real existence. And since this assumption is spontaneously and universally made, it is incumbent upon the sceptic to show that such is not the case. The bare possibility of doubting my neighbor's existence leads to nothing; the same possibility of doubting things' existence is in logic equally barren.

Further, it is to be noted that a dogmatic denial of knowledge based upon the subjectivity of the laws of thought is not only illogical but self-destructive. It is illogical, because the fact only makes doubt possible; it does not compel it, and still less does it warrant denial. It is self-destructive, because when no law of thought is allowed to be valid for things, the things themselves become not only unaffirmable, but also meaningless and empty of all contents. If all the categories are subjective to us, then the independent reality is neither one nor many; for unity and plurality are categories. It is then neither a thing in itself nor things in themselves; for either phrase supposes number, which is ruled out by hypothesis. The reality also is neither cause nor effect; for these too are categories, and hence without application to objective reality. Reality, again, is neither substance nor attribute, neither thing nor quality; for these also are categories. Finally, it is not even real or unreal; for reality and negation are categories, and hence without application. What, then, is it? If these denials are to be taken strictly it is nothing, either subjectively or objectively. It is neither a thing nor a thought: it is only a verbal phrase, to which neither reality nor conception corresponds. If we relax the denial sufficiently to bring it under the general head of existence, even then we have no positive thought or thing; we have only the bare category of being "suspended *in vacuo* by the imagination." As such it has only the abstract conceptual existence of class terms, and, like them, is objectively nothing. The unknowable reality then vanishes, leaving only verbal phrases in its place. With this result the scepticism based thereon also vanishes, for there being nothing to know we cannot be expected to know it.

To this result every doctrine of unknowability must come which is based upon a denial of the objective validity of the laws of thought. It must finally reject its unknowable as only a form of words, and must reinstate knowledge by leaving known phenomena the only reality to be known. The theory, too, in its best estate introduces an unmanageable dualism into philosophy. On the one hand are things utterly unrelated to thought, and on the other is thought utterly unrelated to things. Neither accounts for the other, neither can do anything with the other. They stand on opposite sides of an impassable gulf without any means of communication. This Manichæism of philosophy results from uncritically adopting the assumed opposition of thought and thing which rules in spontaneous thought and making it universal. The relation of thought and thing in finite thought cannot be determined without some theory of their relation in fundamental being. The adoption of the crude realistic view produces only the most inconsistent of scepticisms. It must affirm things, and can find no reason for so doing. It is equally impossible to give any articulate contents to the things which it affirms. It is not surprising that reason, seeing itself in such straits, denied the irrational reality outright and took refuge in idealism. This it did do historically, and this it must do in logic. Reality must either come within the reach of thought or go out of existence.

To what extent Kant himself accepted these implications of his system is far from clear. When summoned by Fichte to give up the things in themselves under penalty of his disesteem, Kant chose the disesteem. This suggests that Kant meant that his system should be understood from its anti-dogmatic side rather than by a verbal exegesis of his own statements. The dogmatists had unhesitatingly confounded the order and connection of ideas with the order and connection of things, and Kant showed, in opposition, how much there is that is relative and subjective in our thinking. Hence, over against the dogmatists, he maintained the subjectivity of the categories, without thinking overmuch, however, of the consequences and inconsistencies of a thoroughgoing relativity. It remained for his followers to develop these. As a consequence of Kant's work and of later criticism, philosophy has to steer between a naïve dogmatism which criticism has made impossible and an absolute relativity which criticism shows to be self-destructive.

The affirmation of an essentially unknowable is suicidal. Instead of it, scepticism can only affirm an unknown, and that upon two general grounds. We may claim that the evidence is so conflicting that we are unable to reach any conclusion, or we may fall back upon the strict sense of knowledge, and deny that anything is known which is not either self-evident or demonstrated.

In the first claim we return to the position of the ancient sceptics, and abandon the attempt to establish scepticism once for all on some general theory of the human mind. This claim would have to be established by examining each special case. For instance, the sceptic would have to show that we have as good reason for thinking that the sun goes round the earth as the converse; that the law of the inverse square of the distance is no better established as the law of gravity than the law of the inverse cube, or any other law whatever. The other claim mentioned is harmless. It only contends, what every one admits, that objective knowledge is not a matter of absolute demonstration or of speculative certainty, but involves certain elements of assumption. This, however, while leaving doubt formally possible, constitutes no practical justification. Here again, to justify any specific and concrete doubt, the sceptic must give specific reasons other than the formal possibility of doubting. Formally I can doubt even my neighbors' existence, but it would not be wise to do so on that account.

Yet this question has been so befogged with phrases that without doubt the question has long been recurring in the reader's mind: Can we, after all, know things in themselves, or anything more than appearances? And if we should once see things as they really are, should we not find them altogether different from what they seem to us? These questions are best answered by asking others. And, first, What is meant by knowing a thing in itself, or as it really is? That we can know things only as they exist for intelligence is manifest, and that all minds are in the same plight is equally manifest. If by knowing things in themselves is meant a knowing in which the mind gets out of itself and becomes the thing, or does something else than form a conception of the thing, the phrase is strictly unintelligible. If we can know things as they exist for intelligence, we can dispense with a knowledge of them as they do not exist for intelligence, especially as this latter existence is an inconsistent fiction. Let the sceptic first show that there is anything in itself beyond the intelligible things which our thought affirms, and then it will be in order to consider its knowability.

But, it is sometimes said, our knowledge extends only to qualities and activities, and never grasps the real essence of the thing or the thing in itself. Thus, we do not know what the soul is in itself, but only its phenomena. That this should be regarded as a limitation of knowledge is a striking testimony to the power of confusion. At bottom it rests upon a fancy that being, to be truly known, should be presented to the senses or in sense forms. But being, in speculative thought, has long since passed over into the unpicturable categories of causation and activity, and hence has no way of manifesting itself except in its activities and laws. But these furnish us a valuable knowledge of the thing, and it would puzzle any one to tell what other knowledge is possible to any intelligence whatever. At all events, before we deplore our loss we ought to be told precisely what it is we miss.

But we know only appearances. This utterance also is unclear. Through the senses, of course, we know only appearances, and these appearances are the data for all further knowledge of things. But if we really knew only appearances the claim itself would be impossible. For these appearances present themselves as things, and it is only as the mind, working over its sense data, comes to the conviction that things are to be conceived as other than they appear, that the distinction between reality and appearance arises. But if this conception be repudiated the appearance resumes its ancient form of thing and becomes all there is to know. Indeed, as already hinted, there is very great obscurity in the current doctrine of phenomenal knowledge and in the current conception of the relation of the phenomenal to the real. A phenomenon as such exists only in relation to a percipient, and is a pure absurdity when conceived as external to intelligence. As used by the positivists, the doctrine is little more than an unconscious juggle with words, whereby a sop is thrown to commonsense and a handy polemical weapon is secured. If it is to be taken in earnest we must determine the perceiving mind for and in which the phenomena exist. If we say the human mind, we remember that the reality of the human mind is a plurality of particular minds. In that case there would be no common world, but only a similarity of presentations in these individuals. If to escape this collapse we make the phenomena independent of all human minds we must assume a cosmic mind as their condition. Failing to do this, we have no new ideas, but only a new terminology. As commonly used, the doctrine represents no clear conception, but only a convenient device for postponing troublesome questions, and for making occasional onslaughts on theology and metaphysics.

The relation of the phenomenal to the real is equally uncertain; indeed, neither term is used with exact and consistent meaning. By the real we may mean the ontological fact, and we may mean the universal in experience. Whatever is neither of these is unreal, fantastic, fictitious. But in the sense of universality phenomena belong to the real. They are not fictions of the individual, but are a part of universal experience. In this sense the whole sense world belongs to reality. And the antithesis of phenomena is not noumena conceived as something which the phenomena mask or vainly seek to reveal, but noumena conceived as the cause of the phenomena. Behind the phenomenal world is the causal world, and this latter can be grasped only in the unpicturable notions of the understanding. Noumena in any other sense are fictitious. Phenomena and their causes exhaust the fact, and both alike are needed to express the full reality. In that case, in knowing phenomena we are knowing reality in its manifestation, and we dismiss the elusive noumenon altogether. But in much of the discussion of the subject the noumenon appears to be something which the mind might grasp if the masking phenomenon did not thrust itself between them. This notion is born of crude realism and the desire to grasp reality in sense forms.

As to our seeing all things to be different if our eyes were opened, this also is an unclear notion. It may mean that we should see different things in the event mentioned, and to this there is no objection. No one contends that we are cognizant of all existence. It may mean that we should see the same things to be different, and this in turn may mean that we should gain a more extensive knowledge of things, should see them to stand in relations unsuspected at present, and it may mean that we should get views of things which contradict our present knowledge. The last meaning is the only one relevant to the problem of scepticism, and if we are to accept it we must have proof. Until proof is furnished the suggestion is only the ever-recurring doubt whether, after all, our entire life be not illusion. This, as said, is forever irrefutable and forever irrational. It may be entertained in an academic fashion when there is no demand for action, and life with its brusque contradiction is at a distance; but it is rationally unfruitful, or, rather, non-existent.

In closing this chapter we recall the aim announced at

the beginning. This was not to refute but to understand scepticism. As the result of our study we find scepticism as a system of thought unclear in both its doubts and its denials, and especially so in the reasons given for them. We find the doctrine of the unknowable meaning any one of many things, some truisms and some absurd. The doctrine of relativity is equally confused and indefinite. In popular writers of this school there is no consistent thought, and often no thought whatever, but only a repetition of inherited or remembered phrases. Instead of being presuppositionless, scepticism in most of its forms depends on undemonstrated psychological and metaphysical theories. Its most pretentious form rests upon the assumed truth of the crudest realism of the crudest common-sense. This form is so inconsistent with itself that it is impossible without this realistic assumption; and, in turn, it makes that assumption impossible. The theory is unintelligible without a "thing in itself," and a contradiction with a "thing in itself." Hence, instead of viewing scepticism as the supreme example of logical acumen, the critic can only regard it as a confused compound of instinct and reflection, in which the elements are mutually incompatible, and in which we miss all clear comprehension of the cognitive problem, and all consciousness of logical obligation. This state of affairs will continue until the critical faculty sufficiently recovers from the panicky state to insist that the professional sceptic shall define and defend the unfaith that is in him. This demand would put the matter in its true light, and would reduce scepticism to something like its real dimensions. In short, we must replace scepticism as system by scepticism as rational criticism. The former is indeed more picturesque, but the latter is more useful.

The dependence of traditional scepticism on antecedent theories suggests, what reflection confirms, that the problem of knowledge can never be solved by itself and in advance of all concrete investigation, but only in the actual exercise of all the cognitive powers. We learn that we can walk by walking, and in the same way we learn that we can know by knowing. Academic discussions of the standard of certainty or of the criterion of truth are barren of any valuable result. There is no general standard which the mind can mechanically apply. The standard is the mind itself, dealing with particular and concrete cases; and any given item of knowledge must stand or fall, not because it agrees or disagrees with some assumed standard, but because of the evidence with which it presents itself to the living mind in contact with the facts.

An illustration of the confusion resulting from abstract discussion without bringing it to the test of concrete application is found in the debate concerning the trustworthiness of the senses. We know, on the one hand, that the senses do sometimes mislead us, and we know, on the other, that they are the sources of the highest practical certainty. If this question were discussed academically we should never reach a solution which would not be open to critical cavil; but in practice the problem is easily solved. Motion can always be proved by walking, whatever theoretical difficulties it may involve.

Intelligence, we have said, must assume and accept itself. Rational scepticism can arise only within thought and as a result of rational criticism. The path of progress lies in the following direction:

The aim of thought is to rationalize, and thus to comprehend, experience. In spontaneous thought this end is unclearly conceived and carelessly followed. There is need, then, of a careful and systematic working over of the elements of experience in order to see to what results thought really leads us. Such work involves a careful study of the given facts and a careful criticism of our inferences from them. When we have at last determined the results to which thought and experience lead we have done all that we can do. If these results should prove inconsistent, and should defy all attempts to harmonize them, then scepticism would be finally installed, for reason would be found in contradiction with itself; but if they should be necessary inferences from the facts, and also consistent among themselves, then scepticism would be gratuitous.

What the outcome of such an investigation would be can be known only by making it. The inquiry would doubtless compel many changes in our spontaneous convictions. It might reveal that many features in our thinking are relative to ourselves, and have nothing corresponding to them in reality. Critical inspection might show that many aspects of human thinking can lay no claim to strict universality. Criticism would then have the task of separating the formal and relative elements from the real and universal. But, in any case, rational scepticism must come at the end and not at the beginning of such a study.

The theory of knowledge, therefore, must exchange the question, Is knowledge possible? for this other, How is knowledge possible? That is, assuming the possibility of knowledge, we may study the implications of the assumption. The validity of knowledge is pretty sure to get itself recognized in the long-run in spite of the sceptic, and philosophy does well to push on to consider what is involved in the assumption of a knowable universe and a valid knowledge. The fact that scepticism is so often the result of antecedent theories shows that trust in the mind is not compatible with every theory of thought and being. We have abundantly seen, in treating of sensationalism and the problem of error, that a consistent empiricism or necessitarianism must end in the overthrow of reason and the destruction of knowledge. This may not prove them false, but it does impose upon every one who believes in the reality or even the possibility of knowledge the logical obligation of rejecting them.

CHAPTER II

THOUGHT AND THING

FROM the standpoint of the Absolute, things may possibly be conceptions; but from the human standpoint it is impossible to identify things with our conceptions. Their conceptual existence in our thought is not their real existence. They do not begin to exist when we conceive them, nor do they cease to be when we go to sleep. From the human standpoint, then, there is an ineradicable dualism of thought and thing. The traditional debate on their relation has been hopelessly confused by the failure to keep distinct the human and the absolute points of view. If any result is to be reached we must keep them distinct and discuss them in their order.

The necessary antithesis of thought and thing in human experience when combined with the results of our previous study reveals knowledge to be a highly complex process with far-reaching implications. The general trustworthiness of reason presupposes that thought is a free activity based on rational insight. Objects exist for us only as the mind builds up valid conceptions within itself. The forms of knowledge are primarily forms of thought, and we can have no knowledge which is not determined by those forms. Hence it follows that our apparent knowledge can have no objective validity unless our objects themselves are cast in the moulds of thought, or unless the laws and categories of thought are also laws and categories of being. Without this essential identity, or, at least, parallelism, between our thought and things, there must be a parallax between the conception and the reality, and a resulting failure of knowledge. Without assuming, at least implicitly, that the laws of thought are valid for reality, knowledge is impossible, and the theory of knowledge vanishes in absurdity.

But from the dualistic standpoint we here find ourselves in very great complexity which soon passes into corresponding perplexity. We seem to have a parallelism of two mutually independent series: the thing series and the thought series. Neither is the other, and neither implies the other; yet both agree. This fact itself constitutes a new problem. That two mutually independent series should yet be under the necessity of agreeing is a conception not easily admitted as an ultimate fact, and there has been a very general agreement among all speculators for whom knowledge is a problem at all that this dualism must in some way be removed. Very queer things have been said about the subject and the object, and the necessity of mediating their antithesis. Sometimes the two have been united in a transcendent third, but more commonly the aim has been to reduce one of the series to the other, or to an effect of the other. Thought has been presented as an effect of things, or things have been viewed as produced by thought. The former view has lost itself in the superficialities of sense thinking, and the latter has erred and strayed from the way from the confounding of the absolute and the human point of view.

Let us now see if the dualism of thought and thing can be removed in this way. And, not to lose ourselves in abstractions, we once more point out that our present concern is with the relation of our human thinking to its cosmic objects. This may lead us to the more general problem of the relation of thought and being in the fundamental reality, but for the present we deal with the former question.

The first view mentioned is materialism. Things produce thought. The laws of things are first and essential; those of thought are secondary and derived. Instead of saying that the former agree with the latter we must rather say that the latter are copies or shadows of the former. Their agreement or identity, then, does not point to a rational origin of things, but to a material origin of thoughts, and is in no way surprising.

This view has been extensively held, and when criticism is asleep it is not without plausibility. But some difficulties appear on examination. To begin with, things are not to be taken in the phenomenal sense. This chair, this table, this pen, this paper, and no collection of similar things, could ever produce a knowledge of themselves. If any kind of things is to produce thought it must be the invisible things of metaphysical theory. Phenomenal things are altogether out of the question.

But that the invisible things, as atoms and molecules, with their mysterious forces, should do something in this line seems quite possible, until our thought is cleared up. The mystery of the molecule impresses the imagination, and readily leads to the fancy of its all-sufficiency in this matter. But an elementary acquaintance with physics teaches us that the activity of the molecule, so far as known, consists entirely in producing movements and groupings of one kind or another in space; and thought can in no way be identified with such movement or grouping. An equally slight acquaintance with the nature of thought shows that thought can never be put together from the outside in any such way. We must have abiding thinking subjects with highly complex mental activities. There is no thought or knowledge in general, but only specific thoughts and definite acts of knowing.

This view, then, would need to show, first, how things, conceived as impersonal and unthinking, can ever produce personal and thinking subjects. Since the mind is only an abstract term for individual minds, this view, next, would have to show how things can produce minds all of the same rational pattern. It would finally have to show how things can and must produce individual minds able to react upon their cosmic causes and correctly grasp them in thought. These several steps are distinct, and form a graded series. Things might form minds on no fixed pattern, and knowledge would vanish into individualism. And if things formed minds on a common pattern, there would still be no security that the rational nature would be so related to the objective fact as to secure valid cognition. The form of cognition might be given to mental movements which had no objective significance whatever, as in hallucination and dream.

These demands have been met, not so much by ignoring them as by being ignorant of them. There has been, indeed, a deal of polysyllabic utterance about the adjustment of inner relations to outer relations; but few have bethought themselves to inquire into the meaning and implications of this antithesis. There has also been a crude fancy that thought originates in a kind of raw material, "mindstuff," and that this may be variously integrated and differentiated in connection with the organism, and by the aid of association, until the order of conscious thought finally emerges. Hence it has been viewed as a very simple thing to produce a world of conscious persons from a world of things, which are not only unconscious, but are essentially unrelated to consciousness. Recipes for the process abound; but when reduced to their net value they turn out to be purely verbal.

And this is but the beginning of sorrows. Supposing the

work done up to this point, we are at once confronted by the difficulty arising from the relativity of much of our apparent knowledge and from the problem of error. A large part of what is apparently objective is really subjective, and a large part of human thinking in every department is really error. The showiest of these theories respecting the adjustment of inner relations to outer relations reduces the outer relations to phenomena, which thus, in strictness, become inner relations, and declares the real—that is, the truly outer—to be strictly unknowable. Thus the progressive adjustment of the inner to the outer turns out to be a progressive alienation, or, rather, it turns out to have no connection with reality whatever. This is one of the most extraordinary cases of anticlimax in the history of thought.

The difficulty in the problem of error is already familiar to us. Error arises by the same necessity as truth, and by the action of the same causes, and we are left without any standard of distinction between them. We appeal in vain to evolution and natural selection to help us. Such appeals presuppose that thought is not mechanically determined, and that is contrary to the hypothesis. On the plane of natural causation, the ideal distinctions of truth and error, rational and irrational, are meaningless. One notion is as necessary as any other and as good as any other while it lasts. Scepticism, rather than knowledge, is the outcome. No theory of knowledge is possible on this view. The theory is utterly opaque in its possibility, and as soon as it is admitted it proceeds to cancel itself.

Such views result from attempting to solve unpicturable thought problems in terms of the imagination. Hence the notion of "mindstuff," the antithesis of inner and outer, the building up of thought by the mechanical cohesion of sensational units. They show the unconscious working of a philosophical principle, with no suspicion, however, of its true nature. In this respect they resemble the crude beginnings of Greek speculation, in which genuine rational principles were latent, but not understood.

That things, considered as external to thought and antithetical to thought, should, nevertheless, produce thought is an unmanageable thesis. The dualism of experience can never be removed in that way. Let us, then, try the opposite view, and say that thought makes things. Possibly here we may be more successful.

But here, too, we meet with confusion. In itself the view is unclear. It may mean that things are nothing but a system of presentations, as in the common view of Berkeley's theory, and it may mean that thought is the cause and source of things. Both of these views again are unclear. In the first view it is not plain where and for whom the order of presentations exists. If it be independent of finite minds our knowledge of it is not explained, and we unwittingly and to no purpose stumble out of epistemology into metaphysics. If it depend on finite minds, then each mind makes its own world. Either alternative has its special embarrassments.

In the second view mentioned, it is not plain whether finite thought or absolute thought be the cause of things. The former view is absurd, and the latter does not advance the problem. No finite person would say, My thought is the creator of all I mean by earth, and sky, and stars; and even if one should say so it would not matter much. Some have indeed thought it worth while to say that we create our thoughts, and thus do create our objects: but this is a very cheap wisdom. In this sense, the worshipper creates God himself; but there is still a difference between creating the thought of a thing and creating the thing which the thought reports or apprehends.

The other view, that absolute thought is the source and cause of things, is incomplete, and, however true it may be, it is also irrelevant to the present discussion. It is incomplete; for thought itself is only an abstraction from the living activity of a personal spirit, and the reference of anything to thought must at last mean its reference to a rational agent. It is irrelevant; for if we should refer things to an absolute spirit the problem of finite knowing would remain unsolved, and the dualism of our knowledge would be untouched. We have once more the perennial confusion so often referred to, of finite thought and knowing with an assumed absolute thought and knowing, or of the relation of thought and being in our experience with their relation in an assumed absolute reason. Whenever idealists speak of thought as creating its objects, or of consciousness as embracing all reality, they implicitly occupy the standpoint of "Thought" or "Consciousness." These are supposed to be universal and altogether superior to anything occurring in the "history of the individual." Unfortunately, it has never been made clear how these high considerations solve the problem of human knowing, and this is the question of immediate interest. In fact, we have merely stumbled once more out of epistemology into metaphysics. We shall see, hereafter, that these considerations have an important place in the theory of knowledge, but they in no way remove the dualism from human knowing.

The most elaborate attempt to overcome this dualism and identify thought and thing is found in the system of absolute idealism. To understand this system we must note its origin in the Kantian philosophy. Kant showed that all knowledge must be relative to our faculties. But he assumed, with common-sense, that things are external and antithetical to thought, and these things in themselves he pronounced unknowable. At most, all that follows from experience, or from the Kantian premises, is that things are external to our thought; that is, are independent of our thought. It does not follow that they are independent of all thought, or that they are incommensurate with our thought. But the independence of our thought was mistaken for an independence of all thought, and the doctrine of the unknowable followed as a matter of course. Such things, if they exist, are indeed unknowable.

If they exist, that is; but do they exist? Fichte soon showed conclusively that such things are not only unknowable, but also unaffirmable. The same argument which proves them unknowable proves them unreal. Here, again, the true conclusion should have been not that we may not affirm things independent of our thought, but that we may not affirm things independent of all thought and unrelated to thought. But the ambiguous conclusion was drawn instead that thought can recognize nothing beyond itself, without telling us whose thought or what thought is meant. Specification on this point would have been embarrassing. In this way reality became thought, and thought became all-embracing and all in all. The idle mystery of the "thing in itself" vanished along with the uncritical prejudice on which it rested.

This was the second stage of the development. We are clear of all existence beyond thought. It only remains to develop everything within thought itself as a necessary consequence of reason. In that case we shall not only know the world, but we shall also understand its genesis and creation. This was Hegel's aim. He sought to show principles of movement and development in thought itself, whereby it must necessarily pass through the various forms of existence until it emerges as absolute spirit. Such was the genesis of the system of absolute idealism.

It requires patience to unravel the abstractions and ambiguities involved in this doctrine. It derives all its plausibility from confounding the absolute and the human standpoint. From the former point of view conclusions not altogether unlike these might be drawn, but we must deal with the latter first. And here, unless we allow the hypostasis of the human reason, the Kantian doctrine leads at once to pure individualism. Kant's transcendental ego forthwith became the universal ego with Fichte; and thus apparently an all-embracing reality was secured. Then, by an analysis of the notion of egoity, Fichte proceeded to deduce the forms and facts of the actual world. Hegel carried the abstraction a step further. Fichte starts with the self-positing ego; but at that time, or in that stage of speculative development, this was thought to stop short of the true first principle. This Hegel found in thought itself. In the beginning, then, was thought, developing by its essential laws into a world of persons and a world of things. The world movement is but the dialectical unfolding of thought itself. Criticism must direct itself, first, to the alleged identification of thought and being, and, secondly, to the development of pure thought into its concrete forms; that is, to the deduction of the world from thought.

But now we seem to have thought without a thinker, and thought developing itself into a thinker—both of which notions are sheer fictions. Either, then, we must see our view collapse through the vanishing of its most important term, or we must make a distinction. By thought we may mean thinking, or we may mean the rational contents grasped in thinking. The thought of triangle may refer to the mental activity of conception or to the contents apprehended. It is only in the latter sense that thought and being are to be identified. Thought, viewed as the process of conceiving, comparing, reflecting, in which our mental life so largely consists, is in no sense identical with things. No particular occurrence whatever in the individual consciousness is to be mistaken for objective reality. Our thoughts as mental acts, or mental products, are never things; it is only their logical contents which are things. But these contents are all with which the mind can deal, and they are subject to logic. The laws of thought are their laws. There is no distinction; they are strictly the same. Having thus identified thought and reality, it only remains to find in thought some principle of movement whereby it is set a-going, and we shall understand the deepest mysteries of existence.

The possibility of such a claim is not utterly unintelligible. There is a dialectic in our thought whereby we are driven from one position to another, until complete consistency has been reached. There is a logic in events which in the long-run will work itself out. There is a logic in a system which is often more cogent than that of its holders, and which at last forces itself upon its holders. So for reason in general. A thought may be found incomplete or contradictory until another thought is added. The lower categories, upon analysis, may imply the higher. And this may go on until we are led to see that thought itself is organic and forms a systematic whole. If now we can persuade ourselves that thought is the active principle of reality, then this dialectic of thought acquires objective significance, and we seem to be ready to comprehend existence through and through.

But here again it is plain that we have once more exchanged the problem of knowledge for one of metaphysics. Whatever value there might be in this view for a theory of the nature and origin of the world, it has none for our present purpose. We have simply identified the world of things with the contents of an assumed absolute thought; but we have made no provision for our knowledge of them.

Our thoughts as conceptions, as subjective and mental, are not things. Thinghood belongs only to their contents; and these exist apart from the subjective processes of the individual as objectively real. But such a view advances the theory of knowledge very little. Grant that there is a universal reason whose contents are reality, and whose contents are united by rational necessity into an organic whole, the problem of human knowing still remains untouched, unless we show that the objective reason must specialize itself not only into the world of things, but also into the movements of human thought. Supposing, then, that this universal reason means anything, before we can use it we must learn how this universal thought is related to our thinking, and how it secures the validity of our individual conceptions. Some provision must be made for our sharing in this thought, if it is to help us in our theorizing. Unfortunately, this provision has not been made. The metaphysical monism of thought and being for the absolute leaves the epistemological dualism of human thought and cosmic being as undeniable as ever. We conclude, then, that the identification of thought and being is a somewhat obscure doctrine in its best estate, and that it is only indirectly of use in solving the problem of human knowledge.

In truth, this doctrine is purely metaphysical. It is simply a declaration that being is subject to logical laws, and may be comprehended through them in its innermost essence. It only remains to find a principle of development whereby we may trace being from its simplest form to its highest manifestation. When being is conceived as essentially impersonal, the view is atheistic or pantheistic; and the difference between materialism and absolute idealism is only one of words. This brings us to the second subject of criticism, the development of being into manifestation.

By analysis of the space intuition we build up the system of geometry as a necessary implication. It is conceivable that, in like manner, the notion of being implies the whole scheme of concrete existence as a rational necessity, or, what comes to the same thing, that the system of reason implies the actual world with all its concrete details. Analysis, however, fails to reveal the necessity. No reflection upon the bare notion of being will reveal anything beyond the formal categories of quality and causation. Pure being refuses to unfold or differentiate. No formal category enables us to deduce any specific application whatever. Pure space accounts for no figures in space. Pure time explains no events in time. The idea of motion provides for no specific movements. The category of causation alone contains no particular effects. Reason as a system of principles is only a formal outline of possibility, and contains nothing specific and actual. The actual is found, not deduced; it is a fact of experience, not an implication of reason. Within the objective order alone we find three factors which we cannot connect by any logical bond. We have, first, the necessary truths or categories of reason. Their presence as laws, both in the inner and outer world, unites the two realms and makes communication possible. But these categories only outline a possible existence, and do not contain the concrete reality as a necessary implication. We have next certain general laws of cosmic procedure. These cannot be deduced from the categories of reason, though they are specifications under them. For instance, the various forms of force are specifications of the general category of causality, but no consideration of the latter will yield the former. The actual existence and nature of these general laws have to be admitted as a fact without any hope of deducing them as rational necessities. Finally, neither the categories of reason nor the general laws contain any account of the detailed facts of existence. No reflection upon the eternal truths of reason or the general cosmic laws would deduce a boulder or any other concrete fact. These have to be admitted as opaque facts, so far as reason is concerned; and if we will have an explanation, it can be found only in the notion of purpose. The cosmic laws could serve other ends as well as the actual, and for the actual we must have recourse to the idea of plan. Necessary truths, general laws, and specific facts bound up in an all-embracing plan are the elements which our understanding of the system demands.

For us, the system, so far from being a necessity of reason, abounds in contingent elements. It may occur to us, however, that the case is otherwise from the standpoint of the absolute reason, and that the inability to connect all the elements of existence in a necessary logical scheme is due solely to our lack of insight. There is here a certain ambiguity of reason which must be noted. Reason may mean the system of necessary truth involved in the nature of the intellect; and it may be extended to cover design, purpose, fitness, and character. In the latter sense, existence may be rational, or an implication of the highest reason, without being such in the former sense. But the implications of reason in the latter sense are not self-realizing necessities of logic, but imply foresight and will for their realization. It is only in the first sense mentioned that the claim has significance here; and in this sense the claim cannot be allowed without immediate speculative shipwreck. For as the logical implications of a thing coexist with the thing, if the universe as existing were a logical implication of the pure reason it and all its contents would be eternal. There would be no room for change, but all things would rigidly coexist. In this view, also, finite minds with all their contents would be necessary and eternal; and as error and evil are a manifest part of these contents, it follows that they likewise are necessary and eternal. Hence we should have to assume an element of unreason and evil in reason itself, and by this time the collapse of the system would be complete. Freedom and contingency are necessary elements of an intelligible universe.

From our human standpoint the dualism of thought and thing is ineradicable. Our thoughts can never be identified with things or brought into line with them, either as their source or as their product. Experience forces upon us the admission of two orders of movement, one subjective and one objective. The former is our conscious life; the latter is not dependent upon us, but exists for all. Whatever its essential nature, it is not our product. This is the fact which distinguishes the order of our thought from the order of things. But if knowledge is to be possible, then this double order must be harmonious and parallel; otherwise our thought, which is shut up to conceiving according to mental laws, and which indeed can know the world only through conceptions which it internally constructs as a reaction of its own nature, could never grasp reality as it exists apart from our thought. And this general parallelism of the laws of our thought with those of things is only one factor in the possibility of objective knowledge. Since this knowledge is a process with many media between the known object and the knowing mind, it is plain that without a profound and accurate adjustment of the nature of the media to the nature of things, on the one hand, and to the nature of thought, on the other, the resulting knowledge would miss its mark. There is no way of deducing this adjustment. Knowledge as a psychological event is an effect of interacting causes mainly subjective; and no reflection upon it as effect gives the slightest hint of the nature of its objective cause; at least no reflection reveals that the perceived object is the only adequate cause of the perception. Indeed, so far as perception goes, the object is purely passive and does not appear as causal at all; and, so far as theory goes, the object enters causally into the mental effect only at many removes of mediated causation.

The relation of our thought to cosmic being involves, then, a dualism and a parallelism. A dualism, for our thought, though able to grasp objects only through conceptions, is not able to view its conceptions as real, but only as valid for reality. It likewise involves a parallelism, as otherwise thought would not grasp reality. And, finally, the representation of the thing series in the thought series is possible only through a highly complex activity within the latter. But while this is the case for finite thought, it is impossible to view it as expressing the ultimate relation of thought and being in fundamental existence. We have frequently complained of the idealist for overlooking the dualism of our knowing in the interests of a metaphysical monism. It is now in order to complain of our traditional philosophers that they generalize the dualism of our knowing into a necessity of all knowing. Our thoughts are not things, but are valid for things; nevertheless, we must at last come down to a thinker whose thoughts are things; that is, to a thinker whose objects are only his realized thoughts.

If we should posit over against this thinker an independent and eternal cosmic existence as the object of his thought, we should fall into a hopeless metaphysical dualism. Metaphysical considerations compel us to admit one fundamental existence upon which all else depends, and the conception of two entities, mutually independent yet groundlessly parallel, is impossible. If fundamental existence be impersonal, there is no way to thinking existence. If there be a self-existent thinking being and self-existent impersonal being, there is no way of bringing them together without cancelling the self-existence of one or the other. The only way out is to view thinking existence as fundamental, and all impersonal or physical existence as a manifestation or product of the same. At this point we must go with the absolute idealists and hold that thought is all-producing and all-embracing.

In further discussion of the problem we may get some light by calling Kant to our aid. He distinguished three ideas of the reason—the soul, the world, and God. The soul stands for the finite knower, the world stands for the system of objective existence, and God is at once their presupposition and bond of union. In our theory of knowledge we need something of the same sort. We must recognize the objective system as something independent of us. We must also recognize the finite thinker as something which can in no way be identified with the objective system. The subject and the object, in this sense, are in unchangeable antithesis. Here is a dualism which cannot be removed from the finite system, but in which, nevertheless, it is impossible to rest. We must go behind both the finite subject and the finite object to their common ground and bond of union, if any theory of knowledge is to be possible. The dualism of the finite must be both founded and transcended in a monism of the infinite.

In a way this conclusion has been quite generally recognized; and monism, at least in word, has become almost universal. Even materialists are given to calling themselves monists. And this suggests, what is the fact, that while there is pretty general insight into the necessity of a basal monism, there is no corresponding insight into the true nature of monism. Hence many have thought to find an adequate monism in atomistic materialism. Here a certain all-alikeness in the elements is made to cover up the extreme pluralism of the doctrine. A better conception is found in the notion of a fundamental reality with a dualism of nature. The dualism is supposed to provide for the antithetical manifestation in the finite, and also to be transcended in the unity of the fundamental being.

This notion has long been a favorite with speculators. It finds its classical expression in the system of Spinoza, and has been repeated with variations in more modern systems. According to Spinoza the infinite substance is one, but it has two attributes, thought and extension. According to later writers, matter and mind are opposite sides, faces, aspects, manifestations, of the basal reality.

In these utterances all that is clear is the conviction that a basal monism must be reached; but it is very far from clear that we have reached it. Sometimes Spinoza talks of the attributes in such a way that they require thought for their distinction. The attributes are said to represent ways of looking at things. In that case thought would lie behind the dualism of attributes as its source, for the ways of looking would belong to thought and not to the infinite substance. But in general he regards the attributes as separate; and then several questions arise:

First, how can the unity of the substance be maintained when the attributes are incommensurable, especially as each attribute is supposed to express the essence?

Secondly, since knowing as a form of thinking belongs to the thought attribute, how can thought reach things at all?

Thirdly, granting that thought and extension in the abstract are attributes of the basal reality, how can we deduce from the abstract attributes concrete extended bodies and particular and specific conceptions?

To these questions there is no answer. The unity becomes purely formal. We have an unmediated dualism of nature and a groundless parallelism of antithetical manifestations. We might call such a being one, but no one could tell in what its oneness consists. Again, the thought side, being separated from the thing side, could never reach the thing side; and logic would never rest until it had denied the thing altogether. The dualism remains ineradicable until thought is seen to be the source of things, or to be the activity whereby things exist. Finally, if we allow the abstract attributes of thought and extension, they lead to nothing. They are merely class terms which apply to all the members of the class without implying any of them. They imply specific thoughts and things as little as the thought of motion implies any specific movement. We have here the fallacy of the universal.

Similar criticisms apply to the doctrine of a double-faced substance, in whatever form. The monism reached is only verbal. We never escape "the infamous two." And we never shall escape it until thought is allowed to pervade and possess and constitute all the reality which it recognizes. Until then the problem of knowledge remains insoluble.

Thought, then, is the supreme condition of any real monism. But this thought must be more than a passive conception in a mirroring consciousness. It must be a complex activity—must be, in fine, a thinker and a doer. Both elements are needed to meet the case. The production of reality cannot be reached by any analysis of conceptions, but only by a free actualization of conceptions. The conception in the understanding must be completed by the energizing in the will. In other words, creation is the only solution of finite existence in which our thought can rest. The finite subject and the cosmic object must find their common ground and bond of union, not in some one impersonal substance, but in the absolute thought and will.

In this way we escape the impossible, or unintelligible,

identification of thought with being. At the same time we reach a true monism which provides for, while it transcends, the finite dualism. We provide also for the element of freedom or contingency necessary to prevent both speculative and ethical collapse. Finally, we make some provision for the problem of human knowledge. The world itself, though more than a thought, is essentially the expression of a thought, and hence lies open to intelligence. If we assume that the world expresses thought and that our thought has something universal in it, the ground of the parallelism between our thought and the system becomes apparent, and there is no longer any speculative reason why finite minds should not grasp the cosmic fact. Things, as products of the creative thought, are commensurable with our intelligence and are essentially knowable. Both human minds and cosmic things must be traced to a common source in the creative thought and will. Only thus can the antithesis of thought and thing be transcended and mediated. The universe, though not founded in our thought, is yet founded in thought; though independent of our will it is still dependent on will. It is not an hallucination of the individual, and it does not exist in brute lumpishness out of all relation to intelligence.

What wild things have not been said about the relation of subject and object, without first inquiring what subject and what object! In general we have had a confused oscillation between the finite subject and the absolute subject. The impossibility of identifying the finite subject with the cosmic object is fairly apparent; and the impossibility of viewing the cosmic object as independent of the absolute subject is equally clear. Out of a vague perception of this difficulty have arisen many statements, as that thought and thing are opposite sides of the one reality, or that they are the same, but viewed from different standpoints, or that subject and object are identical in the absolute. These views are so unintelligible that Schelling had to demand a special intellectual intuition on the part of those who would grasp the identity of subject and object. Yet one can easily understand the dialectic which produces this view. So long as the cosmic object is separated by any distinction of independent being from the absolute subject, knowledge is not possible; but not having risen to the conception of free creation, there is no way out, except to affirm an unintelligible identification of subject and object, with a resulting impossibility of differentiating them again, except by another act of violence. There is no escape from this deadlock save in the notion of a free creation whereby the cosmic object is produced by the absolute subject, and whereby the cosmic object may be so related to the human subject that each in a sense exists for the other.

The dualism of the human subject and the cosmic object is at once transcended and explained in the unity of the absolute subject. This conclusion we may hold with clear insight and conviction. But a great deep of mystery remains behind. We may ask how creation is possible; and there is no answer except the negative one that it involves no contradiction. We may ask how the fundamental reality gives itself objects or becomes its own object; and again there is no answer that is not purely formal or verbal, as when we say that the selfhood of the absolute depends upon sundry immanent acts of self-distinction, whereby objectivity and otherness are produced. But after even so profound an utterance the psychology of the absolute remains somewhat obscure. Finally, we may inquire into that structure of the absolute reason which implies the possibility of the finite system. Behind all volition we are compelled to assume a rational nature on which possibility itself depends. Here the clue eludes us. To escape the fatalism of the purely logical reason we have to appeal to freedom, and to escape the abyss of chance and arbitrariness we have to unite the fixity of the intellect with the freedom of volition in the notion of purpose, itself fixed and determined by the notion of the good. But we have little insight into the nature and implications of that purpose, or into its relations to the supreme good. The gloom is deep, and we have to walk circumspectly and with great wariness, testing our results not so much by the possibility of positive comprehension as rather by the negative insight that any other view is fatal. The attempt to interpret and deduce the internal and eternal thought life of the absolute as a necessity of logic we have already seen to be a failure, and we have also seen that the notion itself shatters on the problem of error. We must, then, at all events, keep clear of that view, whatever mystery that life may contain. It is also impossible to deduce and interpret the contingent purposes of the system, or to relate the great bulk of experienced facts in any scheme of purpose whatever. At the same time, we cannot abandon the belief in purpose without giving up all hope of ever rationally construing the system. Every theory of knowledge must reach the theistic conclusion or suffer collapse.

At the close of the last chapter it was suggested that, instead of debating the possibility of knowledge with the sceptic, we should rather push on to study the implications of knowledge, or to establish certain fundamental conditions, in accordance with which a theory of knowledge must be worked out. We gather out of our previous work a few points as aids to reflection :

1. If the sensational theory of knowledge leads to the impossibility of knowledge (and Hume showed that it does),

then sensationalism must be eschewed by every one who views knowledge as possible.

2. If materialism has similar consequences (and it certainly has), then materialism must be rejected by every believer in knowledge.

3. If all fatalistic theories, whether of finite minds or of the basal reality, engulf thought in hopeless scepticism (and they unquestionably do), then they also are to be ruled out as fatal to the first condition of all theorizing—trust in our power to know.

4. If, finally, atheism is but another name for some or all of the above-named theories, and hence has the same bearing upon knowledge (and the identity is unquestionable), then atheism is to be rejected as essentially inadmissible, as being the destruction of all theory, itself among the rest.

These subjects for reflection are respectfully submitted. The implications of the theories mentioned may not prove them false, but they do prove that we cannot consistently allow them to be true and retain any system of knowledge. Even the theories themselves would lose all logical foundation as the result of their own consequences. And this is the point we especially emphasize. Not every theory of knowledge is compatible with knowledge, and there can be no speculative progress until this question is consistently settled. For unreflective thought the question does not exist, and knowledge is taken for granted. The basis of instinct is the best possible foundation for practical life; but it cannot do the work of reflective speculation. It is necessary to make the problem of knowledge the subject of special study and to subject our theories of knowledge to a searching criticism. In this way we shall discover the anachronistic and suicidal character of many current theories, and shall definitely place them among the views of which the raising indicates an uninstructed or belated intelligence.

CHAPTER III

REALISM AND IDEALISM

THIS question belongs about equally to epistemology and metaphysics. As a theory of the object it belongs to metaphysics, but the arguments adduced are largely taken from epistemology. Moreover, any sharp distinction of the two realms is impossible, as the previous discussion has abundantly illustrated. Hence we propose to treat of it here, but, as in the case of scepticism, mainly in the way of exposition. We aim to understand the problem and the line of argument. In advance of a final decision from metaphysics, there is some work to be done in clearing up the field. And first we must inquire, What is idealism?

In casting about for an answer to this question we discover that idealism exists in many forms. There is an idealism springing from the sensational philosophy, according to which things are only groups of sensations, real or possible. There is also the Berkeleian idealism, which views things as a system of presented ideas without any material substance. Closely akin to this, with some metaphysical differences, is the doctrine of phenomenalism, which reduces things to phenomena or appearances. In addition, we have the absolute idealism of the Hegelian school, which has been discussed in the previous chapter. These idealisms have many and profound metaphysical and epistemological differences. The name is one, but the thing is manifold.

This fact, that idealism has many forms, explains the

indifference with which reputed idealists often regard the most titanic belaborings of idealism by some realistic Boanerges. If now we look for some common element in these forms we find it in the claim that what we call material things and the whole system of material things exist only for, and in relation to, mind and consciousness. The realistic contention, on the other hand, is that things exist by themselves as material elements and bodies, or at least as impersonal realities of some kind, outside of and apart from mind, and in antithesis to mind and consciousness. At any rate, this is to be the meaning of the terms in the following discussion.

As with so many other speculative problems, the question itself does not exist for spontaneous thought; and if by any chance it should be raised it would be at once dismissed as absurd. Idealists and lunatics are ranked together in popular thought, with the distinction that the lunatic is thought to be the less insane of the two. Things exist and are known as a matter of course. There is nothing obscure in the process; indeed, there is no process, but the mind stands over against the thing, and forthwith knowledge results.

This naïve confidence in perception is invaluable for practical life. It results necessarily from the objectivity of thought when uncritically understood. But a little reflection serves to shake this confidence as a speculative finality. To begin with, perception itself admits of being viewed in two ways. It claims to be an apprehension of something objectively existing, and it is also a mental event. Primarily, and as mental event, it is a psychological reaction against some other action, and it results in placing certain objective presentations before consciousness. But these presentations are purely a product of the percipient mind; and if the appropriate stimulus were given they would be there, even if there were no corresponding facts in reality.

The study of perception as process, or as psychological effect, makes it possible to think of the apparent object in a somewhat idealistic fashion. Many realists have thought to escape the idealistic suggestions of such study by appealing to the law of causation. We find ourselves coerced in our experience. We cannot have or dismiss objects at will. This proves that there is objective reality. We also find that the object itself coerces us, that it has laws and powers of its own; and thus our assurance of the object becomes as immovable as our intuition of causation.

The first part of this claim would be significant if the aim were to disprove solipsism; but it is quite irrelevant to the question respecting the nature and existence of the apparent object. An idealist might admit the claim, and still persist in maintaining the phenomenality of the object. The attempt to demonstrate the object by the law of causation is equally unfortunate. The law only says that perception as mental event must have a cause; but it does not tell us where to seek it, or what it must be. Leibnitz found the cause in the nature of the soul itself, and not in any external action upon the soul. If we are not satisfied with this view, and determine to look for a cause other than the soul, we are quite at a loss to connect the effect with the apparent object as its only possible cause. The object itself does not seem to cause anything, and, so far as causation is concerned, appears to be entirely inactive. The causation in the case is by no means given in the perception, but is imported into the problem by the mind itself.

If, nevertheless, we insist on finding causation in the object, it turns out that the immediate cause is neither the object nor anything like it. The immediate external antecedent of perception is said to be some form of nervous change in the brain; and this is totally unlike the object, on the one hand, and the mental effect, on the other; and, besides, it is itself only hypothetically and very obscurely known. No reflection upon the mental effects shows that it can have only one cause, and that a nervous change. Anything else whatever seems as well fitted to produce the effect. We have next to reason our way from the hypothetical nervous change to the apparent object as its only adequate cause; and by the time we have fairly mastered the conditions of the problem it is seen to be impossible to deduce any necessary connection between the mental effect and the perceived object.

To have perceptions, all that is needed is the appropriate stimulus; and there is no way of necessarily connecting this stimulus with the independent existence of the object. Often the perception takes place when there is nothing really objective, as in dreams, delirium, and insanity. Of course, perception takes place only under the form of subject and object; but this psychological form in no way secures the independent reality of the object. However valid, then, perception may be, and however convinced we may be of its validity, there is no logical or metaphysical way of deducing the object as an independent existence from the psychological experience.

Accordingly, realistic speculators of the better sort have given up attempts to demonstrate the object, and have sought to connect the perception, as mental state, with the object as externally existing by "a law of our nature," of which no further account can be given, or which may be founded on the divine veracity. But the matter is somewhat complicated by the fact that there is very general agreement among theorists, physical and psychological alike, that a good part of the apparent object is purely phenomenal, and has only a subjective existence. The subjectivity of sense qualities has become an abiding part of both physical and psychological theory; and this fact itself is something of a stumbling-block to the "unsophisticated consciousness." We distinctly perceive and are immediately conscious of many qualities as inhering in the object, which, nevertheless, exist only in and for our sensibility. Here, if anywhere, we seem to have an undeniable working of the law of our nature, an immediate utterance of the unsophisticated consciousness; and yet we are led to modify it. This has gone to such an extent that the world of sights and sounds, of heat and cold, of all pleasant and painful sensations—the world of the unsophisticated consciousness, in short—is affirmed to have only a subjective existence, while the truly real is placed beyond the reach of sense altogether. Such realism as remains is very properly called "transfigured realism," and the transfiguration is so foreign to spontaneous thought that Berkeley was not entirely out in his claim that he alone agreed with common-sense. The transfigured view he stigmatized as the parent of all manner of scepticism and unbelief.

But if, to escape the transfigured realism, we fall back on the divine veracity, we are met by the fact that, while a law of our nature leads to spontaneous realism, a still deeper law of our nature leads to the transfiguration, when reflective criticism begins. When the mind comes to work over its experiences, so as to harmonize them with itself and with one another, it finds it impossible to do so without distinguishing between things as they appear and things as they are. This result does not depend upon a distrust of our faculties, but upon a trust in them; and it is only in this way that all the demands of our cognitive nature can be met. And if we are to appeal to the divine veracity, it must be in a larger way than is common in this discussion. That veracity can hardly be held responsible for anything beyond the truth and harmony of our nature as a whole. Certainly it would be a sorry sort of veracity which should leave perception and reflective thought in hopeless contradiction, which would be the case if we are to suppose the impressions of spontaneous thought to be final.

We shall have, then, to admit that our first thought of things may not be the truest, or may not be the final utterance of the mind. And to reach this utterance we shall have to undertake a critical analysis both of the knowing process and of the known object. When this is done, and we have found what our faculties really give us, then we may appeal to some fundamental veracity as the warrant of our trust in the result; but nothing could be more barren, superficial, and impertinent than such an appeal against speculative conclusions because they depart from the unreasoned assumptions of sense experience.

The more we study perception as an effect, the plainer it becomes that the ontological and independent existence of the apparent object is no necessary factor of it. All that is needed is an orderly excitation of sensations; and if our present set of sensations were produced, no matter how, by some law of the soul, as Leibnitz supposed, or by the direct action of God, as Berkeley held, the assumed world of things might fall away without our ever missing it, or without in any way modifying the apparent world. We must, then, allow that idealism, in the sense of the phenomenal or subjective existence of the world of things, is possible, and admits of no decisive refutation. The admission is all the more easily made from the fact that so much of what common-sense regards as undoubtedly objective is confessedly subjective.

Our study of the process of perception has led to the conviction that idealism admits of no direct disproof, and realism admits of no demonstration; but we need to be on our guard against hastily concluding to the truth of idealism. Because the object of perception is primarily the contents of our conceptions projected as real, some idealists have concluded that it is always and only such. Of course the object itself can never pass bodily into the mind, nor can the mind get outside of itself so as to grasp the object otherwise than through the conceptions formed of it. Perception takes place only as the mind projects the contents of its conceptions under the form of reality. In this sense all our objects are primarily a projection of our own conceptions; but to conclude from this that they are nothing more is hasty and leads to absurdity.

The conclusion is hasty because the alleged fact would be true, however real the world of things might be. If things were as real as the veriest rustic thinks them, it would still be true that they become known to us only through the conceptions they awaken in us, and that for our knowledge the thing can only be the contents of our conceptions projected as real. But it would still be possible that our conceptions truly reproduce a reality existing apart from them.

The conclusion is also absurd, for to deny the possibility just mentioned would lead at once to the absurdity of solipsism. For our knowledge of other persons is reached only as we form the conception of personal existence out of the materials of our own consciousness and project it as real. Here the conception is our own product as much as in cases of sense perception, and yet we cannot without absurdity deny that it reproduces for us a reality existing apart from itself.

Again, in our apprehension of another's thought we grasp the thought only by thinking it ourselves, and the only thing we can possibly have in our consciousness is our own thought; and yet, if all personal intercourse and understanding be not delusive, this subjective thought of ours reproduces for us a thought existing beyond the range of our personal consciousness. It is indeed true that we cannot prove that these other persons and thoughts exist apart from our consciousness; and it is also true that a being able to control our sensations could produce for us an apparent world of persons as well as of things without their substantial existence; but, on the other hand, it is equally true that it is strictly impossible for any one to hold to solipsism. No one could ever persuade himself that all past history has occurred only in his own consciousness; that his neighbors exist only as his mental states; that a blizzard is only a tumult among his states of consciousness; that a city with its busy life is only a complex mental state of his own, which vanishes when he goes to sleep. It may be forever impossible for us to tell how our thoughts, which arise and exist only in our consciousness, should yet grasp realities independent of our consciousness, but none the less are we compelled to admit the fact. And if we have to admit it in one case, there is no theoretical reason why it should be denied in any case where the facts seem to call for it.

Without doubt, many of the traditional arguments for idealism are short-sighted. The general claim that the individual mind can know nothing but its own states, which is so often made by idealists, is distinctly false as to psychological form. Objectivity is the universal form of perception; and things are not known as mental states, but as independent objects. The claim can only mean that, however objective and independent things may seem, they are, after all, only our own projected conceptions. In this form the claim rests upon various grounds. There is first the fact, already dwelt upon, that knowing can take place only through subjective conceptions which are products of the mind's own activity; but this fact does not exclude the possibility that those conceptions reproduce an existence independent of the conceptions themselves. Then there is the further fact that we are quite unable to tell how our minds can grasp realities external to ourselves; but this negative impotence decides nothing as to the positive fact. If the fact were given as real, we should have only another instance of the common experience of having to admit as facts things whose full rationale we are unable to give. Admitting the fact as real, however, reflection might reveal certain general metaphysical relations between the mind and its objects as necessary implications of the fact; but those relations would be deduced from the fact, and not the fact from the relations.

The claim that the mind can know only its own states is further supported by the philosophy of sensationalism. In this doctrine the mind is a passive impotency, or, rather, a mere cluster of experiences. But experience in the last analysis reduces to impressions, vivid or faint, and beyond these there is nothing. Of course, a mind which is only a sum of impressions can never transcend the impressions. The impressions being all, it is hard enough to see how they can know themselves; and there being nothing else for them to know, it is needless to inquire how they know it. A nihilistic idealism is the immediate result. This argument has the same value as the sensational philosophy in general, and hence is worthless; and the general claim which we are considering, by whatever arguments supported, leads necessarily to solipsism and must be abandoned.

The conclusion is (1) that both traditional realism and traditional idealism have been hasty and superficial, and (2) that no tenable idealism can be founded on a theory of the knowing process alone. Such idealism must either lapse into solipsism, or it must be arbitrary and inconsistent. In the latter case it would admit that thought sometimes grasps external reality, and it would have no reason for limiting the range of knowledge as demanded by the theory. If any idealism is to be held, therefore, it must be based upon an analysis of the object known, rather than of the knowing process. A study of the object and of the system of objects must show that they are meaningless, and hence impossible, apart from mind and consciousness, in and for which they exist. As a world of ideas demands the conception of a mind as the condition of its being, and as a world of sensations would be absurd when conceived as existing apart from consciousness, so it must be shown that the world of things is so completely a world of ideas as to have no meaning except in relation to mind and consciousness. This is the only idealism worthy of consideration. The vast difference between it and the cheap idealisms of negation and sensationalism is self-evident. It does not dispute our mental competence, or the testimony of our faculties, but aims rather to find what our faculties really give when they become critical and reflective. It takes the apparent as a datum from which to find the real; it accepts the system of experience as a subject of critical analysis, with the aim of finding how much of it is apparent and how much of it is real. And it points out that this inquiry is no private freak of the speculator, for, by common consent, a good part of objectivity has only apparent existence in distinction from ontological reality. The critic only extends the realm of the apparent still further, but by arguments identical in principle.

The difference between this idealism and the traditional conception of idealism is also manifest. The common thought of idealism is that it denies the system of experience altogether as something common to all, and reduces the external world to an atomistic and discontinuous set of impressions in scattered minds, which may possibly be similar, but which have no common object beyond this similarity of distinct impressions. Crude realism always represents reality by the conception of space full, and unreality by space empty, and so its typical conception of idealism is that it affirms a real space, but empty. Yonder where that tree or house is, there is nothing. This is supposed to be the idealist's faith; and hence the ironical exhortations to knock his head against a post or enter a closed door. But the idealist who understands himself is so far from believing in a real space filled with phantoms that he reckons the space itself as a part of the phenomenon, and as without any ontological existence.

But it is not our purpose to deduce the idealism in question, but rather to expound it and give some general idea of its leading arguments. The point of view may best be learned by considering the following questions:

1. Is there anything in existence but myself? The answer is, Yes. To escape the absurdity of solipsism I must admit at least the existence of other persons.

2. Does the world of apparent objects exist for me only? No: it exists for others also, so that we live in a common world.

3. Does this common world consist in anything more than a similarity of impressions in finite minds, so that the world apart from these is nothing? This view cannot be disproved, but it accords so ill with the impression of our total experience that it is practically impossible.

4. Is, then, the world of things a continuous existence of some kind independent of finite thought and consciousness? This claim cannot be demonstrated, but it is the only view which does not involve insuperable difficulties.

5. What is the nature and where is the place of this cosmic existence? That is the question at issue between realism and the idealism under discussion. Realism views things as existing in a real space as true ontological realities. Idealism views both them and the space in which they are supposed to be as existing only in and for a cosmic intelligence, and apart from which they are absurd and contradictory.

If it were not for the last point idealism and realism would seem to agree. And doubtless many a realist would find in the answers to the first four questions a full confession of the realistic faith. A world which we did not make, and which is independent of all finite thought and consciousness, what is this but realism pure and simple? We reply that this is probably all there is in realism; but to make the distinction clear between this and unreasoned realism, we point out that there is a difference between being independent of our thought and being independent of all thought, between existing apart from our consciousness and existing apart from all consciousness in a lumpish materiality, which is the antithesis and negation of consciousness.

There is much uncertainty in the terminology of this subject which needs clearing up. Subjective and objective primarily denote, respectively, appertaining to the subject or to the object, or having the position of a subject or an object. The distinction, moreover, is primarily made by thought itself, and lies within consciousness itself. Objects are first of all whatever we think about; ourselves, our affections, our thoughts, our neighbors, as well as things, may be objects in this sense. Sometimes the distinction is psychological, referring to the antithesis of the thinker and his objects, be they persons or things. Sometimes it is metaphysical, and expresses the antithesis of conscious mind and impersonal thing. Speculation has suffered not a little from confusing these two points of view. Many things might be true of the object conceived as material thing which would not be true of the object conceived as something thought about. The subject itself may be an object in the latter sense.

Again, objective is applied to all the elements of experience to which we give space relations, and subjective applies to the other elements to which we give only time relations. But both classes are subjective in depending on thought for their existence. Objective and subjective here have the same meaning as the familiar antithesis of external and internal. Psychologically, this antithesis must be interpreted in the way suggested; it must not be taken in a spatial sense.

But objective and subjective have still another meaning. Universality is the special mark of truth. The common to all is true, the special to me is illusion. Hence objectivity is identified with universality, and subjectivity is identified with illusion. When this fact is combined with the reference to independent existence implicit in the judgment, the object is easily transformed into an extra-mental reality which exists apart from mind altogether. This multiplicity of meaning warns us to be on our guard in the use of these terms.

We easily understand how spontaneous thought comes to this conception of extra-mental reality as the truly and only real. It is rightly convinced that our objects are not our own products or private property, and it knows of no way of expressing this conviction except by saying that they exist extra-mentally. But the general admission that a large part of apparent objectivity has only phenomenal existence shows that the subjective and the illusory are not always to be identified. We have at length become accustomed to the idea of universality in the phenomenal, and are gradually growing able to distinguish between phenomenality and illusion. This makes it possible to maintain at once the subjectivity and the universality of the world; that is, that it exists only for mind and not in itself, and yet that it exists for all minds.

Moreover, it is extremely doubtful whether the notion of extra-mental objects represents any clear conception. To be sure, the imagination, by means of its space forms and by locating the mind inside of the body, represents the idea with perfect clearness and self-evidence; but when we come to define the idea, it is hard to escape an implicit reference to a percipient mind. The illusory object is such because it is not there for all, and the real object is no illusion because it is there for all. If we suggest that illusion itself might be universal we only grasp the conception by thinking of some universal mind for which the illusion does not exist, or by thinking of a fault in finite experience whereby the continuity of the illusion is broken. In either case its universality is denied. But if the universality be maintained, it is hard to see in what the truly real would be superior to the illusion, or in what its special reality would consist. It is extremely difficult, we repeat, to define the object as either real or unreal without reference to the subject; and hence the notion of strictly extra-mental objects which exist by themselves and without any reference to a conscious subject, while so clear to the imagination, is remarkably difficult to the understanding.

But however this may be, it is plain that one may believe in the subjective existence of the world of things without thereby making it a particular delusion of his own, and may also believe in the universality of the world, or in its existence for all, without admitting its extra-mental existence. Such an idealism would differ from realism only on the one point of this extra-mental existence. Both alike would have an orderly and universal system of objects, and both would be equally far from conceiving this system as an individual delusion. The difference concerns the essential nature of this system, and the place and mode of its existence. The question is a purely speculative one, and lies entirely beyond the jurisdiction of the senses. The attempt to solve it by the customary appeals to common-sense, the unsophisticated consciousness, the divine veracity, etc., indicates complete inability to understand the problem, to say nothing of solving it.

The only way of vindicating an extra-mental existence for perceived objects is to bring them under the category of causation, and to claim that when they are not perceived or thought about they still exist in manifold interaction with one another. This would, indeed, remove the difficulty in defining what we mean by such existence; but it would also make it necessary to find the true realities, not in objects as the senses give them or as spontaneous thought finds them, but in a series of invisible and supersensible things; that is, our realism must be "transfigured."

This conclusion has generally been accepted by realistic speculators, and a "transfigured realism" has been offered instead of the crude realism of common-sense. The sense world has been unhesitatingly handed over to phenomenal—that is, subjective—existence. Light, sound, heat, etc., which seem so manifestly extra-mental, are declared to have existence only in our sensibility. Of course the realist hastens to remark that these qualities have objective realities corresponding to them—namely, vibrations of some sort; and with this fact he fancies he removes the paradox of his view for the unsophisticated consciousness. Indeed, at times he even grows impatient at references to the subjectivity of sense qualities as little more than a fetch on the part of idealists. Heat, sound, light are objective; of course, not as common-sense supposes. But vibrations are objective; and though they are never objects themselves, still they are the reality of the object.

The ease with which this assurance is accepted as a solution of the difficulty is due to the fact that anything which looks like reasoning will do for a foregone conclusion. The unsophisticated consciousness knows nothing of vibrations in sense experiences. It knows qualities directly as properties of the objects. For it the thing is no compound of qualities partly projected from the thinker and partly existing in the thing, but the whole thing is objective and external. Transfigured realism has an altogether different set of objects from common-sense realism. The things of the latter are the phenomena of the former, and the realities of the former are undreamed of by the latter. Each believes in the reality of things, but the things of one are not those of the other. The things of common-sense are the objects of perception, bodies in space with various apparent properties. The things of transfigured realism are sundry deductions of theory which the senses do not give. The former realism believes in what the senses give, and falls back on the unsophisticated consciousness. The latter realism sets aside what the senses give, and allows as real only what the senses do not and cannot give; and yet it too, upon occasion, falls back on the unsophisticated consciousness. All that the two realisms have in common is the conviction that the apparent system is not arbitary and groundless, or a private fiction of the individual; and this conviction they share with idealism.

It is doubtful, as we said in treating of scepticism, if the current doctrine, that we know only phenomena, however true it may be for the objects of sense perception, has been fully apprehended in all its consequences by the rank and file of its holders. If we take it in earnest, it follows that the whole apparent world has only a subjective existence, and that its very nature is to be perceived. If we make this subjectivity individual, the apparent world is only a series of similar presentations in different minds. If we reject this view we must provide some cosmic consciousness as the source and seat of cosmic phenomena; for phenomena apart from a consciousness, for and in which they exist, are nonsense.

We are no better off if we say that the apparent world is the form under which the cosmic realities appear, for appearance also presupposes a mind to which things appear. Besides, it is hard to see in what sense phenomena are the appearances of the alleged realities. These realities may be the cause of the appearance, but they can hardly be said to appear in the effect. The sensation of light may be caused by a vibrating ether; but the ether cannot be said to appear in the sensation, or to be in any sense an object of perception. A mind which should see the ether as it is would see no light, and one which saw light would see no ether. Thus the actual object of experience becomes inevitably subjective, while the reality is put beyond any range of the senses.

Nor do we much mend the matter by deciding that the object is partly mental and partly extra-mental, as in the distinction of primary and secondary qualities; for the line between the subjective and the objective is hard to draw, and the distinction itself seems like an affront to the unsophisticated consciousness. Supposing it made, however, it is not clear how the subjective qualities are to be regarded. If they are to be excluded from reality, reality itself begins to seem poverty-stricken, so much so as to be only a bare skeleton of existence without life or meaning. In that case a knowledge of the real would reveal very little worth knowing, and all the value and significance of existence would be in the unreal subjective world. The subjective qualities which are supposed to be nothing apart from consciousness do, nevertheless, appear as an important system of objects for consciousness and have the utmost practical value. This difficulty can never be escaped as long as we make the distinction of real and unreal depend upon the antithesis of mental and non-mental. In that case the real must ever grow poorer and poorer, and less and less worth knowing; for the solid things of crude realism are perpetually vanishing into phenomena.

By this time the realism of spontaneous thought has vanished almost entirely. Transfigured realism has reduced all apparent realities and properties to manifestations of hidden realities; and these it regards only under the causal categories of force, energy, etc. Whether the hidden reality be one or many is not decided. Many will have it that it is only one, and that so-called things are but relatively constant phases of an all-embracing power. When we follow this doctrine into its consequences we find that it has nothing in common with crude realism beyond the general belief in an extra-mental existence, and possibly the additional assumption that this existence is in objective and independent space.

Before proceeding to consider this question, attention must be called to a fundamental change in the problem itself, as the result of the previous considerations. We have seen that the antithesis of phenomenal and noumenal leads to the notion of a noumenon behind or within the phenomenon, which is ever trying to manifest itself, but ever failing because masked by the phenomenon. We have also seen the impropriety of regarding the phenomenon as a manifestation of the noumenon unless it really manifests it. We have further seen that transfigured realism, from seeking the real only in the extra-mental, can at best reach only a real of growing poverty and worthlessness. All of these difficulties are outgrowths of the uncritical common-sense notions of knowledge. These notions are built on the assumption of a reality beyond and antithetical to thought; and when criticism shows the phenomenality of much that is apparently real, instead of revising the definition of reality, superficial thought takes the direction of transfigured realism with its elusive or unknowable noumena, or things in themselves. Again, there is complete oversight of the fact that mind and life also are in some sense parts of reality, and hence the attempt to constitute reality in complete separation from them, and to form a theory of knowledge without any theistic reference, solely on the basis of our crude native realism, brightened up by a little not very profound reflection. The result is the incongruous collection of notions we have been considering.

Our thought in this field can be brought into harmony with itself and with experience only by a restatement of the problem. Phenomena and noumena must be replaced by phenomena and their causes. And phenomena must be taken for what they report themselves to be, and not as the mask of hidden noumena which they ought to reveal but only distort. The truth and reality of phenomena are the phenomena themselves, and the only remaining question concerns their cause or causes. Behind the apparent light or sound there is no noumenal light or sound, but certain conditions or causes. Thus in an important sense we save the truth of appearances, as Berkeley claimed that he did; for we accept the sense report, and go behind it, not in the way of denial, but of explanation.

In the next place, reality must be seen to be double. By objective reality we may mean the common to all in external experience, and we may mean ontological or metaphysical reality. The former is phenomenal reality, and is distinguished from individual illusion by the fact of its universality. The sense world is an illustration. This world has only phenomenal existence, and yet it is the great field of common experience. Concerning it, the true question is not, Is it real? but, What kind of reality does it have? or, In what does its reality consist? Common-sense insists that the sense world is real. Criticism shows that it is neither an ontological fact nor a property of ontological facts, but rather a constant effect of unseen causes. Its reality is simply its universality. Metaphysical reality, on the other hand, consists in causality. In this sense only the causal is real.

With this elimination of noumena as misleading or fictitious, and with this distinction of phenomenal from ontological reality, we escape many of the misunderstandings which have infested this region, and even bring idealism into some kind of harmony with common-sense; at least, we show common-sense that idealism does not mean to deny any reality that experience gives, but only to inquire what kind of reality our objects have. We have seen that there is no resting in the sense world as a finality. We are compelled, not to modify it, but to supplement it by going behind it. We find transfigured realism handing over the whole world of sense qualities to phenomenal existence, and idealism suggests that the whole world of spatial objects in like manner has only phenomenal existence.

And now there seems to be no escape from an excursion into metaphysics. The theory of knowledge cannot be settled by simply studying the psychological process of perception, and by appealing to the intuitions of the unsophisticated consciousness. We must leave the standpoint of the finite and particular individual, and form some conception of the general relation of thought and being in the fundamental reality. In the previous chapter we have seen that the absolute reality must be viewed as a free intelligence, and that all other existence must depend on it. Combining this result with the realistic view of space, we should have three kinds of reality : (1) Independent thinking existence, (2) dependent things, and (3) space as something quite distinct from the others, and as *sui generis* in its existence.

That this view of space seems self-evident is unquestionable; indeed, it stands high among the traditional intuitions; but that it can be harmonized with reason is not so plain. And, first, we need to know what is the relation of space as existing to that fundamental reality which is the source of things. If the two be independent we collide with the demand of reason for unity in the fundamental reality. We should be equally at a loss to express the ontological relation of these two independent existences. The space which is declared to be real would at the same time be so like the negation of existence that the only possible relation between the two would be that space contains the reality, or the reality is in space. But here again we should be unable to tell what difference such a relation would make to either, and hence to tell what we mean by it. If the space does nothing to the being, and the being does nothing to space, the two seem to be out of all real relation. Moreover, if we allow the fundamental reality to be in space, we collide also with its unity; for whatever is in space must be subject to the laws of space, must be extended, therefore, and hence has parts, and is no proper unit. The affirmation, then, of the mutual independence of space and being makes it absurd to predicate any relation between them. On the other hand, it is impossible to view space as the source of being, or being as the creator of space, viewed as something real. It is ontologically so near a negation that many have identified it outright with non-existence; at the same time, they have not scrupled to furnish it with divers geometrical properties, and to insist upon its reality, as if the non-existent did nevertheless exist. All that such persons really mean is to affirm that space is not an illusion, and they know of no way of expressing themselves except by contradiction and nonsense.

It seems, then, that the existence of an ontological space cannot be maintained, whether we view it as containing and conditioning the fundamental reality, or as produced or created by it. In the former case the necessary unity of the first principle would be violated, and creative reality is made subject to an hypostasized negation. We should have a something which is nothing, and a nothing which is yet something; and this something-nothing would be law-giving for the causal reality itself. In the other case, we should first find it impossible to get any positive notion of our own meaning, and then we should have an infinite regress on our hands, as each created space either would need another to hold it, or would be preceded by another quite as good as itself.

Now, rational idealism never dreams of questioning the existence of space as the form of external experience. It never tries, therefore, to conceive external objects apart from space relations. Those objects are so largely constituted by space-relations that they would be nothing intelligible when abstracted from them. Neither need idealism deny that this form of space is universal for all intelligence, so that the same objects have the same space-rules and space-relations for all. This question lies in another field, and must be debated there. The essential denial of idealism touches the existence of an ontological space, separate from, and yet containing, all active reality. And the essential affirmation is that space is only the form of experience or the form of phenomena, and hence is absurd and impossible when abstracted from consciousness as its fundamental condition. The world, then, as universal, may have a universal space-form, or one which is valid for all. Hence it is no individual delusion; at the same time, it has no extra-mental existence, and in this sense is subjective. These considerations remove much of the paradox from the idealistic view.

The subjectivity of space carries with it, of course, complete idealism as to all that appears in space, or that is spatially determined. Hence, not only the world of sense-qualities, the world of sounds and colors and odors and temperature, but also the world of form and extension, the world of apparent things, in short, are to be viewed as having only subjective existence; that is, as existing only for and in consciousness. By this time not a shred of every-day realism remains. The entire world of objects has become phenomenal. Their laws and inter-relations remain as important subjects of study, and they may express a universal order; but neither the phenomena nor their laws have any significance except with reference to intelligence. And if it be absurd to suppose that these phenomena exist only for our intelligence, and equally absurd to suppose that they exist apart from all intelligence, it only remains to infer that an all-embracing intelligence is the condition of cosmic being, not only its original cause but its constitutive condition, apart from which it would not even have meaning, to say nothing of existence.

Locke's conclusion was that relations are the work of intelligence, and hence represent nothing extra-mental. In this conclusion he was certainly correct so far as the formal relations are concerned. Such are the relations of space, of formal logic, of classification, etc. No one can tell what is meant by these relations except as the objects are related in consciousness. But Locke was led by the prejudice of extra-mental existence to overlook the fact that such formal relations may still have a universal element in them, so that, while meaningless apart from intelligence, they are still true for all intelligence. He was also led to look for the real in something quite unrelated, and hence able to exist on its own account. But as our objects as known are known only as related, and can be known only as such, this view leads at once to the conclusion that the real is unknowable. Reality and intelligence are opposed beyond any possibility of reconciliation. The reality as unrelated cannot be known or even affirmed, and if affirmed it can in no way be used as a basis of our cognitive system. To such contradiction we are sure to come when we exclude intelligence as a constitutive factor of the cosmos, and seek to found it upon an extra-mental reality. But possibly Locke was right only for the formal relations of things. Their metaphysical relations of causation and interaction may be supposed to exist among non-spatial and extra-mental realities. Here would be the last stand even of the most transfigured realism.

The study of this question would take us far into the metaphysics of being and interaction, and it would at length appear that between the phenomena and the fundamental spiritual reality there is no place for any dependent impersonal existence. We should find all such being vanishing into law and process without any proper substantiality beyond continuity, uniformity, and universality. But into this field we forbear to enter. Nor is it necessary for our purpose. After we have reduced the world of apparent things with all its space-relations to phenomena, the chief speculative question remaining, even for realistic thought, concerns the cause of phenomena. This cause cannot be thought of as spatial or mechanical, but must be of an essentially spiritual or rational nature, in order to prevent our theory of knowledge from falling into contradiction with itself. For just so surely as the world of things in space is phenomenal, just so surely can it have its existence only in intelligence; and just so surely as it does not depend upon our intelligence, just so surely must we affirm a cosmic intelligence as its abiding seat and condition.

The world exists only in and for a supreme mind; but how? We may conceive it to be merely a conception in that mind, just as any conception may exist in the imagination. There is, then, no cosmic activity, no world process, but only a passive conception in the divine mind. This view, which is often presented as the teaching of idealism, is hopelessly poverty-stricken, and little less than a speculative collapse. Berkeley seems not to have had a very clear conception of the relation of his ideal world to the divine mind, and much that he says leads to this view; but idealism is by no means shut up to it. For the fundamental reality is not merely mind or understanding; it is also will or agent. We may say, then, that the world is not merely an idea; it is also an act. It exists not only as a conception in the divine understanding, but also as a form of activity in the divine will. It is this fact which constitutes its real existence in distinction from a purely conceptional one. In traditional thought this reality is secured by the world's being outside of God, external to God, etc., but these phrases lose all intelligible meaning when space itself is seen to be only the form of the world. And even if space were real they could not be taken in earnest without making God a being with space limits. Let us say, then, that the world is essentially a going forth of divine causality under the forms of space and time, and in accordance with a rational plan. The outcome of this activity is the phenomenal world, which is neither outside nor inside of God in a spatial sense, but which exists in unpicturable dependence upon the divine will; as our thoughts are neither outside nor inside of the mind in a spatial sense, but depend upon the mind as their cause and subject. This world, being independent of us, has all the continuity, uniformity, and objectivity which an extra-mental system could have; and, as distinct from individual delusion, is real and universal. Indeed, it is hard to say what this view should be called. In distinction from the idealism of sensationalism, it is realism. In distinction from the idealism which reduces the world to a set of similar but discontinuous presentations, it is realism. It is realistic, also, in affirming an objective cosmic system independent of finite thinking. It is idealistic, on the other hand, in maintaining that this system is essentially phenomenal, and exists only in and for, as well as through, intelligence. Over against the human reason whereby nature exists for us is a supreme reason, through and in which nature has its real existence.

Thus we have sought to give the meaning of idealism, and also an idea of the general arguments by which it is supported. The discussion can be completed only by metaphysics. Epistemology prepares the way and opens the case.

CHAPTER IV

APRIORISM AND EMPIRICISM

KNOWLEDGE has two factors, form and matter, or principles furnished by the mind and raw material given in the sensibility. Without the former, thought is chaotic; without the latter, thought is vacuous. The former is the apriori, the latter is the empirical element. Philosophers have been distinguished as apriori or empirical, according as they emphasized one or the other of these elements. Sometimes, with the natural one-sidedness of the human mind, the attempt has been made to eliminate one or the other of these elements entirely. This has been the case especially with the empiricists. They have claimed to find in experience a sufficient account of all knowledge, whether of things or principles. Matter and form alike are to be traced to experience.

This question has been implicitly treated in much of our previous discussion. Little remains to be done except to gather up into connected statement the conclusions already reached.

The debate between the two schools has been marked historically by great unclearness of thought on both sides. Each party has had a clear conviction of the error of the opposing view, but neither party has always had a clear conception of its own position. Apriorism has often been put forth as a doctrine of innate ideas, a doctrine which easily lends itself to misunderstanding, and which in its obvious sense is false. The empiricists, on the other hand, have seldom had any clear idea of what experience is, and have even been led by the association of words to think that they are inductive philosophers, while their opponents, by force of the antithesis, appear as deductive dreamers of the palæontological type. In truth, empiricism never proceeds on properly inductive principles. A truly inductive philosophy would be concerned only to know what the mind is, not what it must be. It would aim at an exact determination of our mental powers, operations, principles, ideas, without distorting or explaining them away. Empiricism, on the other hand, has been a speculative theory of mind, and actual experience has had few rights that empiricism felt bound to respect.

The earlier empiricists, as Locke, held that all knowledge is from experience. We find all the categories given in experience. Time, space, number, identity, causation are objects of direct experience, and by abstraction we get the corresponding general ideas. The mind is purely passive and receptive, and simply reads off what is imposed or impressed upon it.

This claim is almost self-evident to superficial reflection. Thought is so quick and spontaneous that only trained and developed thought can detect itself. It is, then, perfectly easy for crude thought to mistake its own products for something found without. Again, we might ask, where can any object of knowledge whatever be given but in experience? Does not any and everything, so far as known, thereby become an object of experience, and hence is not experience manifestly the only source of knowledge?

With this extension of the term, of course the question itself would vanish. In some sense experience is all-embracing. But experience as Locke used it, and as it must be used to give the question any meaning, is that in which the mind is purely passive and receptive. The mind was supposed to be a blank tablet, a sheet of white paper, and marks were supposed to be made on this tablet from without. Those marks, singly and collectively, are experience. Its distinguishing feature is that the mind is passive therein. It adds nothing, but only receives.

But this view had a double criticism to meet. First, Hume showed that the categories of thought could never be found in a passive experience, and that, assuming the mind to be passive, experience must be cut down to sense impressions. All else must be illusion, and even the illusion can be explained only by assuming in the mind a mysterious propensity to feign. This propensity is the real source of the fictitious categories of the understanding. With this result the possibility even of any rational experience vanished altogether. In the next place, Kant said that we do indeed have an articulate experience, but that it is possible only because the ideas supposed to be abstracted from it are immanent in the mind as conditions of experience. We may, then, abstract the categories as formal ideas from experience, but only because the categories are the immanent principles which make experience possible.

The empiricist, then, has two leading questions of about equal difficulty to answer. If by experience he means that in which the mind is purely passive, he must consider how to escape Hume's results. If by experience he means anything rationally articulate, he must answer the Kantian question, How is experience possible? The impossibility of answering these questions so as to save empiricism is already familiar to us. We have seen that experience, apart from the constitutive action of the mind, is an elusive phantasmagoria without intelligible contents, and that articulate experience is possible only as the mind imposes its own rational forms on the sense matter.

These considerations definitely vacate empiricism as a

tenable theory. Any further interest in it must be such as we have in tracing the genesis of any error and superstition. We look for the grounds of its plausibility in the naïve oversights of spontaneous thought and the crudeness of superficial reflection. From this point of view it is an interesting and profitable subject of study.

Historically, empiricism has been in a state of chronic uncertainty as to the meaning of experience. Sometimes it has meant an unqualified impression in the sensibility, and sometimes it has meant such impression as variously qualified by reference to both the mental subject and the external object. Empiricism is about equally unclear as to the meaning of our mental passivity. The mind is spoken of as passively receptive, and the notion has been thought perfectly clear. This clearness, however, is entirely due to the imagination. The mind is conceived as an extended substance, and marks or impressions are made on it. But even if we allowed this grotesque notion we should have to affirm some kind of action to make even this possible. The material lump itself exercises a reaction equal to the action. Or, and this is the more common fancy, knowledge is conceived as something that can be handed along, and that can be received by the mind as a vessel receives material poured into it from without. Or, again, sensations may be conceived as originating in the nerves and brought by them to the mind, which simply receives them ready-made, and in which they combine according to the laws of association. All such notions vanish as soon as we see that nothing can exist for the mind except through the mind's own action, that even sensation is nothing put into the mind from without, but is properly a reaction of the mind against external action.

If there be any mind, the mental nature must be a determining factor in knowledge; and the denial of such nature leaves the mind so nearly nothing that the next thing is to pass on to its denial altogether. This tendency appears throughout the history of empiricism. The mind vanishes when all its functions are determined from without. Reflection shows that such a being is nothing; and thus, finally, mind disappears, and only body and nerves are left. This tendency is strengthened by the desire to conceive the subject in terms of the imagination. Even sensation and association become at last too elusive for the empirical thinker, and he proceeds to steady his thought by substituting for them some physical fact and process. These are the physical basis of the sensations and their association. These also admit of easy construction in imagination, and all is clear—at least, to the imagination.

The road from empiricism to materialism seems easy, and has often been travelled. But this is one of the chronic superficialities of the doctrine. There is really no thoroughfare in either direction. Since the time of Berkeley and Hume it has been patent to all critical thinkers that consistent empiricism must destroy materialism altogether. The world of things and laws to which materialism so confidently appeals turns out to be something which empiricism makes impossible as an object of knowledge, or even of faith. And, to make matters worse, consistent materialism, on the other hand, overthrows empiricism. For materialism, so far as it claims to be scientific, must build on the notion of fixed elements with fixed forces and fixed laws; and hence, if matter should attain to thought, the laws of thought must be viewed as a part of the nature of things, as much so as the laws of physics and chemistry. The mental manifestation, when it comes, is as much rooted in the nature of matter as any physical manifestation. In that case antecedent experience is as little needed for intellectual insight as for chemical action. Both alike are expressions of the essential nature of matter under the circumstances, and all that is needed for either is the appropriate physical condition. This is so much the case that, if we suppose the physical double of any person produced directly from the inorganic, his mental double would also be produced. There would be the same insight, memory, and expectation in both cases. Thus the empirical deductions and explanations by reference to experience would vanish altogether. But in crude thought this is entirely unsuspected, and materialism and empiricism live along together on the best of terms, and without the slightest suspicion of their mutual contradiction.

A vast deal of irrelevant argument on the part of empiricists has arisen from a misunderstanding of their opponents' view. That view was long called the doctrine of innate ideas, which, we have said, readily lends itself to misconception. It was supposed to mean that these ideas are in all minds unconditionally, irresistibly, and antecedent to all experience. Accordingly, all that was necessary to test the theory was to look into experience and see if the ideas were really there. Under the influence of this illusion Locke set to rummaging in the minds of babies, idiots, and savages, and had rare success in finding failing cases. In this monstrous *ignoratio elenchi* he has had many followers.

Before Locke's time, Descartes, whom Locke had especially in mind, had explained that innate ideas were not to be understood in any such way. Leibnitz afterwards set the matter in a clear light in commenting on the maxim that there is nothing in the intellect which was not previously in sense. To this he added the clause, "Except the intellect itself." That is, the intellect is organic, and when it acts it acts in accordance with its own constitution and laws. But this notion of an organic law, though having its analogue in all laws of growth and development, has been hard to grasp for the average empiricist. His implicit notion that knowledge can be handed along, that sensations and experience can be poured into the mind from without, leads to the fancy that to see what is native to the mind we must look in upon it anterior to experience, or, as Mr. Mill has it, we must look into "the mind of the infant as it lies in the nurse's arms." To one who regards the analogies of growth this is like claiming either that we must find the oak sensuously present in the acorn, or else that we must view the oak as the accidental product of the acorn without any governing law. The real question is whether we can understand mental activity and unfolding without the thought of a conditioning rational nature which manifests itself in both.

The demonstrable impossibility that anything should exist for the mind except through the activity of the mind rules out once for all the notion of a purely passive intellect. The generally received doctrine of the subjectivity of sense qualities puts an end to the fancy that the mind merely reflects and reads off what is there. The empirical claim when modified to meet this fact would be that the only reaction of the mind is that to which sensations are due, and that all else is due to the modification and combination of the sensations according to the laws of association. The mind, then, is able to have sensations. This is a primary and irreducible quality; but nothing more is needed beyond the mechanics of sensation. All else in mind is product.

Underlying this view is the analogy of molecular physics. We analyze masses into molecules and atoms, and we combine atoms and molecules into masses. After a fashion, too, we analyze complex mental states into simple states, and we combine the simple states into the complex states. Indeed, what is judgment in general but such a combination? Thus a mind on the sense plane is easily led to fancy that thought can be construed after the analogies of molecular mechanics. The simple sensations are the data; all else is but their combination.

This view is perfectly clear to the imagination, and is highly plausible in the picturing stage of thinking. With deepening reflection, however, it becomes doubtful if the doctrine be anything more than an exegesis of misleading metaphors and analogies. A more careful study reveals the unique and lonely nature of the mental facts, and the impossibility of grasping them through any of the categories of sense.

In the further discussion two questions are to be distinguished: (1) the origin of articulate experience and intellectual forms, and (2) the ultimate warrant of knowledge and belief. The first question is psychological, the second philosophical. On the first question the doctrine of empiricism is that the sufficient origin of the higher mental forms is to be found in sensation. The doctrine of apriorism is that while the occasion of their manifestation is found in sense, the forms themselves are the expressions of principles immanent in the mind. On the second question empiricism holds that experience is the only ground for believing anything. Apriorism holds that experience is the warrant for believing many things, and that the mind has the warrant in its own insight for believing some other things. These two questions are quite distinct.

In treating of the categories and of the way in which the mind gets objects we have sufficiently discussed the origin of experience from the positive side. We recall the main difficulties in the empirical view.

Experience, reduced to its true dimensions on this view, sinks to impressions on the sensibility. These are supposed to be united by association into various groups of coexistent and sequent clusters, and when they are sufficiently compacted by repetition they form the complete contents of consciousness. But this work, we saw, is possible only through and for a mental subject whose consciousness unites and comprehends the impressions. A consciousness composed of impressions externally juxtaposed would be no consciousness at all.

The theory commonly identifies the impression with sensation, and hence is called sensationalism; and as the principle of movement and synthesis is found in association, it is called associationalism. But we saw the impossibility of passing from the impression as occurring to the sensation as anything articulate, without an activity of fixation and generalization. Particular impressions or sensations are perishing existences. There is nothing in them that abides or that can be recalled. It is not the particular sensation that recurs or that is associated, but rather the logical universal. Before the theory can move at all there must be a logical activity above and upon sensation. Without doubt the fact of association has great significance for our mental development. It is of the nature of habit; and, like habit in general, is a condition of growing facility in the use of our powers. But when the universalizing intellect is not presupposed the doctrine vanishes either into grotesque psychological mythology, or into a physiological function of the nerves. Associationalism is absurd without the universals which it sets out to generate.

Omitting to press this difficulty, we next note that association working upon sensations cannot make anything new out of them except by appealing to some other principle. Since, by hypothesis, we have only sensations, association can only give us associated sensations. If we put only sensations in we can get only sensations out—sensations variously grouped, perhaps, but sensations, after all. With only such data no one can assign the least reason why the product should ever be anything but associated associations. Not even a fictitious objectivity or fictitious rational connection is possible on this view. Just as little can we give any reason why the homogeneous sense data should build up such various mental forms, unless we assume somewhere a peculiar ground for those forms. Hume, as we have so often said, found the theory would not work without assuming on the part of the mind a special "propensity to feign," and this propensity turned out to be the real source of rational categories.

That a rationally passive mind could never attain to articulate consciousness at all is clear, but certain naïve oversights have shielded the theory from its own fatuity :

1. The distinction between the particular sensation and the logical universal has been overlooked. Unwittingly the theory has operated with the latter, and thus has not seemed to talk manifest nonsense in its theory of association, recurrent sensation, etc.

2. There has been a perpetual and unsuspected shuffle between sensation as unqualified impression and sensation as various qualified by reference to both a subject and an object. With sensation qualified as a state of a subject, and as a quality or effect of an object in space, it would not be difficult to deduce several rational categories.

3. Growing out of this uncertainty is still another as to the place of the outer world in the theory. For the more thorough-going, as Mr. Mill, the world is simply a function of sensation, and they lapse into solipsism unless they make sensation independent of the particular consciousness, and attribute to it a species of universality. Others, as Mr. Spencer, assume the world of things and laws as a matter of course, and suppose that the only problem is to generate in consciousness a mental reproduction of that world. But this view presupposes the whole set of rational ideas for its

understanding, and its account of knowledge all depends on our knowing beforehand what is to be done. Its theory of thought makes the knowledge of such a world impossible, and if we have real knowledge of such a world its theory of thought is thereby overthrown.

4. There is also an oversight of the objective intention of the judgment, and of the distinction between the conjunctions of association and the connections of reason. The former are always particular events in a particular consciousness, and can never take us beyond solipsism. The common to all slips in unobserved—a piece of great good-fortune to the theory.

5. The constructive part of the theory depends on assuming the ideas it rejects. With its denial of connection all further speculation should cease. Instead of this the speculator next proceeds to deduce the ideas of reason. But this deduction consists entirely in telling how the ideas are produced. But as efficiency is not a sense impression, and the mind may not contribute anything, this is hopelessly inconsistent. There is no production. Nothing is due to anything. Everything is groundless. Beliefs, as well as other things, come and go, and for no reason whatever. Some things were, and some other things are, but there is no connection. In that case all the deductions, explanations, and geneses vanish, and by sheer excess of empiricism we transcend it altogether, and come back to a queer kind of apriorism. We cannot be even empiricists without assuming the unpicturable reality of causation.

6. The same inconsistency appears in the account of sensations. If they are not produced by anything a curious solipsistic phantasmagoria results. If they are produced we have the very idea which is to be deduced invoked to explain its own production.

For the sake of clearness and progress at this point

the empiricist should wrestle with the following questions:

1. What does he mean by experience? If only affections of sense, how can the laws and categories of thought be generated? If he means the articulate experience of common-sense, how is experience possible?

2. What is the place of the outer world in his theory? real or unreal, a determining ground of our sensations, or only a projection of our sensitive states? If the former, whence the notion of determination? If the latter, how does he escape solipsism? If there is no determination anywhere, what becomes of his own view?

3. How can the subjective grouping of sensitive states in a particular consciousness ever transform itself into the affirmation of the existence and rational connection of objects beyond the particular consciousness.

While he is puzzling over these points we will go on to the second leading question mentioned: the warrant of knowledge.

Knowledge exists in the form of the judgment, and is expressed in propositions. But the judgment affirms some kind of connection between subject and predicate. How do we know that there is any connection? Empiricism says, by experience. Apart from experience the mind could affirm nothing. The only reason we have for saying that any elements belong together is that we find them coming together in experience.

The plausibility of this view is largely due to its ambiguity. It may mean that conjunction is the mark of rational connection, and it may mean that conjunction is the true meaning of connection. In the latter case we fall a prey to Hume's destructive criticism, and reason vanishes entirely. In the former case we say nothing to the purpose. Of course a rational mind, one impelled by its nature to seek connection, will surely take a continuous coming together as a mark of belonging together. But this is not to deduce connection from conjunction; it is to apply the principle of rational connection to the explanation of empirical conjunctions. The truths of inductive science are, indeed, in a way, won from experience; but not by simply reading off what is given in sense, but rather by transforming the sense data through the application of a rational idea.

But all this is possible only to the rational mind, and not to the passive and receptive mind. For the latter continuous recurrence can be no warrant for expectation, for expectation can only rest on the idea of fixed law and connection. Without this the data lie rationally dead and motionless, however they may be whisked about by association. For the passive mind there is no way from external adherence to inner connection, and the active mind finds it, not in experience but in itself. It is a principle which it brings with it for the interpretation of experience.

Any further plausibility the view may have is due to the assumption, implied or expressed, of a fixed objective order. This independent order has its uniformities of connection; and these reproduce themselves in uniformities of experience, and these in turn become uniformities of thought. This view has all the superficialities of empiricism in general; and in addition, as we have already pointed out, it has its own special inconsistencies, in that it dogmatically assumes a system of metaphysics impossible to empiricism. Nevertheless, this has become the prevailing form of empirical doctrine, and in the form of mental heredity has introduced a novelty into the discussion. This we have now to consider.

The aim of empiricism is to generate the conviction of connection by recurrent association. The strength of association varies with frequency, and hence invariable and uniform association must, it was claimed, generate necessities of thought and belief. To this the rather superficial answer was given that the most assured beliefs often appear very early in the experience of the individual, and that the time was too short for association to work its wonders. To be sure, the empiricists ground away at the associational mill with the utmost briskness, but they found it increasingly difficult to furnish a full set of faculties in the early years of infancy and childhood. When, in addition, the various facts of mental heredity became prominent, the bankruptcy of the doctrine became manifest.

But this particular argument had the misfortune to mislead criticism by a side issue. It contained the suggestion that the great difficulty with empiricism is the lack of time for working its transformations, which is a sad mistake. The essential difficulty with the doctrine is the complete incommensurability between its data and its assumed products, and the longest time is as powerless as the shortest to remove this fact. When the doctrine is taken in earnest it is intelligible only because it is false. But the misleading suggestion having been made that lack of time is the chief shortcoming, it was natural to look about to see if this failing could not be remedied. And a remedy was found. By combining the facts of mental heredity with the current theory of biological evolution, it seemed possible to substitute for the experience of the individual the experience of the race, and even the experience of all our prehuman and subhuman ancestors. Thus an immense extension of time was secured, and with the new capital acquired by the brilliant stroke empiricism set up business again, and is now operating almost exclusively on this basis.

The new conception of a race experience has been especially emphasized by Mr. Spencer, and has been put forward by him as reconciling apriorism and empiricism. The former is true for the individual; the latter is true for the race. There is a great deal in the individual which cannot be explained by his own experience. His experience is preformed in its great outlines, and in this sense is innate. But there is nothing in the individual which cannot be explained by the experience of the race; for these inborn outlines in the individual are but the net result of all ancestral experience, consolidated by indefinite repetition and handed on by heredity.

Protests were not wanting from the more logical empiricists when this doctrine was first put forth. It seemed to them to be a surrender of empiricism in the only field where it can be tested, in order to recover it again by the aid of an uncertain biological speculation. Moreover, the new view had a most formidable metaphysical basis, and one which consistent empiricism could never reach or justify. But these protests, though well-founded in logic, had little effect. Empiricism in general, being largely a product of sense thinking, needs no argument beyond metaphors which can be readily grasped by the imagination. Hence the notion of a race experience was so peculiarly satisfying and all-explaining that it was taken up without criticism, and even without understanding, by the great majority of empiricists. The result is a great falling off in mental precision in the present generation of empirical philosophers. We seem to have fallen back into the pre-Kantian and pre-Humian empirical dogmatism. No one cares to inquire what experience is to mean, or how experience is possible. The important thing is to say that experience, whatever it may mean and no matter what it may mean, is the sole source of knowledge. The proof of this proposition is no longer to be found in careful logical and psychological analysis, but in biological speculations of uncertain meaning, set forth in an exceedingly profuse vocabulary of polysyllabic terms of classical origin.

The truth or falsehood of the biological doctrine of descent is not here in question, but only whether it has any significance for philosophical empiricism; and the answer is that it has no significance. Consciousness by its very nature must depend on a unitary activity which organically unfolds from within. It can never be produced by any mechanical juxtaposition of particular states from without. Knowledge, also, by its very nature can never be handed along, but must exist for the knower only in and through his own act. More or less time is irrelevant. If we conceive an individual living through all past time, there would be no way of lifting him from sense to thought by the mechanical operations of association. The seeming significance of the doctrine of descent lies in its appeal to the imagination, and in the mistaken fancy that with time enough association might do anything. The imagination can readily see that knowledge may be passed along, and thus the experience of the race may be integrated for posterity to any desired extent.

For thought, in distinction from imagination, the doctrine alters the case for empiricism in no respect, except in the apparent increase of time. This is reached by the notion of a race experience. This notion deserves closer inspection.

A race experience is a perfectly clear notion so long as thought is quiescent; but a brief reflection serves to show that the race is composed of an indefinite number of individuals, and that the experience of the race can only be the experiences of these individuals. At once the appearance of unity and identity vanishes into indefinite plurality. Or if we take a genealogical line, of which A, B, C, and D

are successive members, it is plain that the line is nothing and that the members are all. There is no common experience, and, except in a figurative sense, there is no transmitted experience. If the members are only phenomenal phases of an ontological movement there is no transmission of any kind, but only succession, as in a series of sounds. The mental manifestations are not the result or integral of anything that has been, but simply the appropriate expression of their ontological ground in its actual phase. If the members are real, transmission is only a metaphor. Experience is inalienable. It cannot pass from A and it cannot pass into B.

We commonly hide these difficulties from ourselves by a word. Heredity is their solution. The later members of the series inherit the experience of the earlier members. But heredity is another metaphor. The facts for which it stands are the problem itself rather than its solution. Even if it were not so, empiricism is not helped; for heredity can only transmit what is possessed; it can produce nothing. Making a will creates no property. Thus the tranformation has to be worked, after all, in the experience of the individual, where analysis shows it to be impossible.

Again, in what sense does B inherit the experience of A? Seeing that experience cannot be separated from its subject and that knowledge cannot be passed bodily along, we must say that B in no sense inherits A's experience. If A and B are only phenomena, then, as we have just pointed out, there is nothing but succession of experiences; there is no connection in experience. If A and B are real subjects, then the fact is that the power which posits both A and B posits B with a measure of similarity to A and also with a measure of dissimilarity. The similarity is the fact in what we call heredity; the dissimilarity is the fact in what we call variation. The ultimate reason for this order must be sought in the nature or plan of the fundamental reality itself. While, then, we must seek the ultimate ground for the likeness of A and B in their relations in the world-ground or world-plan, the actual experience of B must always be immediately founded in B's own nature, and can never be looked upon as anything transmitted from without. Hence, finally, whatever the nature and number of any one's ancestors, his experience is his own, and is determined by his own mental nature.

The popular appeal to biology has the full sanction of the *Zeitgeist*, and has also been ably supported by another great empirical philosopher, *Ignoratio Elenchi*. Nevertheless, on critical inspection, empiricism is seen to derive no real logical advantage from this appeal. Question-begging metaphors and cloudy imaginations abound, largely owing to the efforts of that prince of empiricists, *Petitio Principii;* but when these are reduced to their net value only a zero result emerges. The question remains what it always has been—a question for logical and psychological analysis.

Are there, then, any truths of reason which are intuitively discerned, or which the mind takes on its own warrant? This question divides into two: (1) Are there any universal truths? and (2) How do we discover them? From failure to separate these questions, the doctrine of empiricism has always been vague and unsteady. Many empiricists have held that there are universal truths, but that we gather them from experience. Others hold that we know nothing of universal truth, but only of empirically discovered rules which are valid only within the limits of experience with what has pleasantly been called "a reasonable degree of extension to adjacent cases." In the former view we have the naïve dogmatism of Locke and all who hold his ambiguous notions of what experience is; in the latter view we have implicit the scepticism which emerged in Hume.

The former view is forced to pass over into the latter. For since the truth is not known by direct insight, it must in some way be derived from experience, and we have to show how the particular experience itself is possible, and how it can prove a universal truth. And even supposing the experience possible, it could not carry us beyond itself without the aid of some general principle; and if that principle itself is not self-evident, it also needs proof. Strict proof, then, is impossible without some principles somewhere which the mind takes on its own warrant; for in that case proof would never come to an end, and nothing would be proved. Hence, either we must credit the mind with a power of knowing some things on its own account and warrant, or we must pass on to the second phase of empiricism, and hold that we have no ground for holding that any truth is strictly universal.

But once started on this road it is not easy to stop short of denying truth outright. "A reasonable degree of extension to adjacent cases" seems to be an illuminating formula until we bethink ourselves to ask what degree of extension and adjacency would be reasonable, and then it leaves us in the lurch. When all principles are eliminated from experience, experience itself vanishes, and leaves nothing articulate, not even a rack, behind. A passive mind can have no rational experience of any sort, particular or universal. Hence the second form of empiricism must end in the denial of truth altogether, and the dissolution of consciousness into a series of vanishing and meaningless shadows.

To empiricism in all forms mathematics has been a perennial stumbling-block. The attempts to deduce it from experience rest upon a superficial notion of both experience and mathematics. It has been supposed that a passive experience of number and of space forms and relations is possible, and that by abstraction from this experience we get the elementary notions of mathematics. The error of the first part of the supposition is already familiar to us, and the error of the second is manifest upon inspection. The elements of mathematics exist nowhere in external experience in the pure form which the science demands. All mathematical conceptions in their pure form are generated by the mind itself, and most of them have no analogue whatever in experience. Roots, powers, logarithms, differentials, integrals, functions, are examples. The mind evolves all such notions out of itself and for itself, and tests them by its own insight. And even in cases where the conceptions admit of representation, objective experiment is still unable to deal with them because of their vastness, or the fineness of perception and measurement required. The products of large numbers, the properties of curves, the ratio of the circumference of the circle to its diameter are illustrations. In all these cases the mind works by methods of its own invention, and tests these methods by its own insight. Proof and disproof are alike impossible to any form of sense experience. That 10 raised to the power .301030 equals 2 is a proposition which a passively registering intellect would have difficulty both in comprehending and establishing.

Consistent empiricism cannot explain mathematics even as a form of error without imputing to the mind a very active propensity to feign. The truth of mathematics it cannot allow at all. This was admitted by Mr. Mill in a moment of special frankness. For aught we know, he said, two and two may make five in some other planet. But why five rather than fifty, or five hundred, or three, or nothing, would be hard to say; or why in another planet, and not in another street, or another moment, or for another person, would be equally hard to say. Indeed, it would be hard to give any good reason why it should not be equal to all of these things at once, and a good many more besides. The condition of absurdity is the existence of a rational standard, and when the standard is gone there is no longer anything irrational or absurd.

That articulate experience is impossible without a constitutive action of the mind whereby the sense elements are given a rational form is clear. That this activity must proceed according to principles immanent in intellect itself is equally plain. That the source of these principles cannot be found in anything external to the mind is likewise manifest. They are not conscious possessions of the mind prior to all experience, but they reveal themselves in and through the experience which they alone make possible. In this sense we may look upon apriorism as established.

If the apriori truths covered the whole field of knowledge no more need be said. In fact, however, the apriori only outlines a possible, and does not determine what shall be actual within the limits of the possible. If experience is to be possible it must take on certain forms, but those forms are compatible with an indefinite variety of experience. This is the contingent element of experience, and it can never be deduced from apriori principles. It must be learned from experience itself. This is the true field of induction and experiment, and nothing can replace it. If empiricism has often been narrow in ignoring the apriori element in experience, apriorism has often been equally narrow in ignoring the contingent element in experience. The necessity of both elements is evident.

In this field of the contingent we come upon a special difficulty. Necessary connection can be affirmed only where logical necessity can be discovered. What shall we make of those connections where no such necessity can be discovered? Most of the laws of nature are of this sort. They are given only as uniformities of happening, but the mind cannot regard them as only uniformities of happening. We must find some reason for them. We cannot turn them into logical necessities without speculative disaster; and when we view them as ontological necessities we not only lose ourselves in words, but we get no real relief.

If we affirm such ontological necessity and persuade ourselves that we know what we mean, we are at a loss to understand its implications. What warrant have we for thinking that this necessity will always remain the same in manifestation? So far as we can see, it may take any direction whatever within the outlines of possibility drawn by the pure reason. That the necessity is compatible with change we know from experience, and how much change it may involve is quite beyond us. Even the most determined apriorist, so long as he refrains from volitional dogmatism, must allow that we have no speculative security that the laws of nature are eternal. And so finally it turns out that both apriorism and empiricism leave a very important question unanswered; namely, Can the nature of things be practically trusted? or, Can we depend on the nature of things? For concrete knowledge this question is as important as the more general one of empiricism.

To this question no answer can be found in the field of the speculative reason. Empiricism leaves us hopelessly in the lurch, but apriorism does not bring us far. It contains no security for any of the contingent elements of knowledge, and these elements make up the bulk of practical life. Indeed, we cannot extend apriorism to them without turning them into necessities, and then we make shipwreck of reason. The only way of escaping the speculative disaster involved in the notion of necessity, and the lawless irrationality attaching to the notion of chance, is to look upon the cosmic uniformities as noted in purpose and maintained by freedom. But then, for any absolute science, we should need to know what that purpose is and what it implies; and as no one can pretend to any such knowledge, it follows that we have no absolute concrete science whatever, and that such science as we have has a considerable element of assumption attached to it. How far it is valid and how long it will remain valid is known only to the uncritical dogmatist, who mistakes the monotonies of his thinking for the changeless laws of existence.

The conclusion of the whole matter is that we must keep clear of dogmatic finalities in the concrete realm, and must confine our concrete science to "a reasonable degree of extension to adjacent cases." Having made merry over this phrase as applied to the formal sciences, it is now in order to reinstate it as the sum of our wisdom in the concrete sciences. And if we are asked to explain it and tell what degree of extension is reasonable, and what constitutes adjacency, the answer must be found in the range of practical interest; that is, our faith must be practical rather than speculative, and must become vague and uncertain when the matter is far and permanently removed from any practical interest. Of course the dogmatist is likely long to be with us, and magazine science with its clear knowledge of the infinities and eternities will abound. The sceptic, on the other hand, will perennially assure us that he has succeeded in destroying knowledge. Meanwhile life will go on its way, and the wise man, like *Candide*, will continue to cultivate his garden. As Pascal has it, criticism confounds the dogmatists, and nature is too strong for the sceptics.

CHAPTER V

KNOWLEDGE AND BELIEF

Our previous conclusions represent only the general conditions of reproducing reality in any form for our consciousness. Given a world, or an order of fact or reason, which we do not make but find, what are the general conditions of its being an object for us? The answer has been given in the previous discussion. A word must now be said about knowledge from the subjective side.

From this side our convictions may vary all the way from opinion to certainty. They all agree in this, that they are held for true; and hence the objective reality and connection affirmed is the same in all these cases. This fact constitutes their objectivity. The difference lies in the attitude of the mind towards them, or in the nature of the grounds on which they are held.

Now with regard to propositions held for true the subjective assurance is highly variable. The degree of certainty is not constant even in the same case, and it varies greatly from one case to another. And when the assurance is complete it may be well or ill founded, ranging all the way from rational conviction to superstition and infatuation. Hence propositions held for true form diverse classes according to the measure of assurance, or the nature and cogency of the grounds. Thus we have knowledge, belief, faith, opinion, assumption, postulate, and, finally, whim, prejudice, and superstition.

These classes exist only subjectively. Apart from our thought only the reality exists, and this shows none of the distinctions which emerge on the subjective side. Again, no perfectly sharp distinction can be drawn between these classes. They shade into one another. Popular language also is very variable and uncertain. Leaving out the irrational classes, we might distinguish as fundamental knowledge and belief. Some would incline to distinguish faith as a special type of belief because of the æsthetic and ethical character of its grounds and the religious nature of its object.

If we thus distinguish knowledge and belief, knowledge must be defined as that which is self-evident in the nature of reason, or which is immediately given in experience, or which is cogently inferred from the given. The subjective form of knowledge is certainty of the truth of its contents; but this certainty is so often the product of thoughtlessness that we have to test it by denying the alleged knowledge, and seeing if the mind can entertain the denial. If it can, then we have at best only probability. If it cannot, then we have the highest objective certainty possible. It is illuminating sometimes to apply this test. We find to our surprise that pure thought can entertain without shock the denial of a great many items of supposed knowledge.

The certainty of knowledge is inexpugnable in the case of the truths of reason and the facts of immediate experience. The matter is not so clear when we come to interpret these facts. For instance, the Copernican theory, the wave theory of light, the atomic theory of matter, shade away from knowledge into belief. Even if such interpretation were necessary from the side of the present facts, we have seen, in treating of explanation, that it rests upon postulates concerning nature which are everything but objects of knowledge. There is, then, even in the realm of objective knowledge, no fixed frontier between knowledge and belief. From the definition of knowledge it is plain that only a small part of our convictions can lay claim to be matter of knowledge. In every field the bulk of our supposed knowledge is properly belief.

The general character of rational belief, in distinction from knowledge, is that it is a conviction based on reasons which lend some support, but do not compel it. These may make it probable, but do not prove it. When we cannot separate and accurately express our reasons, as is often the case, we have the informal reasoning of common-sense on which daily life so largely depends.

The grounds of belief may be both subjective and objective. Many beliefs make no appeal to subjective interest, and their grounds may be objectively set forth. This is the case with most scientific beliefs, and with matters of historical fact. Such beliefs, so far as they are rational, are based upon objective facts and evidence. To be sure, a deal of subjective bias can be shown in connection even with such matters; but every one sees that this bias is irrelevant as proof. Whether a given scientific theory is correct, or whether a given historical statement is true, could never be decided by the state of our feelings. But many beliefs are not thus objective in their grounds. They have their roots in feeling and our system of mental interests. Their grounds, then, cannot be objectively presented, but must be sought rather in life itself.

Beliefs of the former class are both logically and psychologically simple, and they offer no difficulty. Beliefs of the latter class have been largely misunderstood. They have often been set aside as groundless, and have been variously stigmatized. There is some reason for this in the fact that feeling and sentiment are frequently put forward as grounds of belief when they are totally irrelevant. Lofty feelings and beautiful sentiments have often clustered around irrational conceptions, and have been appealed to hide, or save, the irrationality. Historically, there has been a good deal to justify suspicion of and impatience with appeals to feeling in any form as reasons for belief.

But this impatience is itself short-sighted. First, it overlooks the fact that there are feelings and feelings. There are particular fancies, and there are the great catholic sentiments of the race. There are individual desires, and there are the great fundamental human interests in which life itself roots. Feelings of the former class might have no significance, while feelings of the latter class might express the very substance of the soul. No doubt there are many beliefs whose grounds must be purely objective; but that does not decide that there may not be other beliefs, even more important, whose grounds may be subjective.

Secondly, this impatience is at least equally open to the charge of bad logic. The assumption that subjective grounds are no reasons for belief is quite as illogical as the opposite assumption. And considering the assumption of a parallelism and harmony between our mental nature and the nature of things, which is implicit in every theory of knowledge, we may even say that the rejection of subjective grounds of belief is far more illogical than their acceptance. The mind itself, its nature and needs, are certainly parts and products of reality, and we are not to suppose them misleading without good reason.

Thirdly, the objection overlooks the practical nature of belief. There is here a tacit assumption that the mind is pure intellect, without practical interests and necessities, and that it has nothing to do but argue and weigh evidence. This is an ancient superstition of intellectualism which is due to treating this subject academically, and which is almost ludicrous in its inapplicability to human conditions. Man is not only nor mainly intellect. He is also and chiefly a practical being; and his thought is determined less by speculative reflection than by the pressure of practical necessities. Belief is a means rather than an end. It is valuable for what it helps us to, and its grounds lie quite as much in its practical necessity as in its speculative foundation. Evidently we need a profounder study of the nature and grounds of belief.

It is often easier to maintain an extreme than a moderate doctrine. The extreme is clear, while the moderate doctrine has an air of vagueness and compromise about it. This makes the latter obnoxious to all those who crave finality and sharp definition, forgetting that reality declines to be too sharply defined. In the present case it would be simpler to maintain that belief is either speculative or practical, whereas it is both speculative and practical; and it is not easy to draw any sharp line of distinction. We must seek to bring both aspects into view.

If we were looking about for an ideal conception of mental method it would run something like this: Let us first find some invincible fact or principle, something which cannot be doubted or denied without absurdity, and from this let us deduce by cogent logic whatever it may imply. When we reach the end of our logic let us stop. In other words, admit nothing that can be doubted. Make no assumptions and take no step which is not compelled by rigorous logic. And, above all, let no feeling or sentiment or desire have any voice in determining belief.

This is certainly a method of rigor and vigor, as Matthew Arnold would call it, and commends itself to closet thinkers and debating youths. It is also exceedingly effective in polemic, as it makes it easy to show what sorry stuff anything we may dislike is. But there is a doubt whether this be a counsel of perfection for rare souls, or whether all alike are to follow this method. As soon as we come out of the closet we perceive that we have not to deal with an abstract man or with abstract mind, but with human beings in all grades of development and with the most various mental powers. The mass of human beings, in the nature of the case, must always live intellectually by hearsay. This is manifestly the case with children and largely the case with men. Nothing could be more absurd than to require the great majority of human beings to think for themselves in any field whatever. They have neither the knowledge nor the faculty required. Instead of advising them to think for themselves, the only safe and wise advice, both for them and for the community, is to think like other people. And even the wisest man, because of the shortness of life and its practical necessities, must take a very large part of his knowledge on trust. The intellect of the community—that is, the conceptions and customs which represent the net result of the thought and experience of the community—must always be the great law of the individual. On no other condition can he or society exist.

It is this fact which constitutes the great significance of institutions for human development. They conserve the experience and wisdom of the past, and form the bond of continuity between the ages. They furnish the channels of custom along which the individual may develop in every department of thought and action. Language, the social order, the customs and conventions and the gathered knowledge of the community are the mental and moral matrix of the individual; and he finds his way into life not so much by reasoning as by instinctive imitation and submission to social authority. If we were laying down a rule for the procedure of an abstract and non-embodied intellect it might do to talk of taking nothing for granted; but if we are to deal with human beings we must take account of their actual conditions, and, taking these into account, nothing could well be more absurd than the mental method proposed.

This is self-evident as soon as it is brought to our attention. Men in general must live by authority. It is only the use of such abstractions as thought or reason which hides it from us. But still we may think that the things to be believed must admit of demonstration somewhere. I may accept a mathematical or physical truth on authority, but I must believe, nevertheless, that the authorities themselves have demonstrated it. This is the condition in which most of our knowledge exists. We accept it on authority, but we believe that the authority is based on reason. Reason, then, must be the final test of truth, and thus the method of rigor and vigor is once more set up.

In this claim there is implicit the ideal of a transparent rational connection in the system of truth. If we knew all we should find everything to be reasonable. The unreasonable would be the unreal and fictitious. We might possibly allow this claim as an ideal, and we might also insist that the ideal is realized from the standpoint of the absolute reason, but it would not follow that we had anything of practical value for ourselves. For it might be that our limitations are such that we have to follow other than the high apriori road. And this is the case.

If man were a purely speculative being he would not get far by the way of demonstration. This applies only to the formal sciences, and these are subjective. They can never be applied to reality without certain postulates or assumptions. At the beginning of the modern speculative era Descartes applied the method of doubting everything that could be doubted, and found only one invincible fact: that he, the doubter, existed doubting. But this single premise led to no conclusion beyond solipsism. The world of things, persons, and laws lay among the doubtful matters. And we have seen in our previous study how large an element of assumption runs through our cognitive procedure. We assume that things form a rational and intelligible whole, that the system of law is all-embracing, that the laws of our thought are parallel with the laws of things; but we cannot be said to demonstrate any of these things.

Again, we never rest in things as they appear, but work them over in highly complex ways, until we get a realizing sense of the truth that things are not what they seem. But this interpreting activity proceeds on the assumption that what we must think about things is the truth of things, and that what we need to make things intelligible to us is really necessary to their existence. Thus, our thought makes itself very much at home in the world, and will allow nothing to be real until it has brought it into a form satisfactory to itself. Our entire cognitive procedure rests upon postulates of this sort, and these are so far from being demonstrated that, when abstractly stated, many of them seem almost self-evidently false. They spring out of our cognitive nature and cognitive interests, and if we ask for their ultimate ground we find that they have no other than the energy of the mental life itself. The abstract understanding can entertain their denial without any shock of contradiction; but the living mind rejects the denial, because its own life is thereby rendered futile and meaningless.

A more abstract statement would be as follows: The test of formal truth is the law of contradiction. Matter of which the mind can conceive the contradiction is not founded in the nature of intelligence. The test of concrete truth is practical absurdity. Solipsism involves no contradiction, and is easily conceivable, so far as logic goes. The irrationality and uninterpretability of nature are by no means difficult conceptions. That nature is the abode and manifestation of the ugly, the stupid, the non-moral, rather than the beautiful, the rational, and the good, does not traverse the law of contradiction. The absurdity which emerges is practical rather than speculative. Life is crippled. Thought has no object, action no aim. There is a practical contradiction of our nature and interests, but there is no formal contradiction of the laws of thought. The test is æsthetic, ethical, practical, not theoretical. The argument in such cases consists entirely in analyzing and setting forth the feelings and interests involved, and in pointing out the æsthetic and practical bearings of the question. Such argument has cogency only for one who has the appropriate sentiments. Unless we keep these two tests distinct, the procedure of the living mind must remain a sealed book unto us.

The method of rigor and vigor would doubt everything that can be doubted. The actual method is to assume the truthfulness of our own nature and the nature of things, and to doubt nothing until we are compelled to doubt, to assume that everything is what it reports itself until specific reasons for doubt appear. The law of rigor and vigor is this: Nothing may be believed which is not proved. The law the mind actually follows is this: The apparent truth of things, physical and mental alike, must never be departed from without specific reasons other than the formal possibility of doubting. All fruitful work proceeds under the latter law; most speculative criticism and closet philosophy proceed under the former. Hence their perennial barrenness.

The system of belief exists as a great social fact, and there can be no question of beginning from the start. All that the critic can do is to criticise it. Applying to it the method of demonstration of which the law of contradiction is the test, the critic, if at all keen, finds himself condemned to a barren subjectivity and a lifeless registration of his own experiences. This is the end of rigor and vigor.

Underlying this rigorous method is the tacit assumption that belief is always the product of formal logical processes. This is one of the superstitions of a superficial intellectualism. Man has been considered solely as an intellect or understanding, whereas he is a great deal more. Man is will, conscience, emotion, aspiration; and these are far more powerful factors than the logical understanding. Man is also a practical being, in highly complex interaction with his fellows and with the system of things. Before he argues he must live; before he speculates he must come to some sort of practical understanding with himself, with his neighbors, and with the physical order. This practical life has been the great source of human belief and the constant test of its practical validity; that is, of its truth. The beliefs of a community — scientific, moral, and religious alike — have a very complex psychological and historical origin and a sort of organic growth. While reason may be implicit in them, the reflective, analytic, and self-conscious reason commonly has little to do with their production. A good description of their origin would often be: they grew. This growing is the mind's reaction against its total experience, internal and external; it is the mental resultant of life; it is the mind's movement along lines of least resistance. The product is not a set of reasoned principles, but a body of practical postulates and customs which were born in life, which express life, and in which the fundamental interests and tendencies of the mind find their expression and recognition. There is no one specific reason on which they are founded, and no one root from which they spring. In this respect they have been compared to a large sum of money which has been raised by small subscriptions, and of which the original list of subscribers has been lost.

Insight into this fact is gradually producing an important change in our way of regarding the great organism of belief. As long as we viewed belief as consciously wrought out by formal logical processes it seemed permissible, and even obligatory, to test it by syllogistic forms and the law of contradiction. But when it is seen that belief is made for us as well as by us, that it is wrought out in action rather than in speculation, that the great outlines of belief are the products of life itself, then the basal catholic beliefs of humanity and the unfolding tendencies to believe begin to acquire the significance of any other great natural product. They show the direction of the evolving movement, the trend of the universe of mind. They are no longer accidents or whims of the individual, but are as much entitled to be viewed as belonging to the nature of things as the law of gravitation itself.

But, it may be said, this only describes the psychological origin of belief; it does not decide its logical value. No doubt beliefs spring up as a kind of natural-history product, but logic must try the beliefs as well as the spirits. And have not we ourselves made the distinction between rational and irrational beliefs to consist in this, that while all beliefs have psychological causes, rational beliefs have logical grounds?

This is indeed true, and in a system of necessity it is fatal, as we have seen. We must find in human freedom, in our wilfulness and carelessness, an explanation in principle of the whims and aberrations of thought. But when we have done this we cannot discredit the great catholic beliefs and tendencies of humanity without involving the whole system of knowledge in disaster. Their universality and necessity in human life are the best of grounds for belief. Even the higher moral and religious beliefs can be questioned only by a gratuitous scepticism based on the suicidal principles of mechanical atheism, or on the thoughtless assumption that the five senses exhaust reality, and that anything beyond them is a dream.

But the general assumption, implicit in every theory of knowledge, of the essential harmony of thought with reality forbids any such notion. On a theistic basis it is altogether incredible that the human mind should be so badly made as necessarily to wander off into delusion, and on any scheme such a view can only lead to the destruction of knowledge. That evolution should have produced the correspondence of thought and thing in the sense life, and non-correspondence and alienation in the higher life of the spirit, is something absolutely incredible to one who has not first dementalized himself by making sense the supreme arbiter of truth and test of reality. When we provide in freedom a sufficient explanation of error there is much to be gained by viewing beliefs from the standpoint of their history and origin. Then they are often seen to be no whim of the individual, but something which the power behind the universe is producing for us and in us. And when we see that thought, as it develops and lifts itself above its own crude beginnings, moves along certain lines and towards certain conclusions, we cannot fail to find in such an historical fact a very significant ground of belief.

In this development the implicit aim of the mind has been to adjust itself to reality and reality to itself, so that the fullest and largest life possible may be attained, or so that the fundamental interests of the mind shall be recognized and secured. And these interests have always secured recognition, and, no doubt, always will. History shows that so long as any such interest is overlooked or ignored there can be no lasting peace. The intellect and the heart, conscience and religion, the life that now is and that which is to come have alike made good their claims to recognition. This has often been done with violence and in one-sided ways, but it has been done nevertheless. The civil war of the faculties which has often thus arisen has not sprung from any logical contradiction, but from the necessity the mind is under of making itself, with all its interests, at home in the universe. And as life grows more complex in manifestation and richer in contents the system of belief progresses to correspond. Even where the forms and terms of belief remain the same the contents vary nevertheless. Christian theology is in form and outline-conception a fairly constant quantity, but Christian thought varies from age to age. The child and the saint, the savage and the philosopher, alike say "God," but the one term secures no identity of conception. The thought is the expression of the thinker, and varies with his life. It is by this contact with life and reality that thought grows, and not by a barren logic-chopping or verbal haggling about proof. Science grows, not by debates with the sceptic, but by throwing itself upon the system of things, in the trust that it will not be led astray. And religion grows, not by philosophies of the infinite, but by active faith in God and righteousness.

Thought unfolds itself in life, and justifies itself in life. We begin with the sense world and attain to practical unanimity. We advance to the world of the unseen, and here there is pretty general unanimity as to its existence, with the utmost diversity as to its contents. Those on the sense plane think of it chiefly in terms of sense or of a crude anthropomorphism. But as life develops and reflection becomes conscious of its aims and ideals we find thought rising above these crude conceptions of the unseen, and replacing them by others higher and more refined. And in this growing elevation thought is perfectly clear that it is approaching nearer and nearer the truth. The demands of life, the interest in the ideal, the belief in the perfect, are the driving force of the development, and our satisfaction with the result, or the mind's ability to rest in it, is our chief logical warrant. As an academic thesis, or logical exercise, it would be possible to maintain that the Venus of Milo is really no fairer than the Hottentot Venus, but it is not possible elsewhere. So, as a logical exercise, we might claim that the mind's highest conceptions are no truer than its lowest, but man will not long listen to us. Nevertheless, these conceptions find their warrant far less in any objective contemplation of inductively discovered facts than in the energy of the life which produces them. But by studying the history of this movement we get an idea of the essential tendencies of the mind from which the narrowness and one-sidedness of the individual are eliminated.

A large part of belief has its origin in life. In addition we must note that a large part becomes real only in life. The understanding is unable to give any substance to many beliefs until they are put into practice. If man were not will, as well as understanding, his system of belief would be very different. In the preceding chapter we have seen that by way of speculation we can attain to no certainty in the contingent matters of life. Nor is it altogether clear what a purely contemplative mind would make of probability in general. There would be nothing in the circumstances of such a mind that would call for a closing of the case, and with the case forever open the mind would remain forever in balance. Cases of this kind are not entirely lacking in human experience. The mind can reach no decision. It is the will rather than the understanding which declares the case closed, and it is the practical necessity of doing something which precipitates or compels the conclusion. In such cases probability means at bottom a willingness to act in accordance with the conclusion. It may be said that we act on the probability, and that the perception of the probability precedes the act; but whoever will enter into himself will see that probability, except as a calculation of ratios, is a very elusive notion, until we bring it into connection with a possible action.

And, conversely, this relation of belief to action furnishes a test of real beliefs in distinction from mere assent. In the hearsay stage of mental development our beliefs are largely verbal assents to the thought of the community. They become real beliefs only as they are wrought into life, or as life is built around them. Every one's beliefs are to some extent in the stage of formal and verbal assent, and they pass slowly into living convictions. These are not the product of speculation; they have to be achieved, or conquered, in life itself. And many a thing which, as a play of logic, can be speculatively denied imposes itself irresistibly upon us in practice; and many another thing, for which much might be argumentatively offered, floats in the air like a dream because it has no practical bearing.

The uniformity of nature is hard to define as a speculative principle, and harder still to defend. Here the practical necessities of life come to our aid, and make it impossible to doubt the principle in practical application. And that suffices for practical purposes. And even if we should go to the extreme of denying the speculative competency of reason altogether, all that would follow would be that, by way of speculation, truth could not be attained. But life and its practical needs would remain, and there would be nothing to forbid our making any practical assumption whatever which might be found necessary in order to live, and to live our best and highest life. The fearful logical inferences which might be drawn in such a case would have significance only on the assumption that logic still has jurisdiction, and this assumption is the very thing denied. The speculative faculty having shown itself incompetent, we are under no further obligation to regard it. Knowledge is destroyed, but there is more room than ever for practical belief. Indeed, logic never objects to our making any assumptions or postulates whatever, provided we do not set them forth as demonstrated. We may venture beyond knowledge as far as we will, if we do it at our own risk and with our eyes open.

Hume and Kant differed greatly in their psychology and epistemology, but they were not so far apart in their practical results. Hume claimed that reason is a weak and contradictory faculty, and, left to itself, gets nowhere. Kant claimed that the pure reason, left to itself, falls into contradiction, and can speculatively determine nothing. But both alike pointed out that we cannot practically rest in such a conclusion. Hume referred us to Nature or instinct as sufficiently disposing of the sceptical doubt in relation to practice, and Kant fell back on the "practical reason." Life will always make its practical postulates with an amount of extension to adjacent cases sufficient for practical purposes; and as any case by the time it is a real one will always be adjacent, these postulates suffice for living, which is the main thing, after all.

This reference to Hume and Kant is made not to express agreement with them, but to illustrate the difference between a practical postulate and a speculative principle, and to show the hasty logic of those who reason from the speculative incompetence of reason to the abandonment of the practical principles by which humanity lives. It was also worth while to point out that credit has been very unequally distributed between Hume and Kant in this matter. Such distinction as is made must be based on the character of the men, or on the historical associations of their doctrines, rather than on any essential difference in the practical outcome.

We see, then, that belief has a very complex root. The living mind, reacting against its total experience and under the influence of its own essential tendencies and interests, has built up the great organism of belief. What now is the function of the logical understanding in the case? Are we to stop reasoning, and accept every belief as it comes or as it is historically evolved?

To do this would be the abandonment of reason altogether, and a more excellent way exists. This question, of course, has no application to those beliefs which are admittedly based on objective evidence which must be objectively presented. But even in the case of beliefs based on mental interests and tendencies, logic has a very important function. This function is not to create life or even to justify it, but to formulate it, to understand it, and to help it to self-knowledge. The justification of life must be left to life itself. But our mental postulates and interests exist primarily as implicit tendencies, and not as clearly defined principles. In this state they readily lose their way. The cognitive, the ethical, the religious consciousness are developed into self-possession only by a long mental labor and experience extending over centuries. Left to themselves and without the guidance of criticism, they often fail to recognize their own implications, and sometimes even contradict themselves. Many a scientist's theory of knowledge makes knowledge impossible. Many an ethical theory cancels ethics, and many a theological doctrine has unwittingly passed into blasphemy. Hence the need of a critical procedure which shall help the mind to self-knowledge, define and clarify its aims, secure consistency in the development of its practical postulates, and adjust their mutual relations. This is the field of logic; and in this work of development, adjustment, and rectification logic has its inalienable rights and a function of supreme importance.

The claim that all belief should be rational seems to announce something self-evident, but in truth it has so many meanings as to admit of no fruitful discussion. Rational belief from the side of the subject may mean that which is demonstrated, or at least made probable by objective evidence. Rational belief in its contents may mean harmony with the general laws of thought; or it may have reference to purpose; or it may refer to the quality of the purpose, as one worthy of a rational person; or, finally, it may mean something which we are now able to comprehend. A rational world may be one in which the categories of thought are valid, or which expresses a worthy purpose, or which is transparent to our intelligence. A question of such uncertainty can never be safely answered. We replace it, therefore, by other questions, as follows:

What must we believe? The necessary truths of intelligence.

What must we not believe? Whatever contradicts those truths.

What may we believe? All of those practical principles which are necessary for the realization of our highest and fullest life.

Of course these questions apply only to those beliefs which root in life, and not to those multitudinous beliefs concerning matters of detailed fact which can only be established by objective evidence. It is also to be noted in the case of beliefs founded in life that they become real only as they become controlling. As purely speculative principles, they will always be open to cavil, if not to question. Life itself must furnish the conviction.

These facts in the natural history of belief must be kept in mind if we would understand our mental procedure and development. They explain how it is that we have many beliefs which are not held because we have proved them, but which we try to prove because we hold them. They also explain the barrenness of purely logical criticism. Further, they throw light on the peculiar variations of belief to which all are subject. Since the roots of belief often lie in the sub-logical realm of emotion, interest, aspiration, our conviction will vary as the tides of feeling rise or fall. All of this will be very disturbing to persons in the dogmatic stage of development. They will feel that things are left at very loose ends, and will look anxiously about for a standard. But they must learn that there is no simple and compendious standard which will give the truth by mechanical application. The living mind dealing with the concrete facts is the only standard, and to know what this is it is not enough to construct syllogisms in the closet, but we must also come out into the open field of the world and life and history; for there is where, **in matters of practice, the decisive debate is carried on.**

CHAPTER VI

THE FORMAL AND RELATIVE ELEMENTS IN THOUGHT

THOUGHT as product claims to have objective validity, or to produce for us the independent fact. Thought as process is a subjective activity, many of whose phases are instrumental only and reproduce nothing in the fact itself. In this process we reflect, distinguish, compare, and infer; but we find nothing of this sort in the things themselves. The thinking is the ladder by which we climb to knowledge, but it makes no part of the knowledge when we reach it. Inference, we have seen, is a mark of a finite understanding. The same may be said of thinking in general—at least, of human thinking. For perfect insight truth would lie open and revealed without a process. But whatever may be true of "Thought," our thinking cannot claim to be in all respects the double of reality itself. When, then, we affirm the identity of the laws of thought and those of things, this must not be taken to mean that the processes of our thinking are repetitions of objective fact, but only that things exist in rational forms and relations.

Our thought contains two elements: a certain rational content or insight, and a variety of processes by which this insight is reached. The former is the objective and universal element of thought; the latter is formal only, and it may be related to us. On this account our reason is said to be discursive, and has been opposed to the supreme reason, which, because it possesses truth in immediate vision, is said to be intuitive. The community and universality of intellect or reason does not consist in methods or processes, but in the rational contents.

The distinction may be illustrated by the propositions of geometry and their demonstrations. The former belong to reason; the latter are devices of our own. The former exist in their own right, independently of any demonstration; the latter are simply means of reaching an insight which we do not possess. The demonstration makes no part of the truth, and has significance only for the thinking subject who needs it. We must, then, distinguish between the truth itself and our method of reaching it. The methods may be many. It is only the truth that is one.

The possibility of reaching objective truth by subjective devices may be illustrated by a case in astronomy. Thus, given the circumstances of a planet's motion at one time we deduce its path and its position at another time. Our work is done by diagrams and various devices of mathematics and mechanics, which are totally unlike anything in actuality; and yet we expect the planet to justify the calculation. Such an expectation, of course, implies the essential harmony of the laws of thought and things; but, nevertheless, how much there is in the calculation of a purely formal character, leading, indeed, to results which are objectively valid, but without likeness to any process in reality.

The formal aspect of thought and its relation to reality is illustrated by another case in mathematics. Take, say, the ellipse. By a great variety of devices we succeed in proving various truths about this curve. Starting from a given standpoint we reason to many conclusions, and when the curve is drawn we find them justified. But the curve is plainly independent of these devices, and they are just as plainly the subjective devices by which we reach the truth. This is shown by the fact that these conclusions may be reached in any one of several ways. We may regard the ellipse as a conic section, or as a plane curve, or as the locus of a point moving under peculiar conditions. We may express its equation in various ways and according to various systems of co-ordinates, and may get the same results by the most diverse methods. Hence it is plain that the nature of the thing is really indifferent to all our methods. They have reference only to us. They are the ground of our knowing, but not the grounds of the being and nature of the ellipse itself. These are found in the nature of reason and the space-intuition.

The same is true for a large part of our logical procedure in general. It is relative to ourselves, and repeats nothing in the thing. Things themselves are largely formal, being in many cases only hypostasized phenomena. Even the distinction of subject and predicate is mainly formal without any metaphysical significance. Reasoning is formal. Classifying as a process is of course subjective, and the classes themselves are largely relative to us. The analyses and syntheses of scientific procedure are equally relative. They are a kind of substituted equivalent for the fact, whereby we seek to make it amenable to our calculus when it eludes our direct apprehension. In this respect they are something like the trigonometrical functions whereby we are enabled to calculate indirectly values which cannot be directly measured. Even the laws of things have an element of abstraction about them which warns us against identifying them with reality without careful inspection.

If, then, we should make a careful and critical inventory of knowledge we should find a great deal that is not universal, but only relative to ourselves—a shadow of our mental processes rather than an apprehension of the independent fact. We might still believe that the system of reality is an expression of the absolute reason, and that its factors are all found together in transparent rational order. But however firmly we might maintain that this ideal is realized somewhere or for some one, there is nothing in it which frees us from exercising due critical caution and looking well to our logical goings. Such transparent connection of things may exist from the standpoint of the absolute, and we may conceivably approximate indefinitely towards it. But we are not now at the centre of things. The order of our learning is in no way the order of existence. We have to find our way from fact to fact as best we can, not by the highway of the absolute reason, but by the by-paths of our human intelligence. We maintain our faith in perfect knowledge as an ideal, but we recognize our human limitations. We have here simply the reappearance of the familiar fact that our thought has to find its way between extremes without any simple and compendious rule for deciding where the golden mean lies. Pure subjectivity is self-destructive; naïve dogmatism is no longer possible. There is need, then, of a critical procedure which shall unite these antitheses in the truth which comprehends them both, and which, by separating the formal and relative from the real and universal, shall teach us how to think of reality, not merely as it appears, but as it truly is. This is the task of metaphysics. Accepting the results of logic and epistemology, metaphysics applies them to this highest question of philosophy: How shall we think about reality?

THE END

INTRODUCTION TO POLITICAL SCIENCE

By JAMES WILFORD GARNER, Ph. D., Professor of Political Science, University of Illinois

$2.50

THIS systematic treatise on the science of government covers a wider range of topics on the nature, origin, organization, and functions of the state than is found in any other college textbook published in the English language. The unusually comprehensive treatment of the various topics is based on a wide reading of the best literature on the subject in English, German, French, and Italian, and the student has opportunity to profit by this research work through the bibliographies placed at the head of each chapter, as well as by means of many additional references in the footnotes.

¶ An introductory chapter is followed by chapters on the nature and essential elements of the state; on the various theories concerning the origin of the state; on the forms of the state; on the forms of government, including a discussion of the elements of strength and weakness of each; on sovereignty, its nature, its essential characteristics, and its abiding place in the state; on the functions and sphere of the state, including the various theories of state activity; and on the organization of the state. In addition there are chapters on constitutions, their nature, forms, and development; on the distribution of the powers of government; on the electorate; and on citizenship and nationality.

¶ Before stating his own conclusions the author gives an impartial discussion of the more important theories of the origin, nature, and functions of the state, and analyzes and criticises them in the light of the best scientific thought and practice. Thus the pupil becomes familiar with the history of the science as well as with its principles as recognized to-day.

AMERICAN BOOK COMPANY

EDUCATION IN THE UNITED STATES

Edited by NICHOLAS MURRAY BUTLER, President of Columbia University, in the City of New York

$2.50

THE frequently expressed need for a book giving a complete view of American education in outline is satisfactorily met in this volume entitled "Education in the United States."
¶ The volume consists of the twenty careful monographs, each written by an eminent specialist, on various phases of American education, which were originally planned as part of the American educational exhibit at the International Expositions held at Paris in 1900 and at St. Louis in 1904.
¶ The introduction by the editor sets forth the underlying principles governing American educational activity to the present time. Among the authors of the various monographs are: Commissioner Draper of the State of New York, the late Dr. William T. Harris, formerly Commissioner of Education of the United States, Dr. Elmer Ellsworth Brown, Dr. Harris's successor in the Commissionership, Professor Edward Delavan Perry of Columbia University, Professor Andrew F. West of Princeton University, President M. Carey Thomas of Bryn Mawr College, etc., etc.
¶ The subjects of the monographs include such important topics as Educational Organization and Administration, Training of Teachers, School Architecture and Hygiene, Professional Education, Education of Defectives, and Summer Schools and University Extension.
¶ For the benefit of teachers, reading circles, and classes in universities, colleges and normal schools, each monograph will be published separately at 20 cents and will be furnished in quantities at $15.00 per hundred (net).

AMERICAN BOOK COMPANY

HISTORY OF EDUCATION
By LEVI SEELEY, Ph.D., Professor of Pedagogy
New Jersey State Normal School

$1.25

SEELEY'S History of Education is a working book, clear, comprehensive, and accurate, and sufficient in itself to furnish all the material on the subject that is required by any examining board, or that may be demanded in a normal or college course.

¶ Each educational system that has influenced the world is taken up and summarized in turn, its development shown, and its important lesson pointed out. The fullest information obtainable is presented in simple form and expressed in concise language. The topics are arranged on a well defined plan, everything being practical, useful, and directly to the point.

¶ In addition, the book includes biographical sketches of the great educators with an illuminating account of their systems of pedagogy. It also provides a general outline of the educational history of ancient countries, and affords comparisons of the educational systems of the leading countries down to the present time. In short, the volume gives the student an accurate view in perspective of the educational progress of the world. Extensive bibliographies of works for reference are provided.

¶ The work presents for study many of the great pedagogical problems that have interested thoughtful men in every age. It shows how some of these have been solved in the past and points out the way to the solution of others of no less importance in the near future.

¶ It should form an indispensable volume in every teacher's library, for it not only is inspiring, but furnishes valuable information. Every well informed teacher must know how the past has taught in order to cope intelligently with the educational problems of today.

AMERICAN BOOK COMPANY

GRAY'S NEW MANUAL OF BOTANY—SEVENTH EDITION

Thoroughly revised and largely rewritten by BENJAMIN LINCOLN ROBINSON, Ph.D., Asa Gray Professor of Systematic Botany, and MERRITT LYNDON FERNALD, S.B., Assistant Professor of Botany, Harvard University, assisted by specialists in certain groups.

Regular edition. Cloth, 926 pages $2.50
Tourist's edition. Flexible leather, 926 pages 3.00

AMERICAN botanists, who had been impatiently awaiting the revision of this indispensable work, will be delighted to know that a seventh, completely revised, and copiously illustrated edition has now been issued. The revision has entailed years of work by skilled specialists. No effort has been spared to attain the highest degree of clearness, terseness, and accuracy. The plant families have been rearranged in a manner to show the latest view of their affinities, and hundreds of species have been added. The synonomy is copious, and the ranges are stated in considerable detail. ¶ The nomenclature has been brought into thorough accord with the important international rules recently established—a feature of great significance. Indeed, the Manual is the only work of its scope which in the matter of nomenclature is free from provincialism and rests upon a cosmopolitan basis of international agreement. Nearly a thousand figures, specially designed for this edition, have been added, and scores of brief and lucid keys have been introduced in a manner which greatly simplifies the problem of plant identification. The work has been extended to include Ontario, Quebec, and the maritime provinces of Canada.

AMERICAN BOOK COMPANY

SCIENTIFIC MEMOIRS

Edited by JOSEPH S. AMES, Ph.D., Johns Hopkins University

THE FREE EXPANSION OF GASES. Memoirs by Gay-Lussac, Joule, and Joule and Thomson. Edited by Dr. J. S. Ames. $0.75.

PRISMATIC AND DIFFRACTION SPECTRA. Memoirs by Joseph von Fraunhofer. Edited by Dr. J. S. Ames. $0.60.

RÖNTGEN RAYS. Memoirs by Röntgen, Stokes, and J. J. Thomson. Edited by Dr. George F. Barker. $0.60.

THE MODERN THEORY OF SOLUTION. Memoirs by Pfeffer, Van't Hoff, Arrhenius, and Raoult. Edited by Dr. H. C. Jones. $1.00.

THE LAWS OF GASES. Memoirs by Boyle and Amagat. Edited by Dr. Carl Barus. $0.75.

THE SECOND LAW OF THERMODYNAMICS. Memoirs by Carnot, Clausius, and Thomson. Edited by Dr. W. F. Magie. $0.90.

THE FUNDAMENTAL LAWS OF ELECTROLYTIC CONDUCTION. Memoirs by Faraday, Hittorf, and Kohlrausch. Edited by Dr. H. M. Goodwin. $0.75.

THE EFFECTS OF A MAGNETIC FIELD ON RADIATION. Memoirs by Faraday, Kerr, and Zeeman. Edited by Dr. E. P. Lewis. $0.75.

THE LAWS OF GRAVITATION. Memoirs by Newton, Bouguer, and Cavendish. Edited by Dr. A. S. Mackenzie. $1.00.

THE WAVE THEORY OF LIGHT. Memoirs by Huygens, Young, and Fresnel. Edited by Dr. Henry Crew. $1.00.

THE DISCOVERY OF INDUCED ELECTRIC CURRENTS. Vol. I. Memoirs by Joseph Henry. Edited by Dr. J. S. Ames. $0.75.

THE DISCOVERY OF INDUCED ELECTRIC CURRENTS. Vol. II. Memoirs by Michael Faraday. Edited by Dr. J. S. Ames. $0.75.

THE FOUNDATIONS OF STEREO-CHEMISTRY. Memoirs by Pasteur, Le Bel, and Van't Hoff, together with selections from later memoirs by Wislicenus, and others. Edited by Dr. G. M. Richardson. $1.00.

THE EXPANSION OF GASES. Memoirs by Gay-Lussac and Regnault. Edited by Prof. W. W. Randall. $1.00.

RADIATION AND ABSORPTION. Memoirs by Prévost, Balfour Stewart, Kirchhoff, and Kirchhoff and Bunsen. Edited by Dr. DeWitt B. Brace. $1.00.

AMERICAN BOOK COMPANY

FISHER'S BRIEF HISTORY OF THE NATIONS

By GEORGE PARK FISHER, LL.D., Emeritus Professor
in Yale University

$1.50

THIS is an entirely independent work, written expressly to meet the demand for a compact and acceptable textbook on General History for secondary schools and lower classes in colleges. Some of the distinctive qualities which will commend this book to teachers and students are as follows :
¶ It narrates in fresh, vigorous, and attractive style the most important facts of history in their due order and connection. It explains the nature of historical evidence, and records only well established judgments respecting persons and events. It delineates the progress of peoples and nations in civilization as well as the rise and succession of dynasties.
¶ It connects, in a single chain of narration, events related to each other in the contemporary history of different nations and countries. It is written from the standpoint of the present, and incorporates the latest discoveries of historical explorers and writers.
¶ It is illustrated by numerous colored maps, genealogical tables, and artistic reproductions of architecture, sculpture, painting, and portraits of celebrated men, representing every period of the world's history.

FISHER'S OUTLINES OF UNIVERSAL HISTORY
Revised, $2.40
Also published in three parts, price, each, $1.00. Part I, Ancient History.
Part II, Mediaeval History. Part III, Modern History.

A NEW and revised edition of this standard work. Soon after the publication of the first edition of this history the author was honored by the University of Edinburgh with the degree of Doctor of Laws, in recognition of his services in the cause of historical research. In this edition the book is brought fully up to date in all particulars.

AMERICAN BOOK COMPANY

NINETEENTH CENTURY ENGLISH PROSE
Critical Essays

Edited with Introductions and Notes by THOMAS H. DICKINSON, Ph.D., and FREDERICK W. ROE, A.M., Assistant Professors of English, University of Wisconsin.

$1.00

THIS book for college classes presents a series of ten selected essays, which are intended to trace the development of English criticism in the nineteenth century. The choice of material has been influenced by something more than mere style. An underlying coherence in content, typical of the thought of the era in question, may be traced throughout. With but few exceptions the selections are given in their entirety.

¶ The essays cover a definite period, and exhibit the individuality of each author's method of criticism. In each case they are those most typical of the author's critical principles, and at the same time representative of the critical tendencies of his age. The subject-matter provides interesting material for intensive study and class room discussion, and each essay is an example of excellent, though varying, style.

¶ They represent not only the authors who write, but the authors who are treated. The essays provide the best things that have been said by England's critics on Swift, on Scott, on Macaulay, and on Emerson.

¶ The introductions and notes provide the necessary biographical matter, suggestive points for the use of the teacher in stimulating discussion of the form or content of the essays, and such aids as will eliminate those matters of detail that might prove stumbling blocks to the student. Though the essays are in chronological order, they may be treated at random according to the purposes of the teacher.

AMERICAN BOOK COMPANY

MASTERPIECES OF THE ENGLISH DRAMA

Edited under the supervision of FELIX E. SCHELLING, Ph. D., LL. D., Professor of History and English Literature, University of Pennsylvania

Marlowe (Phelps)
Chapman (Ellis)
Beaumont and Fletcher (Schelling)
Jonson (Rhys)
Middleton (Sampson)
Massinger (Sherman)
Webster and Tourneur (Thorndike)
Congreve (Archer)
Goldsmith and Sheridan (Demmon)

Each, 70 cents

THIS series presents the principal dramatists, covering English dramatic history from Marlowe's Tamburlaine in 1587 to Sheridan's School for Scandal in 1777. Each volume contains four or five plays, selected with reference to their actual worth and general interest, and also because they represent the best efforts of their author in the different varieties of dramas chosen.

¶ The texts follow the authoritative old editions, but with such occasional departures as the results of recent critical scholarship demand. Spelling and punctuation have been modernized, and obsolete and occasional words referred to the glossaries. This makes the volumes suitable for the average reader as well as for the advanced scholar.

¶ Each volume is furnished with an introduction by a British or an American scholar of rank dealing with the dramatist and his work, with special reference to the plays selected. Each volume contains a brief biographical note, and each play is preceded by an historical note, its source, date of composition, and other kindred matters. Adequate notes are furnished at the end, explaining difficult passages in Elizabethan grammar, historical and literary allusions, and other points that seem obscure. Besides obsolete and unusual terms the glossaries include exceptional meanings of common words. Over-annotation, however, has been carefully avoided.

¶ The books are printed in good clear type, are of convenient size (12mo), and are handsomely bound in uniform cloth.

AMERICAN BOOK COMPANY

AN INTRODUCTORY COURSE IN ARGUMENTATION $1.00

By FRANCES M. PERRY, Associate Professor of Rhetoric and Composition, Wellesley College.

SIMPLIFIED to suit the understanding of students in the first years of college or the last years of the secondary school without lessening its educative value. Each successive step is given explicit exposition and fully illustrated, and carefully graded exercises are provided to test the student's understanding of an idea and fix it in his memory. The beginner is set to work to exercise his reasoning power on familiar material and without the added difficulty of research. The brief-drawing method and the syllogistic method have been combined so that the one will help the student to understand the other. Though the course calls for a sustained piece of work, its preparation and criticism by installments are provided for, so that there is no dearth of work during the course and no accumulation of work at its close.

PERRY'S INTRODUCTORY COURSE IN EXPOSITION $1.00

A SYSTEMATIZED course in the theory and practice of expository writing. The student will acquire from its study a clear understanding of exposition—its nature; its two processes; its three functions; and the special application of exposition in literary criticism. He will also gain through the practice required by the course facility in writing in a clear and attractive way the various types of exposition. The volume includes an interesting section on literary criticism. The method used is direct exposition, amply reinforced by examples and exercises. The illustrative matter is taken from many and varied sources, but much of it is necessarily modern. The book meets the needs of students in the final years of secondary schools, or the first years of college.

AMERICAN BOOK COMPANY

HISTORY OF ENGLISH AND AMERICAN LITERATURE
$1.25

By CHARLES F. JOHNSON, L.H.D., Professor of English Literature, Trinity College, Hartford

A TEXT-BOOK for a year's course in schools and colleges, in which English literary history is regarded as composed of periods, each marked by a definite tone of thought and manner of expression. The treatment follows the divisions logically and systematically, without any of the perplexing cross-divisions so frequently made. It is based on the historic method of study, and refers briefly to events in each period bearing on social development, to changes in religious and political theory, and even to advances in the industrial arts. These all receive due consideration, for each author, if not entirely the product of social conditions, is at least molded by them. In addition, the book contains critiques, general surveys, summaries, biographical sketches, bibliographies, and suggestive questions. The examples have been chosen from poems which are generally familiar, and of an illustrative character.

JOHNSON'S FORMS OF ENGLISH POETRY
$1.00

THIS book contains nothing more than every young person should know about the construction of English verse, and its main divisions, both by forms and by subject-matter. The historical development of the main divisions is sketched, and briefly illustrated by representative examples; but the true character of poetry as an art and a social force has always been in the writer's mind. Only the elements of prosody are given. The aim has been not to make the study too technical, but to interest the student in poetry, and to aid him in acquiring a well rooted taste for good literature.

AMERICAN BOOK COMPANY

DESCRIPTIVE CATALOGUE OF HIGH SCHOOL AND COLLEGE TEXTBOOKS

Published Complete and in Sections

WE issue a Catalogue of High School and College Textbooks, which we have tried to make as valuable and as useful to teachers as possible. In this catalogue are set forth briefly and clearly the scope and leading characteristics of each of our best textbooks. In most cases there are also given testimonials from well-known teachers, which have been selected quite as much for their descriptive qualities as for their value as commendations.

¶ For the convenience of teachers this Catalogue is also published in separate sections treating of the various branches of study. These pamphlets are entitled: English, Mathematics, History and Political Science, Science, Modern Foreign Languages, Ancient Languages, Commercial Subjects, and Philosophy and Education. A single pamphlet is devoted to the Newest Books in all subjects.

¶ Teachers seeking the newest and best books for their classes are invited to send for our Complete High School and College Catalogue, or for such sections as may be of greatest interest.

¶ Copies of our price lists, or of special circulars, in which these books are described at greater length than the space limitations of the catalogue permit, will be mailed to any address on request.

¶ All correspondence should be addressed to the nearest of the following offices of the company: New York, Cincinnati, Chicago, Boston, Atlanta, San Francisco.

AMERICAN BOOK COMPANY

www.ingramcontent.com/pod-product-compliance
Lightning Source LLC
Chambersburg PA
CBHW050848300426
44111CB00010B/1171